大学英语立体化网络化系列教材·拓展课程教材

Selected Readings in Education
教育学专业英语教程

马丽雅 主编

马丽雅 李 颖 王晓玲
张 颖 刘春明 李 挺 编注

图书在版编目(CIP)数据

教育学专业英语教程/ 马丽雅主编. —北京：北京大学出版社，2004.10
（大学英语立体化网络化系列教材·拓展课程教材）
ISBN 978-7-301-07526-5

Ⅰ.①教… Ⅱ.①马… Ⅲ.①教育学—英语—高等学校—教材 Ⅳ.①H31

中国版本图书馆CIP数据核字(2004)第 057341 号

书　　　名：	教育学专业英语教程
著作责任者：	马丽雅　主编
责 任 编 辑：	汪晓丹
标 准 书 号：	ISBN 978-7-301-07526-5/H·1027
出 版 发 行：	北京大学出版社
地　　　址：	北京市海淀区成府路205号　100871
网　　　址：	http://www.pup.cn　新浪官方微博：@北京大学出版社
电 子 信 箱：	zbing@pup.pku.edu.cn
电　　　话：	邮购部 62752015　发行部 62750672　编辑部 62754382　出版部 62754962
印 　刷 　者：	三河市博文印刷有限公司
经 　销 　者：	新华书店
	787毫米×1092毫米　16开本　13.75印张　352千字
	2004年10月第1版　2022年4月第12次印刷
定　　　价：	32.00元

未经许可，不得以任何方式复制或抄袭本书之部分或全部内容。
版权所有，侵权必究
举报电话：010-62752024　电子信箱：fd@pup.pku.edu.cn

内容简介

　　本书选编了西方近代教育学史上十二名著名教育学家的十五篇精彩篇章,它们所反映的是近代教育史上不同时期的不同流派的教育思想。每篇课文配有较详细的语言点注释,对《大学英语教学大纲》四级词汇的超纲词汇作出讲解,并有针对性地精心设计了阅读理解、词汇、语法、写作等练习,有助于读者在学习掌握教育学专业知识的同时,提高自己的英语水平。

大学英语立体化网络化系列教材

总 顾 问　李赋宁　胡壮麟
总 主 编　黄必康
网络版主编　李建华

编委会名单 (以姓氏笔画为序)

王海啸 (南京大学)　　　　　王明舟 (北京大学出版社)
王焱华 (北京师范大学)　　　工惠玲 (西北大学)
刘红中 (北京大学)　　　　　刘龙根 (吉林大学)
孙建民 (河北师范大学)　　　孙秋丹 (北京大学)
余渭深 (重庆大学)　　　　　吴松江 (福州大学)
宋　黎 (大连理工大学)　　　李建华 (中国农业大学)
李养龙 (北京航空航天大学)　李霄翔 (东南大学)
杨　跃 (西安电子科技大学)　柯彦玢 (北京大学)
赵　雯 (东北大学)　　　　　夏纪梅 (中山大学)
贾国栋 (华南理工大学)　　　梁育全 (云南大学)
黄必康 (北京大学)　　　　　蒋学清 (北京交通大学)
蔡基刚 (复旦大学)　　　　　黎　宏 (四川大学)

总 序

辜正坤

西学东渐给东方的外语出版界造成一种奇特的景观：在相当短的时间内，外语出版物的数量扶摇直上，使它种民族语出版物相对汗颜，这是可以理解的。日本明治维新之后，新出现过类似的情形，外语（尤其是英语）原著注释读物动辄一套就是数百本，洋洋大观。毫无疑问，这对推进日本的外语教学起到了非常重要的作用。时至今日，其效应已经明显昭示出来：当今的中国各大学发表的论文为 SCI 所收录者，最多者一年达 500 篇，而东京大学一年就达 40,000 篇，两者相距 80 倍！如果以为日本的论文数量必与其科学水平成正比，因而中国大学的科学研究水平就落后了东大 80 倍的话，恐怕是一种很大的误解。其中的奥妙之一，就在于日本学者的英语水平普遍较高，许多论文是直接用英文写成，因此容易被世界各地的媒体注意到，其入选 SCI 的机会也就相对增多。反观中国学者的论文，绝大多数用汉语写成，少量靠懂英语的学者翻译，只有极少量的学者能够自己用英文直接写作。因此，大多数的中国论文是难以进入西方学者的视野的。当然入选 SCI 的机会也就相对少得多了。当然，这并非是说，中国的科研水平就反过来比日本高，而是说，由于中国学者英语写作水平普遍偏低的原因，其实际的科研水平未能在英语世界的文献中充分显示出来。由此可以明白，提高中国学者的英语能力（尤其是阅读文献与用英语写作的能力）是一件非常迫切的事。

然而，改革开放 20 多年来的英语学习大潮虽然使许多中国人在英语学习方面获得了较高的造诣，上了一个较为理想的台阶，但是有更多的人却老在一个水平上徘徊不前：要学的教材已经学了，该考的科目已经通过了，但是，面对英语的殿堂，人们并没有登堂入室的感觉。听说能力未能应付裕如或许情有可原，因为学习者可以抱怨没有相应的可以一试身手的客观条件，但是在阅读方面，例如阅读文史哲数理化的专业文献方面，却仍是磕磕绊绊、跋前踬后，字典不离手，冷汗不离身。这种处于瓶颈地带，欲罢不可、欲进不能的促迫感，源于一个关键的原因：缺乏专业外语文献阅读训练。学校里使用的基础英语教材编得再好，也只能解决基础问题，不能解决超过基础的专业阅读问题。正如要做游泳健儿的人只在游泳池里按照游泳要领奋力拨拉了一阵池水，自觉亦有劈波斩浪之感，但与真正的河涛海潮相比，终究属于两重洞天。

于是，就产生了这一整套专业英语阅读教程。

它的目标非常明确，无非是要把英语知识与技能的培训和高层次系统知识的灌输二者有机结合起来，达到既学语言又学知识的目的；即温故，又知新。照我看来，这是最有效率的学习与巩固方略。

如前所述可以明白，这套教程不只是对一般想要提高英语实际水平的人有用，对于专家学者或研究人员，也有很大的好处。一个人无论多么博学多才，也不太可能对各个专业的英语经典文献和地道表达都了然于胸，因此，当需要在尽可以短的时间内对某专业的英语经典文献或概念有所把握时,这一整套书无疑不会使人们失望。

这套书的编选思路最初萌发于1991年,当时称作《注释本英文世界文化简明百科文库》。编者当时曾会同北京大学英语系大学英语教研室教师和北京大学出版社若干编辑共商过具体编选事宜,并由北京大学出版社出版。尔后还进行过多次类似的讨论。文库分上、中、下三编,每编含精选名著一百种左右。在编选思路上,力求达到雅俗共赏,深入浅出,系统全面。在系统性方面,注意参照《大英百科全书》和《中国大百科全书》的知识框架,用英文把更为完备的知识系统介绍给读者。在实用性方面,亦注意选材的内容与词汇量同现行的英语教材、实际英语教学水平相呼应。

本编为上编,除可供大学英语分科专业阅读选用教材之用外,亦可供社会上一般读者提高英语水平、直接经由阅读原著而掌握某一专业知识之用。基本的编辑方针是1) 选目必须系统、广泛,尽可能把大学的重要专业都包容进去(包括人文社会科学和理工科专业);2) 选目可大致分三类:A. 简史类;B. 名篇、名著类;C. 比较规范的或经典的西方专业教材类;3) 每册书的字数最好在20万字上下(个别可以例外)。至于其他具体事项,则随书说明。

教育部在1999年亦强调大学英语教学不能停留在基础英语教学上,而要逐步过渡到教授专业分科英语,使学生尽可能进入阅读专业英语文献的水平。因此这套教材的产生是适得其时的。

当然,它的具体效果如何,还有待检验。好在这套教材的编注与出版都是一个较长的过程,这期间可望获得有关方面的建议与批评,以期使它精益求精,日臻完善。

是为序。

2001年于北京大学英语系

Contents
目　录

Ⅰ. Pragmatism Education 实用主义教育

1. My Pedagogic Greed ·········· John Dewey 3
   我的教育信条　　　　　　　　　　约翰·杜威
2. The School and Social Progress ·········· John Dewey 14
   学校与社会进步　　　　　　　　　　约翰·杜威
3. Democracy and Education ·········· John Dewey 26
   民主主义与教育　　　　　　　　　　约翰·杜威

Ⅱ. New Education 新教育

4. The Secret of Childhood ·········· Maria Montessori 39
   童年的秘密　　　　　　　　　玛丽亚·蒙台梭利
5. Education and Good Life ·········· Bertrand Russell 50
   教育与美好生活　　　　　　　　　伯特兰·罗素
6. The Aims of Education ·········· Alfred North Whitehead 60
   教育的目的　　　　　　　　艾尔弗雷德·诺思·怀特海

Ⅲ. Essentialism Education 要素主义教育

7. The Wasteland of Education ·········· Arthur Bestor 73
   教育的荒地　　　　　　　　　　　阿瑟·贝斯特
8. Education and Freedom ·········· H.G. Rickove 84
   教育与自由　　　　　　　　　　　H.G.里科弗

Ⅳ. Perennialism Education 永恒主义教育

9. General Education ·········· Robert Hutchins 97
   普通教育　　　　　　　　　　　罗伯特·赫钦斯
10. How to Read a Book ·········· Mortimer Adler 107
    怎样读一本书　　　　　　　　　莫蒂默·艾德勒

Ⅴ. Existialism Education 存在主义教育

11. The Education of Character ·················· Martin Buber 121
    品格教育   马丁·布贝尔

Ⅵ. New Behavorism Education 新行为主义教育

12. The Science of Learning and the Art of Teaching ·················· B.F. Skinner 133
    学习的科学和教学的艺术   B.F.斯金纳

Ⅶ. Structualism Education 结构主义教育

13. Educational Principles and Psychological Data ·················· Jean Piaget 147
    教育的原则与心理学的论据   让·皮亚杰
14. The Process of Education ·················· Jerome S. Bruner 159
    教育过程   杰罗姆·S.布鲁纳
15. Nature of a Theory of Instruction ·················· Jerome S. Bruner 171
    教学论的性质   杰罗姆·S.布鲁纳

练习参考答案·· 179
词汇表·· 201

Pragmatism Education
实用主义教育

　　实用主义教育是杜威所创立的现代西方教育思潮的一个重要流派。它不仅以反对所谓"传统教育"为己任,而且在二十世纪以来流行的各种进步主义教育思潮中,它还自居于领导地位,在世界范围内产生了较大的影响。十九世纪末,南北战争后美国结束了大规模的工业技术改造,开始迅速发展大型工业联合企业,但在教育领域里,仍沿袭欧洲的旧传统,学校制度、课程和教材、教学方法,这与社会实际生活严重脱离。杜威实用主义教育理论就是在这样的历史背景下提出来并经过他所创办的芝加哥实验学校的长期试验。主要代表人物有约翰·杜威、克伯屈、胡克等。

　　实用主义教育流派是以实用主义哲学为基础的,杜威对教育性质判定的三个核心命题:教育即经验的不断改造;教育即生活;教育即生长。他创立了"在做中学"理论,认为一切"从活动中学","从经验中学",给儿童创设各种活动的情境,指导儿童利用各种材料和工具,进行探究式的学习。教学过程阶段论的内容是:(1)疑难的情境;(2)确定疑难之所在,并提出问题;(3)提出假设;(4)进行推理。

　　实用主义教育理论主张把学校办成雏形社会,用设计活动和直接经验取代知识的系统学习,这是不足取的。另外,实用主义教育家基于生物学的本能论,过分侧重儿童的兴趣和自由,这些导致了学校组织松散、学生缺乏系统的具有内在逻辑顺序的知识和技能的训练,使得教育质量下降,这也是二十世纪五十年代后实用主义教育受到众人责难,并在要素主义教育、结构主义教育等的冲击下日益衰微的主要原因之一。

1. My Pedagogic Creed
我的教育信条

John Dewey
约翰·杜威

约翰·杜威(1859—1952),美国唯心主义哲学家、教育家,被誉为"实用主义神圣家族的家长",实用主义的主要代表人物。他生于佛蒙特州柏林顿市附近的农村,1879年在佛蒙特大学毕业后任中学教师。1884年在霍布金大学获博士学位,后在密执安大学、明尼苏达大学讲授哲学。1894—1904年任芝加哥大学哲学、心理学和教育系主任。1896—1903年主办芝加哥大学试验学校。1904—1930年任芝加哥大学哲学教授。杜威于1919年"五四"运动时曾到中国,传播实用主义教育思想。1928年曾访问苏联。

主要著作有:《我的教育信条》、《学校与社会》、《民主主义和教育》、《明日之学校》、《经验与教育》、《人的问题》等。

《我的教育信条》(1920)是一篇鼓舞人心,并且具有预见性的论文,它预示了杜威以后发表的大部分论文的主要内容,而其中主要谈了作者的五个有关教育方面的信念。第一个信条是他对教育过程下的定义,他认为"教育必须从心理学上探索儿童的能量、兴趣和习惯开始"。第二个信条体现了杜威对于学校的看法,学校确实存在于社会之中,无论是教育与受教育者都与我们的生活息息相关,把学生引进到新的领域,发现和探索新的奥妙,获取新的能力,这些更是教育的真谛。在第三个信条中,杜威谈到教育中的教材。他反对以获取知识为目的的教学,认为"学校科目相互联系的真正中心,不是科学,不是文学,不是历史,不是地理,而是儿童本身相关的社会生活"。杜威的第四个信条是他对于教育方法的见解。方法的最后问题可以归结为儿童的能力和兴趣发展的顺序问题,以活动来促成发展,具有进步的意义。杜威的第五个信条认为"教育是社会进步和社会改革的基本方法",他注意到当时学校教育的贫乏、方法呆板,学校教学根本不顾儿童的本性,因此强调直接经验和活动课程的重要性。这种对教育空洞形式主义的批判,对教育方面不足的矫正有很大的作用。

ARTICLE ONE
What Education Is

I believe that all education proceeds by the participation of the individual in the social consciousness of the race[1]. This process begins unconsciously almost at birth, and is continually shaping the individual's powers, saturating his consciousness, forming his habits, training his ideas, and arousing his feelings and emotions[2]. Through this unconscious education the individual gradually comes to share in the intellectual and moral resources which humanity has succeeded in getting together. He becomes an inheritor of the funded capital of civilization. The most formal and technical education in the world cannot safely depart from this general process.[3] It can only organize it; or differentiate it in some particular direction.[4]

I believe that the only true education comes through the stimulation of the child's powers by the demands of the social situations in which he finds himself. Through these demands he is stimulated to act as a member of a unity, to emerge from his original narrowness of action and feeling and to conceive of himself from the standpoint of the welfare of the group to which he belongs.[5] Through the responses which others make to his own activities he comes to know what these mean in social terms.[6] The value which they have is reflected back into them. For instance, through the response which is made to the child's instinctive babblings the child comes to know what those babblings mean; they are transformed into articulate language and thus the child is introduced into the consolidated wealth of ideas and emotions which are now summed up in language.[7]

I believe that this educational process has two sides—one psychological and one sociological, and that neither can be subordinated to the other or neglected without evil results following[8]. Of these two sides, the psychological is the basis. The child's own instincts and powers furnish the material[9] and give the starting point for all education. Save as the efforts of the educator connect with some activity which the child is carrying on of his own initiative independent of the educator, education becomes reduced to a pressure from without.[10] It may, indeed, give certain external results but cannot truly be called educative. Without insight into the psychological structure and activities of the individual, the educative process will, therefore, be haphazard and arbitrary.[11] If it chances to coincide with child's activity it will get a leverage; if it does not, it will result in friction, or disintegration, or arrest of the child nature.[12]

I believe that knowledge of social conditions, of the present state of civilization, is necessary in order properly to interpret the child's powers. The child has his own instincts and tendencies, but we do not know what these mean until we can translate them into their social equivalents.[13] We must be able to carry the back into a social past and see them as the inheritance of previous race activities. We must also be able to project them into the future to see what their outcome and end will be.[14] In the illustration just used, it is the ability to see in the child's babblings the promise and potency of a future social intercourse and conversation which enables one to deal in the proper way with that instinct.[15]

I believe that the psychological and social sides are organically related and that education cannot be regarded as a compromise between the two, or a superimposition of one upon the other.[16] We are told that the psychological definition of education is barren and formal[17]—that it gives us only the idea of a development of all the mental powers without giving us any idea of the use to which these powers are put. On the other hand, it is urged that the social definition of education, as getting adjusted to civilization, makes of it a forced and external process, and results in subordinating the freedom of the individual to a pre-conceived social and political status.[18]

I believe each of these objections is true when urged against one side isolated from the other.[19] In order to know what a power really is we must know what its end, use, or function is; and this we cannot know save as we conceive of the individual as active in social relationships. But, on the other hand, the only possible adjustment which we can give to the child under existing conditions, is that which arises through putting him in complete possession of all his powers. With the advent of democracy and modern industrial conditions, it is impossible to foretell definitely just what civilization will be twenty years from now.[20] Hence it is impossible to prepare the child for any precise set of conditions. To prepare him for the future life means to give him command of himself[21]; it means so to train him that he will have the full and ready use of[22] all his capacities; that his eye and ear and hand may be tools ready to command, that his judgment may be capable of grasping the conditions under which it has to work, and the executive forces be trained to act economically and efficiently. It is impossible to reach this sort of adjustment save as constant regard is had to the individual's own powers, tastes, and interests—say, that is, as education is continually converted into psychological terms.[23] In sum, I believe that the individual who is to be educated is a social individual and that society is an organic union of individuals. If we eliminate the social factor from the child we are left only with an abstraction; if we eliminate the individual factor from society, we are left only with an inert and lifeless mass.[24] Education, therefore, must begin with a psychological insight into the child's capacities, interests, and habits. It must be controlled at every point by reference to these same considerations. These powers, interests, and habits must be continually interpreted—we must know what they mean. They must be translated into terms of their social equivalents—into terms of what they are capable of in the way of social service.

ARTICLE TWO
What the School Is

I believe that the school is primarily a social institution. Education being a social process, the school is simply that form of community life in which all those agencies are concentrated that will be most effective in bringing the child to share in the inherited resources of the race, and to use his own powers for social ends.[25]

I believe that education, therefore, is a process of living and not a preparation for future living.

I believe that the school must represent present life-life as real and vital to the child as that which he carries on in the home, in the neighborhood, or on the play-ground.

I believe that education which does not occur through forms of life, forms that are worth living for their own sake, is always a poor substitute for the genuine reality and tends to cramp and to deaden.[26]

I believe that the school, as an institution, should simplify existing social life; should reduce it, as it were, to abembryonic form. Existing life is so complex that the child cannot be brought into contact with it without either confusion or distraction[27]; he is either overwhelmed by multiplicity of activities which are going on, so that he loses his own power of orderly reaction, or he is so stimulated by these various activities that his power are prematurely called into play and he becomes either unduly specialized or else disintegrated.

I believe that, as such simplified social life, the school life should grow gradually out of the home life; that it should take up and continue the activities with which the child is already familiar in the home.

I believe that it should exhibit these activities to the child, and reproduce them in such ways that the child will gradually learn the meaning of them, and be capable of playing his own part in relation to them.

I believe that this is a psychological necessity, because it is the only way of securing continuity in the child's growth, the only way of giving a background of past experience to the new ideas given in school[28].

I believe it is also a social necessity because the home is the form of social life in which the child has been nurtured and in connection with which he has his moral training. It is the business of the school to deepen and extend his sense of the values bound up in his home life.[29]

I believe that much of present education fails because it neglects this fundamental principle of the school as a form of community life. It conceives the school as a place where certain information is to be given, where certain lessons are to be learned, or where certain habits are to be formed.[30] The value of these is conceived as lying largely in the remote future; the child must do these things for the sake of something else he is to do; they are mere preparation. As a result they do not become apart of the life experience of the child and so are not truly educative.

I believe that moral education centers about this conception of the school as a mode of social life, that the best and deepest moral training is precisely that which one gets through having to enter into proper relations with others in a unity o f work and thought. The present educational systems, so far as they destroy or neglect this unity, render it difficult or impossible to get any genuine, regular moral training.[31]

I believe that the child should be stimulated and controlled in his work through the life of the community.

I believe that under existing conditions far too much of the stimulus and control proceeds from the teacher, because of neglect of the idea of the school as a form of social life.

I believe that the teacher's place and work in the school is to be interpreted from this same basis. The teacher is not in the school to impose certain ideas or to form certain habits in the child, but is there as a member of the community to select the influences which shall affect the child and to assist him in properly responding to these influences.[32]

I believe that the discipline of the school should proceed from the life of the school as a whole and not directly from the teacher.

I believe that the teacher's business is simply to determine on the basis of larger experience and riper wisdom, how the discipline of life shall come to the child.

I believe that all questions of the grading of the child and his promotion should be determined by reference to the same standard. Examinations are of use only so far as they test the child's fitness for social life and reveal the place in which he can be of most service and where he can receive the most help.

注　　释

1 the social consciousness of the race: 人类的社会意识

2 shaping the individual's powers, saturating his consciousness, forming his habits, training his ideas, and arousing his feelings and emotions: 发展个人的能力, 熏染他的意识, 形成他的习惯, 锻炼他的思想, 并激发他的感情和情绪。

3 The most formal and technical education in the world cannot safely depart from this general process. 世界上最正规、最专门的教育确实离不开这个普遍的过程。
depart from: 离开。比如: We departed from London at 10 am. 我们十点钟离开伦敦。

4 It can only organize it; or differentiate it in some particular direction. 教育只能按照某种特定的方向, 组织或者区分这个过程。
第一个代词 it 指代 the most formal and technical education(最正式的、最专门的教育), 后两个代词 it 指代 this general process(这个普遍的过程)。

5 Through these demands he is stimulated to act as a member of a unity, to emerge from his original narrowness of action and feeling and to conceive of himself from the standpoint of the welfare of the group to which he belongs. 这些要求刺激他, 促使他作为集体的一个成员去行事, 从自己行动和感情在原有的狭隘范围里显现出来, 从自己所属的集体利益来考虑自己。
act as sb/sth: 充任某种角色; 担任某工作。比如: I don't understand their language; you'll have to act as my interpreter. 我不懂他们的语言, 你得当翻译了。
conceive of: 设想, 考虑。比如: The ancient conceived of the world as being flat. 古人认为地球是扁的。
from the standpoint of: 从……的角度; 站在……的立场。比如: The store should do its business from the standpoint of the customer. 商家做生意应从顾客的角度考虑。

6 Through the responses which others make to his own activities he comes to know what these mean in social terms. 通过别人对他自己的各种活动所作出的反应, 他便知道这些活动在社会语言中意味着什么。
本句中 which 引导的定语从句修饰 responses。make responses to 指"对……做出反应", 比如: The citizens made a poor response to the appeal for funds. 公民对征集资金的呼吁反应甚微。

7 For instance, through the response which is made to the child's instinctive babblings the child comes to know what those babblings mean; they are transformed into articulate language and thus the child is introduced into the consolidated wealth of ideas and emotions which are now summed up in language. 例如, 儿童由于别人对它的呀呀的声音的反应, 便

渐渐明白那呀呀的声音的意思，这种呀呀的声音又逐渐变化为音节清晰的语言，于是儿童就被引导到现在用语言总结起来的统一的丰富的观念和情绪中去。

be transformed into：被改变。比如：That is the process by which caterpillars are transformed into butterflies. 这就是毛虫变为蝴蝶的过程。

sum up：总结，概括。比如：Now sum up your views in a few words. 现在用几句话把你的观点概括一下。

8 and that neither can be subordinated to the other or neglected without evil results following：它们是平列并重的，哪一方面也不能偏废。否则，将会导致不良的后果。

be subordinated to：次于，附属于。比如：In her book, this issue is subordinated to more general problems. 在她的书中，这个问题处理得不如一般问题重要。

9 furnish the material：提供素材

10 Save as the efforts of the educator connect with some activity which the child is carrying on of his own initiative independent of the educator, education becomes reduced to a pressure from without. 儿童不依赖教育者自己主动地进行一些活动，因为教育者的努力是同这些活动有联系的，除此之外，教育便成外来的压力。

save：除了。比如：We know nothing about her save that her surname is Jones. 我们除了知道她姓琼斯外，对她全不了解。

of one's own initiative 指"主动地、积极地"。be reduced to：处于某种状态。比如：be reduced to begging, borrowing 沦落到得要饭、借债。

without 这里是古语，意指外面。

11 Without insight into the psychological structure and activities of the individual, the educative process will, therefore, be haphazard and arbitrary. 如果对于个人的心理结构和活动缺乏深入的观察，教育的过程将会变成偶然性的、独断性的。

Without insight into the psychological structure and activities of the individual 是介词短语作条件状语。insight into：洞察力，深刻的了解

12 If it chances to coincide with the child's activity it will get a leverage; if it does not, it will result in friction, or disintegration, or arrest of the child nature. 如果它碰巧能与儿童的活动相一致，便可以起到作用；不然的话，那么它将会带来阻力、不协调，或者束缚了儿童的天性。

chance 这里作动词意：偶然发生，碰巧。比如：She chanced to be in/It chanced that she was in when he called. 他打电话时碰巧她在家。

coincide with：与……相符，与……极相似。比如：Her taste in music coincides with her husband's. 她在音乐方面的爱好与她丈夫一致。

coincide with：同时发生。比如：Her arrival coincided with our departure. 她来到时我们正好离开。

get a leverage：起到作用、产生影响。

arrest of the child nature：束缚儿童天性

13 The child has his own instincts and tendencies, but we do not know what these mean until we can translate them into their social equivalents. 儿童具有自己的本能和倾向，但是只有

当我们把这些本能和倾向转化为与它们的社会相当的事物时,我们才会知道它们所指的是什么。

14 We must be able to carry them back into a social past and see them as the inheritance of previous race activities. We must also be able to project them into the future to see what their outcome and end will be. 我们必须能够把它们带到过去的社会中去,并且把他们看做是前代人类活动的遗传。我们还必须能把它们投射到将来,看看它们的结果会是什么。

15 In the illustration just used, it is the ability to see in the child's babblings the promise and potency of a future social intercourse and conversation which enables one to deal in the proper way with that instinct. 在前一个例子中,正是这样能够在儿童的呀呀声里,看出他将来的社会交往和会话的希望和能力,使人们能够正确地对待这种本能。

deal with sth:处理问题等,料理某事。比如:You dealt with an awkward situation very tactfully. 你很巧妙地处理了一个困难的局面。

16 I believe that the psychological and social sides are organically related and that education cannot be regarded as a compromise between the two, or a superimposition of one upon the other. 心理的和社会的两个方面是有机地联系着的,而且不能把教育看作是二者之间的折中或其中之一凌驾于另一个之上而成的。

regard...as:认为,看作。比如:I regard your suggestion as worth considering. 我认为你的建议值得考虑。

a compromise between the two:两者之间的折中。the two 指代 the psychological and social sides;superimpose sth on sth:将某一物置于另一物上

17 barren and formal:空洞的,形式的

18 On the other hand, it is urged that the social definition of education, as getting adjusted to civilization, makes of it a forced and external process, and results in subordinating the freedom of the individual to a pre-conceived social and political status. 另一方面,又有人坚决认为,教育的社会方面的定义(即把教育理解为与文明相适应)会使得教育成为一个强迫的、外在的过程,结果把个人的自由隶属于一个预定的社会和政治状态之下。

be adjusted to:适应,适合。比如:He was quickly adjusted to the hot weather here. 他很快就适应了这儿的炎热天气。

make sth of sb/sth:使某人[某事物]处于某状况或变成某事物。比如:We'll make a footballer of him, despite the fact that he is not a good one now. 虽然他现在不是一个优秀足球运动员,我们会把他造就成的。

19 I believe each of these objections is true when urged against one side isolated from the other. 假如把一个方面看作是与另一个方面孤立不相关而加以反对的话,那么这两种反对的论调都是对的。

be isolated from:与……隔离,被孤立起来。比如:When a person has an infectious disease, he is usually isolated from other people. 人患传染病时通常要与他人隔离。

20 With the advent of democracy and modern industrial conditions, it is impossible to foretell definitely just what civilization will be twenty years from now. 随着民主和现代工业的出现,我们不可能明确地预言二十年后的文化是什么样子。

with the advent of:随着……的到来。比如:With the advent of the new chairman, the company began to prosper. 随着新主席的到来,公司也开始有了起色。

21 command of sth:使用或控制某事物的能力,掌握
22 have the full and ready use of sth:充分和随时使用某事物
23 It is impossible to reach this sort of adjustment save as constant regard is had to the individual's own powers, tastes, and interests—say, that is, as education is continually converted into psychological terms. 除非我们不断地注意到个人的能力、爱好和兴趣,也就是说,除非我们把教育不断地变成心理学的名词,这种适应是不可能达到的。
24 If we eliminate the social factor from the child we are left only with an abstraction; if we eliminate the individual factor from society, we are left only with an inert and lifeless mass. 如果从儿童身上除去社会的因素,我们便只剩下一个抽象的东西;如果我们从社会方面除去个人的因素,我们便只剩下一个死板的没有生命力的集体。
    eliminate...from:清除,排除。比如:The police have eliminated two suspects from their inquiry. 警察从调查中已排查出两名嫌疑犯。
25 Education being a social process, the school is simply that form of community life in which all those agencies are concentrated that will be most effective in bringing the child to share in the inherited resources of the race, and to use his own powers for social ends. 教育既然是一种社会过程,学校便是社会生活的一种形式。在这种社会生活的形式里,集中了凡是能最有效地培养儿童分享人类所继承下来的财富和为了社会目的而运用自己的能力的一切权利。
    education being a social process 是独立主格结构,表示原因的,which 引导的从句是定语从句修饰 life。在 which 引导的定语从句中又有一个由 that 引导的定语从句修饰 agencies。
26 I believe that education which does not occur through forms of life, forms that are worth living for their own sake, is always a poor substitute for the genuine reality and tends to cramp and to deaden. 不通过各种生活形式,或者不通过那些本身就值得生活的生活形式来实现的教育,对于真正的现实来说总是贫乏的代替物,结果将会形成呆板而死气沉沉的局面。
    be a substitute for:是……的代替品。比如:Is margarine a satisfactory substitute for butter? 人造奶油是一种令人满意的奶油代用品吗?
27 Existing life is so complex that the child cannot be brought into contact with it without either confusion or distraction. 现实生活是很复杂,儿童同它接触时会陷于迷乱。
    这是由 so...that 引导的结果状语从句。
28 the only way of giving a background of past experience to the new ideas given in school:惟一方式是对学校所授的新观念赋予旧经验的背景
29 It is the business of the school to deepen and extend his sense of the values bound up in his home life. 学校的任务是加深和扩展他关于与家庭生活联系的价值观念。
    it 是形式主语,真正的主语是后面的不定式结构。
30 It conceives the school as a place where certain information is to be given, where certain lessons are to be learned, or where certain habits are to be formed. 现代教育把学校当作一个传授某些知识,学习某些课业,或养成某些习惯的场所。

31　The present educational systems, so far as they destroy or neglect this unity, render it difficult or impossible to get any genuine, regular moral training. 现在的教育制度,就它对于这种统一的破坏或忽视而论,能使它达到任何真正的、正常的道德训练是困难的或者不可能的。

在此句中,it 是形式宾语,真正的宾语是后面的不定式结构,difficult 和 impossible 作宾语补足语。

32　The teacher is not in the school to impose certain ideas or to form certain habits in the child, but is there as a member of the community to select the influences which shall affect the child and to assist him in properly responding to these influences. 教师在学校中并不是要给儿童强加某种概念,或形成某种习惯,而是作为集体的一个成员来选择影响儿童的教育,并帮助儿童对其做出适当的反应。

not... but...：不是……而是；which 引导的从句作定语修饰 influences。

练　　习

1. 回答问题
　（1）What is the general process which is necessary for all education?
　（2）Why does the only true education come through the stimulation of the child's powers by the demands of the social situations in which he finds himself?
　（3）What will the educative process be if there is no understanding of children's psychological structure and activities?
　（4）How can a child have command of himself?
　（5）What will happen if the social factor is eliminated from the child and the individual factor is eliminated from society?

2. 判断正误
　（1）It is not until a child begins his schooling that he participates in the social consciousness of the race.
　（2）The sociological process is superior to the psychological one in terms of education.
　（3）If education gets adjusted to civilization, then it will be a forced and external process.
　（4）In order to prepare a child for the future life the society must provide him with good education.
　（5）If we want to properly understand the child's power, we should be informed of the knowledge of social conditions, of the present state of civilization.

3. 选词填空
depart from, from the standpoint of, transform... into, sum up, become reduced to, chance to, adjust to, reference to, with the advent of, make of
　（1）Avoid making any _____ his illness.

(2) His parents are determined to _____ a lawyer _____ him, even if he opposes.

(3) The body quickly _____ changes in temperature.

(4) _____ the new chairman, the company began to prosper.

(5) The manager shouldn't always think about the development of the company _____ its profit.

(6) The train to Leeds _____ platform 4.

(7) The complete change of climate _____ the area from a desert _____ a swamp.

(8) The house _____ ashes by a fire.

(9) I _____ meet my old friend on my way home.

(10) Please _____ this passage in a few words.

4. 句型模拟

(1) save as

(2) it is urged that...

5. 英译汉

(1) I believe that this educational process has two sides—one psychological and one sociological; and that neither can be subordinated to the other or neglected without evil results following.

(2) In order to know what a power really is we must know what its end, use, or function is; and this we cannot know save as we conceive of the individual as active in social relationships.

(3) To prepare him for the future life means to give him command of himself, it means so to train him that he will have the full and ready use of all his capacities; that his eye and ear and hand may be tools ready to command, that his judgment may be capable of grasping the conditions under which it has to work, and the executive forces be trained to act economically and efficiently.

(4) In sum, I believe that the individual who is to be educated is a social individual and that society is an organic union of individuals.

(5) Education, therefore, must begin with a psychological insight into the child's capacities, interests, and habits. It must be controlled at every point by reference to these same considerations.

6. 汉译英

(1) 那一击打得他失去了知觉。(consciousness)

(2) 对提高工资的要求大多都能折中解决。(compromise)

(3) 仔细检查以确保消除文字中所有的错误。(eliminate...from)

(4) 这房间由厨房改成了厕所。(convert...to)

(5) 这位老人用了十年使这块贫瘠的土地变成了绿洲。(barren)

1. My Pedagogic Creed 我的教育信条

7. 写作指导

For this part, you are required to write a composition on the topic "What Is Ideal Education". The following points taken from the text are useful expressions for your reference.

- stimulate the child's power by the demands of the social situations
- coincide with the child's activity
- relate the psychological and social sides organically
- give us ideas of the use to which mental powers are put
- put the child in complete possession of all his powers
- give the child command of himself
- begin with a psychological insight into the child's capacities, interests, and habits

2. The School and Social Progress[1]
学校与社会进步

John Dewey
约翰·杜威

杜威在《学校与社会进步》中论述道，我们的社会生活正在经历着一个彻底的和根本的变化。如果我们的教育对于生活应具有一定意义的话，那么它就必须经历一个相应的变革。学校采取主动作业、自然研究、科学常识、艺术、历史，把单纯的符号和形式的课程降低到次要地位，改变学校的道德风尚、师生关系和纪律，引进更生动的、更富有表情的自我指导的各种因素等，都不是偶然发生的，而是出于社会发展的需要。如果把这一切因素都组织起来，把它们所含的观念和理想，彻底地、不妥协地在学校的制度中体现出来，就会把每个学校都成为一种雏形的社会。当学校能在这样一个小社会里引导和训练每个儿童成为社会的成员，用服务的精神熏陶他，并给予有效的指导时，学校便对一个有价值的、可爱的、和谐的大社会提供了最好的保证。

We are apt to look at the school from an individualistic standpoint, as something between teacher and pupil, or between teacher and parent. That which interests us most is naturally the progress made by the individual child of our acquaintance, his normal physical development, his advance in ability to read, write, and figure, his growth in the knowledge of geography and history, improvement in manners, habits of promptness, order, and industry[2]—it is from such standards as these that we judge the work of the school. And rightly so. Yet the range of the outlook needs to be enlarged. What the best and wisest parent wants for his own child, that must the community want for all of its children. Any other ideal for our schools is narrow and unlovely; acted upon, it destroys our democracy[3]. All that society has accomplished for itself is put, through the agency of the school, at the disposal of its future members[4]. All its better thoughts of itself it hopes to realize through the new possibilities thus opened to its future self.[5] Here individualism and socialism are at one. Only by being true to the full growth of all the individuals who make it up, can society by any chance be true to itself. And in the self-direction thus given, nothing counts as much as the school, for, as Horace Mann said, "Where anything is growing, one former is worth a thousand re-formers."[6]

Whenever we have in mind the discussion of a new movement in education, it is especially necessary to take the broader, or social, view. Otherwise, changes in the school institution and tradition will be looked at as the arbitrary inventions of particular teachers, at the worst transitory fads, and at the best merely improvements in certain details[7]—and this is the plane upon which it is too customary to consider school changes. It is as rational to conceive of the locomotive or the telegraph as personal devices[8]. The modification going on in the method and curriculum of education is as much a product of the changed social situation, and as much an effort to meet the needs of the new society that is forming, as are changes in modes of industry and commerce.[9]

No number of object-lessons, got up as object-lessons for the sake of giving information, can afford even the shadow of a substitute for acquaintance with the plants and animals of the farm and garden acquired through actual living among them and caring for them.[10] No training of sense-organs in school, introduced for the sake of training, can begin to compete with the alertness and fullness of sense-life that comes through daily intimacy and interest in familiar occupations.[11] Verbal memory can be trained in committing tasks, a certain discipline of the reasoning powers can be acquired through lessons in science and mathematics; but, after all, this is somewhat remote and shadowy compared with[12] the training of attention and of judgment that is acquired in having to do things with a real motive behind and a real outcome ahead. At present, concentration of industry and division of labor have practically eliminated household and neighborhood occupations[13]—at least for educational purposes. But it is useless to bemoan the departure of the good old days of children's modesty, reverence, and implicit obedience, if we expect merely by bemoaning and by exhortation to bring them back.[14] It is radical conditions which have changed, and only an equally radical change in education suffices. We must recognize our compensations—the increase in toleration, in breadth of social judgment, the larger acquaintance with human nature, the sharpened alertness in reading signs of character and interpreting social situations, greater accuracy of adaptation to differing personalities, contact with greater commercial activities.[15] These considerations mean much to the city-bred child of today. Yet there is a real problem: how shall we retain these advantages, and yet introduce into the school something representing the other side of life—occupations which exact personal responsibilities and which train the child in relation to the physical realities of life?[16]

When we turn to the school, we find that one of the most striking tendencies at present is toward the introduction of so-called manual training, shopwork, and the household arts—sewing and cooking.

This has not been done "on purpose," with a full consciousness that the school must now supply that factor of training formerly taken care of in the home, but rather by instinct, by experimenting and finding that such work takes a vital hold of pupils and gives them something which was not to be got in any other way.[17] Consciousness of its real import is still so weak that the work is often done in a half-hearted, confused, and unrelated way. The reasons assigned to justify it are painfully inadequate or sometimes even positively wrong.

If we were to cross-examine even those who are most favorably disposed to the introduction of this work into our school system, we should, I imagine, generally find the main reasons to be that such work engages the full spontaneous interest and attention of the children.[18] It keeps them alert and active, instead of passive and receptive; it makes them more useful, more capable, and hence more inclined to be helpful at home; it prepares them to some extent for the practical duties of later life[19]—the girls to be more efficient house managers, if not actually cooks and seam-stresses; the boys (were our educational system only adequately rounded out into trade schools) for their future vocations. I do not underestimate the worth of these reasons. Of those indicated by the changed attitude of the children I shall indeed have something to say in my next talk, when speaking directly of the relationship of the school to the child[20]. But the point of view is, upon the whole, unnecessarily narrow. We must conceive of work in wood and metal, of weaving, sewing, and cooking, as methods of living and learning, not as distinct studies.[21]

We must conceive of them in their social significance, as types of the processes by which society keeps itself going, as agencies for bringing home to the child some of the primal necessities of community life, and as ways in which these needs have been met by the growing insight and ingenuity of man[22]; in short, as instrumentalities through which the school itself shall be made a genuine form of active community life, instead of a place set apart in which to learn lessons.

A society is a number of people held together because they are working along common lines, in a common spirit, and with reference to common aims.[23] The common needs and aims demand a growing interchange of thought and growing unity of sympathetic feeling. The radical reason that the present school cannot organize itself as a natural social unit is because just this element of common and productive activity is absent. Upon the playground, in game and sport, social organization takes place spontaneously and inevitably. There is something to do, some activity to be carried on, requiring natural divisions of labor, selection of leaders and followers, mutual cooperation and emulation.[24] In the schoolroom the motive and the cement of social organization are alike wanting. Upon the ethical side, the tragic weakness of the present school is that it endeavors to prepare future members of the social order in a medium in which the conditions of the social spirit are eminently wanting.[25]

The difference that appears when occupations are made the articulating centers of school life is not easy to describe in words; it is a difference in motive, of spirit and atmosphere. As one enters a busy kitchen in which a group of children are actively engaged in the preparation of food, the psychological difference, the change from more or less passive and inert recipiency and restraint to one of buoyant outgoing energy, is so obvious as fairly to strike one in the face.[26] Indeed, to those whose image of the school is rigidly set the change is sure to give a shock. But the change in the social attitude is equally marked. The mere absorbing of facts and truths is so exclusively individual an affair that it tends very naturally to pass into selfishness.[27] There is no obvious social motive for the acquirement of mere learning, there is no clear social gain in success thereat.[28] Indeed, almost the only measure for success is a competitive one, in the bad sense of that term—a comparison of results in the recitation or in the examination to see which child has succeeded in getting ahead of others in storing up, in accumulating, the maximum of information.[29] So thoroughly is this prevailing atmosphere that for one child to help another in his task has become a school crime.[30] Where the school work consists in simply learning lessons, mutual assistance, instead of being the most natural form of co-operation and association, becomes a clandestine effort to relieve one's neighbor of his proper duties.[31] Where active work is going on, all this is changed. Helping others, instead of being a form of charity which impoverishes the recipient, is simply an aid in setting free the powers and furthering the impulse of the one helped.[32] A spirit of free communication, of interchange of ideas, suggestions, results, both successes and failures of previous experiences, becomes the dominating note of the recitation. So far as emulation enters in, it is in the comparison of individuals, not with regard to the quantity of information personally absorbed, but with reference to the quality of work done[33]—the genuine community standard of value. In an informal but all the more pervasive way, the school life organizes itself on a social basis.[34]

Within this organization is found the principle of school discipline or order. Of course, order is simply a thing which is relative to an end. If you have the end in view of forty or fifty children learning certain set lessons, to be recited to a teacher, your discipline must be devoted to securing that result.[35] But if the end in view is the development of a spirit of social co-operation and community life, discipline must grow out of and be relative to such an aim[36]. There is little of one sort of order where things are in process of construction;[37] there is a certain disorder in any busy workshop; there is not silence; persons are not engaged in maintaining certain fixed physical postures; their books thus and so. They are doing a variety of things, and there is the confusion, the bustle, that results from activity. But out of the occupation, out of doing things that are to produce results, and out of doing these in a social and co-operative way, there is born a discipline of its own kind and type. Our whole conception of school discipline changes when we get this point of view. In critical moments we all realize that only discipline that stands by us, the only training that becomes intuition, is that got through life itself.[38] That we learn from experience, and from books or the saying of others only as they are related to experience, are not mere phrases.[39] But the school has been so set apart, so isolated from the ordinary conditions and motives of life,[40] that the place where children are sent for discipline is the one place in the world where it is most difficult to get experience—the mother of all discipline worth the name. It is only when a narrow and fixed image of traditional school discipline dominates that one is in any danger of overlooking that deeper and infinitely wider discipline that comes from having a part to do in constructive work, in contributing to a result which, social in spirit, is none the less obvious and tangible in form[41]—and hence in a form with reference to which responsibility may be exacted and accurate judgment passed.

The great thing to keep in mind, then, regarding the introduction into the school of various forms of active occupation, is that through them the entire spirit of the school is renewed.[42] It has a chance to affiliate itself with life, to become the child's habitat, where he learns through directed living, instead of being only a place to learn lessons having an abstract and remote reference to some possible living to be done in the future.[43] It gets a chance to be a miniature community, an embryonic society. This is the fundamental fact.

注　释

1　本文选自约翰·杜威的《学校与社会进步》。

2   That which interests us most naturally is the progress made by the individual child of our acquaintance, his normal physical development, his advance in ability to read, write, and figure, his growth in the knowledge of geography and history, improvement in manners, habits of promptness, order, and industry. 因此，最令人感兴趣的当然是我们所熟悉的个别儿童的进步，他的体格的正常发展，他的读、写、算能力的提高，他的史地知识的增长，态度以及敏捷、守秩序和勤劳的习惯的改善。

That which interests us most 在句中作主语, is 是系词, the progress 是表语, made by the individual child of our acquaintance, 作 the progress 的定语, his normal physical development, his advance in ability to read, write, and figure, his growth in the knowledge of geography and history, improvement in manners, habits of promptness, order, and industry 都是 the progress 的同位语, 起补充说明作用。

3   acted upon, it destroys our democracy: 如果那样做，就会破坏我们的民主。

act upon/on 意思是"根据某事物"，比如: Acting on information received, the police raided the club. 警方根据所获情报，突然搜查了那个俱乐部。

4   at the disposal of its future members: 交给它的未来的成员去安排

at the disposal of/at one's disposal: 供任意使用，可自行支配。比如: Students have a well-stocked library at their disposal. 学生有个藏书丰富的图书馆，非常方便。

5   All its better thoughts of itself it hopes to realize through the new possibilities thus opened to its future self. 社会所实现的关于它自身的一切美好的想法都希望通过各种新的可能途径提供给自己的未来。

open to: 可利用的。比如: Their whole attitude to these negotiations is open to criticism. 他们对这些谈判的整个态度诚可批判。

6   as Horace Mann said, "Where anything is growing, one former is worth a thousand reformers." 正如贺拉斯·曼说的:"在任何事物生长的地方，一个塑造者胜过一千个再造者。（贺拉斯·曼，1796—1859，美国教育家。）

7   Otherwise, changes in the school institution and tradition will be looked at as the arbitrary inventions of particular teachers, at the worst transitory fads, and at the best merely improvements in certain details. 否则，我们会把学校制度和传统的变革看成是某些教师的任意创造。最坏的是赶时髦，最好的也只是某些细节上的改善。

at (the) worst: 最坏的话; at (the) best: 最好的话。比如: She is at worst corrupt, and at best has been knowingly breaking the rules. 就最坏的话说，她是腐败，就最好的话说，她是故意违反了规定。

8   conceive of the locomotive or the telegraph as the personal devices: 把机车和电报机看成是个人的发明

conceive of...as: 构思，看成。比如: He conceives of society as a jungle where only the finest survive. 他认为社会是一个只有适者才能生存的弱肉强食之地。

9   The modification going on in the method and curriculum of education is as much a product of the changed social situation, and as much an effort to meet the needs of the new society that is forming, as are changes in modes of industry and commerce. 教育方法和课程正在发生的

2. The School and Social Progress　学校与社会进步

变化如同工商业方式的变化一样,是社会情况改变的产物,是适应在形成中的新社会的需要的一种努力。

as much...as:情况(程度)与……相同。后一个 as 引导一个从句。比如：He is as much a stranger in the village today as he was the first summer he arrived.他今天在村里仍是个陌生人,就像他来到村子的第一个夏天那样。

10　No number of object-lessons, got up as object-lessons for the sake of giving information, can afford even the shadow of a substitute for acquaintance with the plants and animals of the farm and garden acquired through actual living among them and caring for them. 为灌输知识而组织的实物教学,不管有多少,绝不能代替关于农场和田园的动植物的直接知识,这种直接知识是通过在动植物中的实际生活,即照料动植物而获得的。

for the sake of/for one's sake:为了……起见,为了……缘故。比如：The company has decided foe economy's sake to close down this department.出于省钱的考虑,公司决定关闭这个部门。

acquaintance with:熟悉,了解。比如：Sadly, my acquaintance with Spain literature is limited. 可悲的是我对西班牙文学的了解是有限的。

11　No training of sense-organs in school, introduced for the sake of training, can begin to compete with the alertness and fullness of sense-life that comes through daily intimacy and interest in familiar occupations. 学校中为了训练而设的感官训练的学科,不能与每天那种生动的、丰富的感官生活相比拟,因为它来自亲切的、有趣味的普通的职业活动。

本句的主干部分是：No training of sense-organs...can begin to compete with..., that 引导的定语从句修饰先行词 sense-life, compete with 意思是竞争、对抗。比如：Several companies are competing with each other for the contract. 几家公司正为争取一项合同而互相竞争。

12　compare with:同……相比较。比如：He cannot compare with Shakespeare as a writer of tragedies.在悲剧写作方面他根本不能与莎士比亚相比。

13　At present, concentration of industry and division of labor have practically eliminated household and neighborhood occupations. 当前,工业的集中和分工,实际上已经消灭了家庭和近邻的各种职业。

eliminate:消除。比如：The police have eliminated two suspects from their enquiry. 警方从调查中已排除了两名嫌疑人。

14　But it is useless to bemoan the departure of the good old days of children's modesty, reverence, and implicit obedience, if we expect merely by bemoaning and by exhortation to bring them back. 但是,哀叹美好往日孩子们质朴、谦恭和绝对服从的品质的消失,一味希望仅靠哀叹和说教把它们挽回来,那是无济于事的。

bemoan:哀叹,抱怨。比如：Researchers at universities are always bemoaning their lack of funds.大学里的研究员总是抱怨自己不足。

15　We must recognize our compensations—the increase in toleration, in breadth of social judgment, the larger acquaintance with human nature, the sharpened alertness in reading signs of character and interpreting social situations, greater accuracy of adaptation to differing per-

19

sonalities, contact with greater commercial activities. 我们必须认识到由于这个根本改变所得到的一些好处：宽容精神的增长，社会见识的扩大，对于人性的更多的了解，从外在的表现识别人的性格和判断社会状况的敏锐性，适应各种不同人格的准确性，接触更多商业上的活动。

  adaptation to：对……适应。比如：Evolution occurs as a result of adaptation to new environments. 进化是对新环境适应的产物。

  contact with：接触。比如：Have you been in contact with anyone with the disease? 你接触过这种病的患者吗？

16. How shall we retain these advantages, and yet introduce into the school something occupations which exact personal responsibilities and which train the child in relation to the physical realities of life? 我们怎样保留这些好处，怎样将严格要求个人负责和培养儿童同外界现实生活有关的各种作业引进到学校中来呢？

  in relation to：与……有关。比如：She used the map to discover where she was in relation to her surroundings. 她对照四周环境看地图来搞清他的位置。

17. This has not been done "on purpose," with a full consciousness that the school must now supply that factor of training formerly taken care of in the home, but rather by instinct, by experimenting and finding that such work takes a vital hold of pupils and gives them something which was not to be got in any other way. 这样做并不是"有目的地"、充分地意识到现在学校必须提供那些过去由家庭负责的教育因素，而是本能地经过试验发现这类作业能生动地吸引住学生，并给予他们以任何其他方式得不到的东西。

  此句中含有 not...but... 结构，在前一句中的第一个 that 引导是 consciousness 的同位语从句，第二个 that 是指示代词，taken 是过去分词作 training 的定语。在后一句中 that 引导的是宾语从句，修饰 which 引导的是定语从句，修饰 something。

18. If we were to cross-examine even those who are most favorably disposed to the introduction of this work into our school system, we should, I imagine, generally find the main reasons to be that such work engages the full spontaneous interest and attention of the children. 如果我们仔细询问那些甚至最乐于把这种作业介绍到我们学校里来的人们，我想，我们就会发现这样做的主要理由是，这种作业能吸引儿童强烈的自发兴趣和注意力。

  本句是一个由 if 引导的虚拟条件句，表示将来时间，本句结构是：If we were to..., we should (would) find... 相同的表示还有：If sb should do/sb did..., sb would do..., 比如：If she were to try harder, she would pass the examination. 如果她再努力写，她会通过考试的。

  I imagine 是插入语。

19. It prepares them to some extent for the practical duties of later life. 在某种程度上，它为他们未来生活的实际责任作好了准备。

  to some extent：达到某种程度。比如：To some extent you are correct. 在某种程度上你是正确的。

20. when speaking directly of the relationship of the school to the child：当谈到学校对儿童的关系时

2. The School and Social Progress 学校与社会进步

speak of:谈到,提到。比如:She didn't speak of her husband at all. 她完全没谈到她的丈夫。

21 We must conceive of work in wood and metal, of weaving, sewing, and cooking, as methods of living and learning, not as distinct studies. 我们必须把木工、金工、纺织、缝纫、烹调看作是生活和学习的方法,而不是各种特殊的科目。

22 as ways in which these needs have been met by the growing insight and ingenuity of man:看作是满足这些日益发展的人的理解力和创造力的需要的方式

which 在这里引导的是定语从句,in the way 是习惯用法,指"以……方式"。比如:The way in which you answered the questions was admirable. 你回答问题的方法令人敬佩。

23 A society is a number of people held together because they are working along common lines, in a common spirit, and with reference to common aims. 社会是由一些循着共同的路线,具有共同的精神,并参照共同的目的而活动的个人聚集在一起而形成的。

24 There is something to do, some activity to be carried on, requiring natural divisions of labor, selection of leaders and followers, mutual cooperation and emulation. 在那里,有些事情要做,有些活动要进行,还要自然的分工,挑选领袖和成员,互相合作和比美竞胜。

25 Upon the ethical side, the tragic weakness of the present school is that it endeavors to prepare future members of the social order in a medium in which the conditions of the social spirit are eminently wanting. 在伦理方面,目前学校可悲的弱点在于他所致力的,在社会精神的条件显得十分缺乏的情况下培养出来的社会秩序的未来成员。

that 引导的是表语从句,in which 引导的是定语从句,修饰先行词 medium。

26 The psychological difference, the change from more or less passive and inert recipiency and restraint to one of buoyant outgoing energy, is so obvious as fairly to strike one in the face. 从多少有点儿被动的、呆板的接受和拘谨变为生气勃勃的状态,这种心理上的差别是那么的显而易见,使人触动。

本句主干部分是:The psychological difference...is so obvious as to strike one in the face. the change...作主语的同位语。

27 It tends very naturally to pass into selfishness. 很显然会变成自私自利。

28 There is no obvious social motive for the acquirement of mere learning, there is no clear social gain in success thereat. 缺乏鲜明的社会动机而只求单纯的学习收获,即使有了成绩,也不能明显地有益于社会。

29 A comparison of results in the recitation or in the examination to see which child has succeeded in getting ahead of others in storing up, in accumulating, the maximum of information. 比较背诵和考试的结果,看看哪个儿童在强记和积储大量的知识方面所取得的成绩优于其他儿童。

succeed in doing:成功地做成某事。比如:The campaign has certainly succeeded in raising public awareness of the issue. 这项活动在唤起公众对这一问题的意识方面肯定是成功的。

30 So thoroughly is this prevailing atmosphere that for one child to help another in his task has become a school crime. 这种流行的风气很普遍,一个儿童对其他儿童的学习作了帮助,就算是犯罪。

此句是由 so...that 引导的结果状语从句，so 带副词提前，句子要求进行倒装。

31 Where the school work consists in simply learning lessons, mutual assistance, instead of being the most natural form of co-operation and association, becomes a clandestine effort to relieve one's neighbor of his proper duties. 在学校的作业只是学习课文的地方，互相帮助就不是一种合作的和联合的自然形式，而变成了接触邻近同学固有的义务的一种秘密行为。
consist in:在于。比如:The beauty of the plan consists in its simplicity. 这计划的好处在于简单易行。

32 Helping others, instead of being a form of charity which impoverishes the recipient, is simply an aid in setting free the powers and furthering the impulse of the one helped. 帮助别人不是使接受者更加依赖别人的一种施舍形式，而是帮助被帮助者发挥能量，继续前进。
本句的主干部分是:helping others...is...an aid. further:促进，推进。比如:He has probably done more to further the cause of interracial harmony than any other person. 他在促进种族和睦的事业上可能做得比其他任何人都要多。

33 not with regard to the quantity of information personally absorbed, but with reference to the quality of work done：这不是关于个人吸取的知识多少的问题，而是按照所完成的作业质量的问题
not...but...:不是……而是;with regard to:关于;with reference to:关于

34 In an informal but all the more pervasive way, the school life organizes itself on a social basis. 在一种非正式的但更普遍深刻的方式下，学校生活是以社会为基础而组织起来的。

35 If you have the end in view of forty or fifty children learning certain set lessons, to be recited to a teacher, your discipline must be devoted to securing that result. 如果你的目的是使40—50个儿童学习某些现成的课文，并在教师面前背诵出来，那么你的训练方法必定力求达到这个结果。
in view of:考虑到，鉴于。比如:In view of what you said, I think we should reconsider our proposed course of action. 听了你的一席话，我认为我们需要重新考虑我们原先提议的行动计划。
be devoted to:致力于，献身于。比如:Over half the speech was devoted to the issue of unemployment. 他的演说用了大半时间讲事业问题。

36 discipline must grow out of and be relative to such an aim. 训练方法必须从这个目的出发并和这个目的相联系。
be relative to:有关，相关。如:The amount of petrol a car uses is relative to its speed. 汽车耗油量与车速有关。

37 There is little of one sort of order where things are in process of construction, 当活动正在进行的时候，就会缺少一定的秩序。
in(the)process of:从事某项活动的过程中。比如:We are in the process of moving house. 我们还正在搬家呢。

38 In critical moments we all realize that only discipline that stands by us, the only training that becomes intuition, is that got through life itself. 在关键时刻我们大家都认识到，我们所依赖的惟一训练，成为了直观的惟一的训练，它是通过生活本身得来的。

stands by 意思是"遵守,信守",比如:She still stands by every word she said. 她仍然信守自己说的每一句话。

39 That we learn from experience, and from books or the saying of others only as they are related to experience, are not mere phrases. 从经验中学习,从与经验有关的书本或别人的言论中学习,并不只是一句空话。
that 引导的是主语从句, only as they are related to experience 作 books or the saying of others 的定语。

40 But the school has been so set apart, so isolated from the ordinary conditions and motives of life: 但是学校却如此地脱离和孤立于社会生活的一般情况和动机。
set apart:使某人/某物与……隔离,使某人/某物独特。比如:His use of language sets him apart from most other modern writers. 他对语言的运用在现代作家中别具一格。

41 It is only when a narrow and fixed image of traditional school discipline dominates that one is in any danger of overlooking that deeper and infinitely wider discipline that comes from having a part to do in constructive work, in contributing to a result which, social in spirit, is none the less obvious and tangible in form. 只有当传统学校训练中狭隘而死板的形象统治一切时,人们才处于轻视更为深刻而无限广泛的训练的危险,这种训练来自参与建造活动,儿童从中贡献出自己的力量并收到一定成果。从精神上说,这成果是社会性的,从形式上说,它仍然是显而易见的,可以感知的。
此句是强调句,状语从句 only when a narrow and fixed image of traditional school discipline dominates 是被强调部分,第一个 that 是引导强调句的,第二个 that 是引导定语从句的,修饰先行词 discipline。

42 The great thing to keep in mind, then, regarding the introduction into the school of various forms of active occupation, is that through them the entire spirit of the school is renewed. 因此,我们应注意学校采用各种不同形式的主动作业这一重大的事情,通过它们,学校的整个精神焕然一新。
此句的主干部分是:The great thing... is...that through them.... regarding:关于,至于。比如:She said nothing regarding your request. 她对你的要求只字不提。

43 It has a chance to affiliate itself with life, to become the child's habitat, where he learns through directed living, instead of being only a place to learn lessons having an abstract and remote reference to some possible living to be done in the future. 在那里,儿童通过直接生活进行学习,而不仅仅是学习课文,这些课文对于他们将来可能从事的生活来说,乃是抽象的和间接的东西。
affiliate itself with/to:隶属于。比如:We are affiliated with the national group. 我们隶属于国营组织。/The school has affiliated itself to a national association of driving school. 这个学校附属于一个全国驾驶学校协会。

练 习

1. 回答问题

   (1) Why are some people most favorably disposed to introduce the occupations which train the child in relation to the physical realities of life into the school system?

   (2) What does the man tend to be like if he is merely absorbed in facts and truths and thinks it's an individual affair?

   (3) What is the spirit of the dominating note of the recitation after the school assigns the students active work?

   (4) How do we get the only discipline that we depend on?

   (5) What is the resource of the rewarding discipline and where is the proper place to get experience?

2. 判断正误

   (1) What the best and wisest parent wants for his own child is not what the community want for all of its children.

   (2) The changes in modes of industry and commerce is a product of the changed social situation, but the method and curriculum of education is not.

   (3) For the sake of giving information, the object-lessons can take the place of the acquaintance with the plants and animals of the farm and guard.

   (4) In an informal and all the more pervasive way, the school life organizes itself on a social basis.

   (5) School is only the place set apart in which to learn lessons.

3. 选词填空

   open to, at worst, compare with, devote to, in (the) process of, eliminate from, at one's disposal, contact with, relative to, compete with

   (1) He has said he will use all weapons _____.

   (2) This library is not _____ the general public.

   (3) _____ we'll have to sell the house so as to settle our debts.

   (4) They found themselves _____ foreign companies for a share of the market.

   (5) _____ our small apartment, our uncle's house seemed like a palace.

   (6) He _____ the contest in the fourth round.

   (7) The report recommends that more resources _____ teaching.

   (8) We are still _____ redecorating the house.

   (9) Your foot keep _____ the pedal at all times.

   (10) The facts he knows are _____ the problem, so he must come here this afternoon.

4. 句型模拟

(1) only + 状语位于句首

(2) if 引导的表示将来时间的虚拟条件句

5. 英译汉

(1) What the best and wisest parent wants for his own child, that must the community want for all of its children.

(2) These considerations mean much to the city-bred child of today.

(3) It keeps them alert and active, instead of passive and receptive; it makes them more useful, more capable, and hence more inclined to be helpful at home.

(4) The common needs and aims demand a growing interchange of thought and growing unity of sympathetic feeling.

(5) Indeed, to those whose image of the school is rigidly set the change is sure to give a shock.

6. 汉译英

(1) 我觉得我舅舅仍把我看成是四岁的小孩子。(conceive of)

(2) 我们不要为了几镑钱闹得不和。(for the sake of)

(3) 恐怕我与他的著作只是泛泛之交。(acquaintance with)

(4) 我们坚信他会成功地完成那项艰巨的任务。(succeed in)

(5) 因天气关系,我们要取消此次郊游。(in view of)

7. 写作指导

For this part, you are required to write a composition on the topic "A Successful School". The following points taken from the text are useful expressions for your reference:

- no training competing with the alertness and fullness of sense-life that comes through daily intimacy and interest in familiar occupation
- introduce the occupations which exact personal responsibilities and which train the child in relation to the physical realities of life
- toward the introduction of so-called manual training, shopwork, and the household arts—sewing and cooking
- have the motive and the cement of social organization
- have obvious social motive
- helping others, co-operating, associating
- a spirit of free communication, of interchange of ideas, suggestions, results, both successes and failures of previous experiences
- learn from experience and from books or the sayings of others as they are related to experience

3. Democracy and Education[1]
民主主义与教育

John Dewey
约翰·杜威

《民主主义与教育》为我们展示了一幅宏大而清晰的教育画面,书中的核心观点教育即社会是这幅巨画的底色。在杜威看来,教育的意义显然不是围墙内的学校教育的范畴,即使是学校教育,杜威也并不认为它应该具有"围墙的局限性"。于是,他的宏大理论向人们清晰地展示了教育、社会与人三者之间互相依存必须具备的大环境,即民主社会中的教育和教育中的民主是人得以完善发展的根基。杜威的这部著作告诉我们,如果不拓宽看待教育的视野,把教育与社会构架成一个互动系统,就会陷入虚无主义的境地或者是功利主义的泥沼之中,即要么构想出纯而又纯的教育理想,要么就使教育成为单纯的谋利工具。教育是一种社会现实,而不是教育本身所引发的现象的这种定位,深信教育的实践需要研究社会。

Applications in Education

There is nothing peculiar about educational aims. They are just like aims in any directed occupation. The educator, like the farmer, has certain things to do, certain resources with which to do, and certain obstacles with which to contend.[2] The conditions with which the farmer deals, whether as obstacles or resources, have their own structure and operation independently of any purpose of his.[3] Seeds sprout, rain falls, the sun shines, insects devour, blight comes, the seasons change. His aim is simply to utilize these various conditions, to make his activities and their energies work together, instead of against one another. It would be absurd if the farmer set up a purpose of farming, without any reference to these conditions of soil, climate, characteristic of plant growth, etc.[4] His purpose is simply a foresight of the consequences of his energies connected with those of the things about him[5], a foresight used to direct his movements from day to day. Foresight of possible consequences leads to more careful and extensive observation of the nature and performances of the things he had to do with, and to laying out a plan—that is, of a certain order in the acts to be performed.[6]

It is the same with the educator, whether parent or teacher. It is as absurd for the latter to set up his "own" aims as the proper objects of the growth of the children as it would be for the farmer to set up an ideal of farming irrespective of conditions.[7] Aims mean acceptance of responsibility for the observations, anticipations, and arrangements required in carrying on a function—whether farming or educating.[8] Any aim is of value so far as it assists observation, choice, and planning in carrying on activity from moment to moment and hour to hour, if it gets in the way of the individual's own common sense (as it will surely do if imposed from without or accepted on authority) it does harm[9].

And it is well to remind ourselves that education as such has no aims.[10] Only persons, parents, and teachers, etc, have aims, not an abstract idea like education. And consequently their purposes are indefinitely varied, differing with different children, changing as children grow and with the growth of experience on the part of the one who teaches.[11] Even the most valid aims which can be put in words will, as words, do more harm than good unless one recognizes that they are not aims, but rather suggestions to educators as to how to observe, how to look ahead, and how to choose in liberating and directing the energies of the concrete situations in which they find themselves.[12] As a recent writer has said: "To lead this boy to read Scott's novels instead of old Sleuth's stories, to teach this girl to sew; to root out the habit of bullying from John's make-up[13]; to prepare this class to study medicine,—these are samples of the millions of aims we have actually before us in the concrete work of education." Bearing these qualifications in mind[14], we shall proceed to state some of the characteristics found in all good educational aims.

(1) An educational aim must be founded upon the intrinsic activities and needs (including original instincts and acquired habits) of the given individual to be educated.[15] The tendency of such an aim as preparation is, as we have seen, to omit existing powers, and find the aim in some remote accomplishment or responsibility.[16] In general, there is a disposition to take considerations which are dear to the hearts of adults and set them up as ends irrespective of the capacities of those educated. There is also an inclination to propound aims which are so uniform as to neglect the specific powers and requirements of an individual, forgetting that all learning is something which happens to an individual at a given time and place.[17] The larger range of perception of the adult is of great value in observing the abilities and weaknesses of the young, in deciding what they may amount to. Thus the artistic capacities of the adult exhibit what certain tendencies of the child are capable of, if we did not have the adult achievements we should be without assurance as to the significance of the drawing, reproducing, modeling, coloring activities of childhood.[18] So if it were not for adult language, we should not be able to see the import of the babbling impulses of infancy.[19] But it is one thing to use adult accomplishments as a context in which to place and survey the doings of childhood and youth, it is quite another to set them up as a fixed aim without regard to the concrete activities of those educated.[20]

(2) An aim must be capable of translation into a method of cooperation with the activities of those undergoing instruction. It must suggest the kind of environment needed to liberate and to organize their capacities.[21] Unless it lends itself to the construction of specific procedures,[22] and unless these procedures test, correct, and amplify the aim, the latter is worthless. Instead of helping the specific task of teaching, it prevents the use of ordinary judgment in observing and sizing up the situation. It operates to exclude recognition of everything except what squares up with the fixed end in view.[23] Every rigid aim just because it is rigidly given seems to render it unnecessary to give careful attention to concrete conditions. Since it must apply anyhow, what is the use of noting details which do not count? The vice of externally imposed ends has deep roots.[24]

Teachers receive them from superior authorities, these authorities accept them from what is current in the community. The teachers impose them upon children.[25] As a first consequence, the intelligence of the teacher is not free, it is confined to receiving the aims laid down from above.[26] Too rarely is the individual teacher so free from the dictation of authoritative supervisor, textbook on methods, prescribed course of study, etc, that he can let his mind come to close quarters with the pupil's mind and the subject matter.[27] This distrust of the teacher's experience is then reflected in lack of confidence in the responses of pupils. The latter receive their aims through a double or treble external imposition, and are constantly confused by the conflict between the aims which are natural to their own experience at the time and those in which they are taught to acquiesce.[28] Until the democratic criterion of the intrinsic significance of every growing experience is recognized, we shall be intellectually confused by the demand for adaptation to external aims.[29]

(3) Educators have to be on their guard against ends that are alleged to be general and ultimate.[30] Every activity, however specific, is, of course, general in its ramified connections, for it leads out indefinitely into other things. So far as a general idea makes us move alive to these connections, it cannot be too general.[31] But "general" also means "abstract," or detached from all specific context[32]. And such abstractness means remoteness, and throws us back, once more, upon teaching and learning as mere means of getting ready for an end disconnected from the means.[33] That education is literally and all the time its own reward means that no alleged study or discipline is educative unless it is worth while in its own immediate having.[34] A truly general aim broadens the outlook, it stimulates one to take more consequences (connections) into account. This means a wider and more flexible observation of means. The more interacting forces, for example, the farmer takes into account, the more varied will be his immediate resources. He will see a greater number of possible starting places, and a greater number of ways of getting at what he wants to do[35]. The fuller one's conception of possible future achievements, the less his present activity is tied down to a small number of alternatives.[36] If one knew enough, one could start almost anywhere and sustain his activities continuously and fruitfully[37].

Understanding then the term general or comprehensive aim simply in the sense of a broad survey of the field of present activities, we shall take up some of the larger ends which have currency in the educational theories of the day, and consider what light they throw upon the immediate concrete and diversified aims which are always the educator's real concern.[38] We premise (as indeed immediately follows from what has been said) that there is no need of making a choice among them or regarding them as competitors. When we come to act in a tangible way we have to select or choose a particular act at a particular time, but any number of comprehensive ends may exits without competition, since they mean simply different ways of looking at the same scene. One cannot climb a number of different mountains simultaneously, but the views had when different mountains are ascended supplement one another: they do not set up incompatible, competing worlds. Or, putting the matter in a slightly different way, one statement of an end may suggest certain questions and observations, and another statement another set of questions, calling for other observations.[39] Then the more general ends we have, the better. One statement will emphasize what another slurs over.⁴⁰ What a plurality of hypotheses does for the scientific investigator, a plurality of stated aims may do for the instructor.

注　释

1. 本文选自约翰·杜威的《民主主义与教育》。
2. The educator, like the farmer, has certain things to do, certain resources with which to do, and certain obstacles with which to contend. 教育者如同农民一样，也有一些事情要做，有一些做事情的手段，有一些障碍要排除。
   句子的主干部分 The educator...has...certain things..., certain resources..., certain obstacles...，动词不定式短语 to do, with which to do, with which to contend 分别作各自所修饰的中心词的定语。
   contend with: 适应，对付。比如：She has a lot of problems to contend with. 她有许多问题要解决。
3. The conditions with which the farmer deals, whether as obstacles or resources, have their own structure and operation independently of any purpose of his. 无论是障碍还是可以使用的资源，农民所要应付的环境，都具有它们自己的结构和作用，与农民的任何目的无关。
   independently: 独立地，经常与 of 连用。比如：Each part of the organization operates independently of the others. 这个组织的每个部分都是独立运作的。
4. It would be absurd if the farmer set up a purpose of farming, without any reference to these conditions of soil, climate, characteristic of plant growth, etc. 如果农民不考虑土壤、气候以及植物生长特性等条件，确定一个农耕目的，那便是荒谬的。
   set up: 确立。比如：The government has set up a working party to look into the problem of drug abuse. 政府已成立工作组调查滥用毒品问题。
   without reference to sb/sth: 不涉及，不顾及。比如：She is used all these invitations without any reference to her superiors. 她没有请示上级擅自把所有这些请柬都发了出去。
5. a foresight of the consequences of his energies connected with those of the things about him: 预见他的能量和他周围各种事物相结合的能量的结果
   本句中 connected 是过去分词修饰 energies。
6. Foresight of possible consequences leads to more careful and extensive observation of the nature and performances of the things he had to do with, and to laying out a plan—that is, of a certain order in the acts to be performed. 预见可能产生的结果，使他对他所要做的事情的性质和运动进行更审慎、更广泛的观察，能够使他拟订一个工作计划，即规定一个运动的程序。
   在 and to laying out a plan 中，and 后面省略了 leads。lay out: 设计，制订。比如：Max listened closely as Linda laid out his plan. 当林达解释她的计划时，麦克斯认真地听。
7. It is as absurd for the latter to set up his "own" aims as the proper objects of the growth of the children as it would be for the farmer to set up an ideal of farming irrespective of conditions. 如果家长或教师提出他们"自己的"目的，作为儿童生长的正式目标，这和农民不顾

环境情况提出一个理想一样,荒谬可笑。

as absurd...as 结构是同级比较状语从句。

irrespective of:不顾,不考虑。比如:We must succeed irrespective of someone's ethnic origins. 不管伤亡多少,我们一定要成功。

8   Aims mean acceptance of responsibility for the observations, anticipations, and arrangements required in carrying on a function—whether farming or educating. 目的就是对所从事的一种事业,不管是农业还是教育,进行的观察、预测和工作安排承担责任。

本句的主要成分是:Aims...mean...acceptance and arrangements. required in carrying on a function 是过去分词短语,作 observations, anticipations, and arrangements 的定语。

9   ...if it gets in the way of the individual's own common sense (as it will surely do if imposed from without or accepted on authority) it does harm. 如果这个目的妨碍个人的常识(如果目的是从外面强加的;如果因迫于威权而接受的,肯定要妨碍个人自己的常识),这个目的就是有害的。

in the way:阻碍。比如:May nothing stand in the way of your future happiness together! 祝愿你们万事如意,未来幸福!

common sense:常识

10 And it is well to remind ourselves that education as such has no aims. 我们要提醒自己教育本身并无目的。

as such:本身。比如:He did not oppose the scheme as such. 他并不反对计划本身。

11 And consequently their purposes are indefinitely varied, differing with different children, changing as children grow and with the growth of experience on the part of the one who teaches. 因此,他们的目的是变化无穷的,因不同儿童而异,随着儿童的生长和教育者经历的增长而异。

on the part of/on one's part:由某人做出……。比如:The agreement has been kept on my part but not on his. 我一直遵守协议,但他并不遵守。

12 Even the most valid aims which can be put in words will, as words, do more harm than good unless one recognizes that they are not aims, but rather suggestions to educators as to how to observe, how to look ahead, and how to choose in liberating and directing the energies of the concrete situations in which they find themselves. 即使是能用文字表达的最合逻辑的目的,除非人们认识到这些并不是目的,而是给教育者的建议,在解放和引导他们所处的具体环境的各种力量时,怎样观察,怎样展望未来,和怎样选择,那么这种目的,作为文字,将是有害无益的。

本句是由 unless 引导的条件状语从句,主句中主干部分是:The most valid aims...will...do more harm than good...more...than 是"与其说……不如说"的意思,more 后不接形容词或副词的比较级形式,than 的前后两项可以跟形容词并用,也可以跟名词、代词、动词、介词短语等。比如:He is more diligent than clever. 与其说他聪明,不如说他勤奋。/It is more a poem than a picture. 与其说这是一幅画,不如说是一首诗。

as to 意思是关于后面可跟名词、动名词、还可接疑问词 what, where...+ 不定式结构,还可接 whether, when, what, where, how 等引导的从句。如:I have no doubt as to his innocence. 对于他的无辜我毫不怀疑。/I am not certain as to when he come back. 我不敢肯定他将什么时候回来。

13　to root out the habit of bullying from John's make-up: 把约翰性格中横行霸道的习惯彻底根除掉

　　root out 意思是"找到并根除"，比如：Ms Li has been appointed to root out inefficiency. 李女士已被任命去彻底根除这家公司中的低效率。

14　bearing these qualifications in mind... 牢记以上这些条件

　　bear...in mind: 记住。比如：Thank you for your advice, I'll bear it in mind. 谢谢你的劝告，我会记住的。

15　An educational aim must be founded upon the intrinsic activities and needs (including original instincts and acquired habits) of the given individual to be educated. 一个教育目的一定要由接受教育的特定个人的固有活动和需要而定(包括原始本能和获得习惯)。

16　The tendency of such an aim as preparation is, as we have seen, to omit existing powers, and find the aim in some remote accomplishment or responsibility. 正如我们前面讲过的那样，把预备作为教育目的，往往会不顾个人享有能力，而把某种遥远的成就或职责作为目的。

17　There is also an inclination to propound aims which are so uniform as to neglect the specific powers and requirements of an individual, forgetting that all learning is something which happens to an individual at a given time and place. 还有一种倾向，就是提出千篇一律的目的，忽视个人的特殊能力和需要，忘记了一切知识都是一个人在特定时间和特定地点获得的。

　　which are so uniform as 作 aims 的定语，to propound aims which are so uniform as to neglect the specific powers and requirements of an individual 是动词不定式短语作 inclination 的定语；forgetting 现在分词表示伴随动作，省略了 There is also an inclination，本句完整的形式应是：There is also an inclination forgetting that all learning is something which happens to an individual at a given time and place.

18　If we did not have the adult achievements we should be without assurance as to the significance of the drawing, reproducing, modeling, coloring activities of childhood. 如果我们没有成人在艺术上的成就，就没有把握了解儿童时期的绘画、复制、塑造和着色活动的意义。

19　So if it were not for adult language, we should not be able to see the import of the babbling impulses of infancy. 同样，如果没有成人的语言，我们就不能了解婴儿咿呀学语的冲动有何意义。

　　if it were not for: 要不是，如果没有。表示同现在事实相反的假设，主句用虚拟语气。比如：If it were not for the rain, the crops should (would) become withered. 要是天不下雨，庄稼就干枯了。

20　But it is one thing to use adult accomplishments as a context in which to place and survey the doings of childhood and youth, it is quite another to set them up as a fixed aim without regard to the concrete activities of those educated. 但是把成人的成就作为一种参考，用以度量和观察儿童和青年的活动，这是一回事；把成人的成就定为固定的目的，不顾受教育者

的具体活动，那完全是另一回事。

one thing...quite another：一回事，另一回事。比如：Feeling guilty for the homeless is one thing, finding cheap secure accommodation for them is quite another thing. 对无家可归者感到内疚是一回事，而为他们提供低廉由安全的住房则又是另一回事。

21 An aim must be capable of translation into a method of cooperation with the activities of those undergoing instruction. 一个教育目的，必须能转化为与受教育者的活动进行合作的方法。

22 It lends itself to the construction of specific procedures：有助于制订具体的进行程序。
lend itself to 意思是"有助于、合适于"，比如：The novel lends itself to dramatization for television. 这部小说适合于拍成电视剧。
sizing up the situation：估量所面临的情境。size up 意思是"打量，估量"，比如：The two cats walked in circles around each other, sizing each other up. 两只猫互相绕着圈，彼此打量着。

23 It operates to exclude recognition of everything except what squares up with the fixed end in view. 这种目的，除了与固定目标相符的事物以外，对其他事物概不承认。
square up with：相符，符合。比如：Your theory doesn't square with the known facts. 你的说法跟已知的事实不符。

24 The vice of externally imposed ends has deep roots. 从外部强加的教育目的的缺陷，根深蒂固。

25 The teachers impose them upon children. 教师把这些目的强加于儿童。
impose upon/on：强加于。比如：Colonial settlers imposed their own culture and religion on the countries that they conquered. 殖民主义者把他们自己的文化和宗教强加与被他们征服的国家。

26 It is confined to receiving the aims laid down from above. 他只许接受上级所规定的目的。
lay down：制定规则。比如：It is laid down that all applicants must sit a written exam. 根据规定，申请者一律要笔试。
be confined to sth, confine sb/sth in/to sth 是"限制在某个空间"的意思，比如：After her operation, she was confined to bed for a week. 手术后，她卧床一周。

27 Too rarely is the individual teacher so free from the dictation of authoritative supervisor, textbook on methods, prescribed course of study, etc, that he can let his mind come to close quarters with the pupil's mind and the subject matter. 教师难免受官厅督学、教学法指导书和规定的课程等等的支配，使他的思想不能和学生的思想以及教材紧密相连。
这是一个由 so...that 引导结果状语从句，否定副词 too rarely 提前，句子要进行倒装。本句可还原为：The individual teacher is too rarely free from.... free from：免受。比如：He wasn't free from punishment even though he neglected his duties. 即使他玩忽职守也未能免于惩罚。
come to/at close quarter with：接近。比如：The young man is at close quarters with the advanced technology. 这位年轻人总是关心先进技术。

28 The latter receive their aims through a double or treble external imposition, and are constant-

ly confused by the conflict between the aims which are natural to their own experience at the time and those in which they are taught to acquiesce. 学生由于外面双重或三重的强迫,接受他们的目的,他们经常处于两种目的冲突之中,无所适从。

The latter 在这里指的是学生,本句的主干是:The latter...receive aims and are constantly confused by the conflict。between...and...引导两个定语从句共同作 the conflict 的定语。acquiesce in 意思是"(不情愿地)接受或同意",比如:He reluctantly acquiesced in the plans. 他勉强同意了计划。

29 Until the democratic criterion of the intrinsic significance of every growing experience is recognized, we shall be intellectually confused by the demand for adaptation to external aims. 当我们承认每个正在发展的经验都具有内在意义这一民主主义的标准时,我们将会由于要适应外来目的的要求而在思想上陷于混乱。

30 Educators have to be on their guard against ends that are alleged to be general and ultimate. 教育者必须警惕所谓一般和终极的目的。

allege:声称。比如:It was alleged that John had struck Mr Liu on the head. 据称约翰打了刘先生的头部。

on one's guard against:警惕。如:It's wise to be on your guard against people who are trying to con you. 提防那些试图骗你的人是明智的。

31 It cannot be too general. 越一般越好。

cannot...too:怎样……也不过分。比如:It cannot be too strongly emphasized that mathematics is the basis of science. 数学是科学的基础,这一点无论怎样强调都不算过分。

32 detached from all specific context:和一切特殊的关系分开

detach...from...意思是"把……和……分开",比如:Detach the lower part of the form from this letter and return it to the above address. 从这封信上撕下表格的下面部分,(填好之后)寄回到上面的地址。

33 And such abstractness means remoteness, and throws us back, once more, upon teaching and learning as mere means of getting ready for an end disconnected from the means. 这种抽象性,又意味着遥远不切实际,这样又使我们返回到教和学,这种教和学仅仅是作为准备达到和它无关的目的的一种手段。

throw sb back upon/on:迫使某人依靠。比如:The television broke down, so we were thrown back on our own resources. 电视机坏了,我们只有自我消遣了。

34 That education is literally and all the time its own reward means that no alleged study or discipline is educative unless it is worth while in its own immediate having. 我们说教育确实而且总是有它自己的酬报,这就是说,除非所说的学习或训练有它自己的直接价值,这种学习或训练就没有教育意义。

be worthwhile (in):值得的。比如:It is worthwhile taking the trouble to explain a job fully to new employees. 给新雇员详细讲解一下工作要求,费点事也是值得的。

35 getting at what he wants to do:熟悉他所要做的事情

get at:熟悉。比如:The truth is sometimes difficult to get at. 有时真相不易搞清。

36 The fuller one's conception of possible future achievements, the less his present activity is

tied down to a small number of alternatives. 一个人对未来可能的成就的认识愈全面,他当前的活动就愈少束缚于少数可供选择的方法。

句型 the more...the more...,意思是"越来……越……"。tie sb down to 是"使某人受到约束"的意思,常用于被动语态 be tied down to。比如:Don't be tied to some petty restrictions. 不要让琐细的规则限制住。

37 sustain his activities continuously and fruitfully: 继续不断地、有成效地把活动持续下去 sustain:继续,维持。比如:We do not have sufficient resources to sustain our campaign for long. 我们没有足够的财力可把运动长期维持下去。

38 Understanding then the term general or comprehensive aim simply in the sense of a broad survey of the field of present activities, we shall take up some of the larger ends which have currency in the educational theories of the day, and consider what light they throw upon the immediate concrete and diversified aims which are always the educator's real concern. 所谓一般的目的或概括性的目的,意思不过是对现在活动的领域进行广泛的观察。有了这种了解,我们将就当代教育理论中流行的比较重大的目的,选取几个来讨论,并且研究这些目的能否使我们明白教育者真正关切的当前各种具体的目的。

39 Or, putting the matter in a slightly different way, one statement of an end may suggest certain questions and observations, and another statement another set of questions, calling for other observations. 或者,用稍稍不同的说法,带有一种目的的说法可以暗示某些问题和观察,带有另一种目的的说法可以暗示另一些问题,唤起别的观察。

put 这里是"讲"、"说"的意思,比如:Let me put it this way. 让我用这种方式。
call for 是"号召"、"呼唤"的意思,比如:The president called to national unity. 总统号召全国人民团结起来。

40 Then the more general ends we have, the better. One statement will emphasize what another slurs over. 因此,我们的目的越一般越好。一种说法可以强调另一种说法所忽略的地方。

练　习

1. 回答问题
   (1) What's the function of the adult language?
   (2) If teachers receive the imposed ends from superior authorities, what's the first consequence?
   (3) Students are constantly confused by the conflict between two aims, what are the two aims?
   (4) How many ends do educators have to be on their guard against?
   (5) What is the function of a truly general aim?

2. 判断正误
   (1) It is absurd for teacher or parent to set up his own aims as the proper objects of the growth of the children irrespective of the children's existing powers.

(2) In general, there is a disposition to take consideration which are dear to the hearts of the children and set them up as ends irrespective of the capacities of those educators.

(3) Even though the educational aim gets in the way of the individual's own common sense, it does no harm.

(4) An educational aim may not be translated into a method of cooperating with the activities of those undergoing instruction.

(5) An educational aim must be founded upon the intrinsic activities and needs of the given individual to be educated.

3. 选词填空

acquiesce in, root out, on the part of, size up, impose...on, lay down, on one's guard against, bear...in mind, as to, square with

(1) It was a mistake _____ Julia.

(2) He is always outspoken _____ what is right and what is wrong.

(3) I suggested you _____ the weeds before they take hold.

(4) We have no vacancies now, but we'll certainly _____ your application _____.

(5) We must _____ the situation before we decide what to do.

(6) The problem is that his story doesn't _____ the evidence.

(7) She _____ her ideas _____ the group.

(8) You can't _____ hard and fast rules.

(9) Her parents will never _____ such an unsuitable marriage.

(10) It's sensible for her to be _____ saying the wrong thing.

4. 句型模拟

(1) more...than

(2) if it were not for

5. 英译汉

(1) His aim is simply to utilize these various conditions, to make his activities and their energies work together, instead of against one another.

(2) Any aim is of value so far as it assists observation, choice, and planning in carrying on activity from moment to moment and hour to hour.

(3) And consequently their purposes are indefinitely varied, differing with different children, changing as children grow and with the growth of experience on the part of the one who teaches.

(4) Instead of helping the specific task of teaching, it prevents the use of ordinary judgment in observing and sizing up the situation.

(5) A truly general aim broadens the outlook; it stimulates one to take more consequences into account.

6. 汉译英

(1) 法律适用于所有的人,不分种族、信仰或肤色。(irrespective of)

(2) 九岁时他就得对付失去双亲之事。(contend with)

(3) 她决心要成功,而且不让任何事妨碍她。(get in one's way)

(4) 金钱本身很少带来幸福。(as such)

(5) 该电脑适合于多种用途。(lends itself to)

7. 写作指导

For this part, you are required to write a composition on the topic "What's the Aim of Education". The following points taken from the text are useful expressions for your reference:

- assist observation, choice, and planning in carrying on activity from moment to moment and hour to hour
- varied, differing with different children, changing as children grow and with the growth of experience on the part of the one who teaches
- be founded upon the intrinsic activities and needs of the given individual to be educated
- take consideration of the capacities of those educated and not neglect the specific powers and requirements of an individual
- lend itself to the construction of specific procedures, and test, correct and amplify the aim
- help the specific task of teaching, and help the teachers to observe and size up the situation
- give the teachers free to use their intelligence
- broaden the outlook; stimulates one to take more consequences into account

II

New Education
新教育

　　新教育是欧洲教育革新运动中的一种教育思潮。它创立于十九世纪末二十世纪初。随着欧洲国家工业化发展,垄断进一步形成而现在欧洲的一种反对传统教育理论和方法,广泛采用新的教育形式、内容和方法,革新已有教育的方方面面的教育运动。这一教育运动在实践上表现为"新学校"的兴起和发展;在理论上则表现为具有深厚自由主义色彩的理论的出现。这一新教育思潮力图使学校教育适应新的社会发展形势,它的理论与实践后来对世界的许多国家,特别是欧美的教育理论以及实践的发展产生了深远的影响。主要代表人物:蒙台梭利、爱伦·凯、罗素等。

　　十九世纪末英国的雷迪,德国的利茨和法国的穆兰,在远离城市的风景区开办一所乡村寄宿学校,破除传统的课程体系,注重近代语,开设农艺、手工劳动课程。1889年,英国的雷迪创办了一所新学校,雷迪认为,他的建校原则和目的是把学生培养成为在能力、智力、体力、个性及手工技巧等方面都能够得到和谐发展的人。他反对死读书本,主张教育与生活相联系,使理论与实践结合起来。1899年瑞士费里埃在日内瓦设立"新教育国际事物局",成为开展新教育运动的联络中心;1901年德穆兰写了《新教育》一书,在国际范围宣传新教育。二十世纪初,比利时的德可乐利,意大利的蒙台梭利"也开创了新学校"。第一次世界大战后,英国开办了萨默尔新学校,一战后,罗素创立了皮肯希尔学校,并发表了《教育与美好生活》一书。1924,由费里埃倡议,在英国加束举行新教育国际会议,成立"国际新教育协会",创立了"新教育原则"。1932年在法国民斯举行的例会上对"新教育原则"进行了修订,1966年改名为"世界教育协会"。这些新学校的教育实践,迅速形成了广泛的新教育运动。新教育运动传入美国后,又从美国的实用主义教育理论得到了论证,进而形成了规模较大的现代教育运动。它的办学实践具有鲜明的自由主义特征。另外,注重幼儿教育的研究是新教育流派区别于其他教育流派的重要特征。

4. The Secret of Childhood
童年的秘密

Maria Montessori
玛丽亚·蒙台梭利

玛丽亚·蒙台梭利(1870—1952)意大利人,是教育史上一位杰出的幼儿教育思想家和改革家。初任罗马大学附属精神病院助理医师,研究、诊疗低能和有智力缺陷的儿童。1900—1907年在罗马大学讲授教育学。于1907年在意大利"贫穷、黑暗、愚昧、悲惨"的罗马圣罗伦佐贫民区创办了"儿童之家",建立了自己独特的幼儿教育理论和方法,引起了社会各界的强烈反响,以及许多教育家和心理学家的广泛讨论,促进了现代幼儿教育的发展。

蒙台梭利认为干涉儿童"自由行动"的教育家太多了,一切都是强制性的,惩罚变成了教育的同义语。她强调教育者必须信任儿童内在的、潜在的力量,为儿童提供一个适当的环境,让儿童"自由活动",才能把学生培养成社会所需要的人材。她特制了许多形式主义的教具,如小型的家具和玻璃、陶瓷等小物件,供儿童进行感官练习。

主要教育著作有:《蒙台梭利教育法》、《童年的秘密》、《新世界的教育》

《童年的秘密》一书是意大利教育家蒙台梭利1936年7月第五次国际蒙台梭利会议在英国牛津举行之际出版的。该书是蒙台梭利对"幼儿之谜"的探索和解答,集中地阐述了他的儿童教育观。全书"导论"外分三个部分,共三十章。《童年的秘密》一书虽然不如《蒙台梭利教育法》这本成名作影响广,但成为在蒙台梭利1914年以后的著作中被最广泛阅读的一本著作。从长远的观点出发,蒙台梭利指出,儿童是人的一生发展中最重要的时期。在不断生长和发展变化的过程中,幼儿的发展包括了生理和心理两个方面的发展。为了促使幼儿的心理发展,儿童的教育应开始于诞生时。教育将帮助儿童的发展,并对他们的自然特性产生影响。幼儿在他的心理发展过程中,如果遇到了一个充满敌意和不相容的环境,加上成人的盲目和压抑以及不适当的干涉,幼儿的心理就会在毫不知觉的情况下出现各种歧变,而且这些心理歧变最初是难以察觉的。在儿童的成长和发展中,尽管成人为儿童作了他们所能做的一切,甚至为了儿童牺牲了自己,但由于成人往往无意识地压抑儿童个性地发展,设置儿童发展心理障碍,从而导致成人与儿童的不断冲突。

Till yesterday, till the beginning of the present century, society showed not the smallest concern for the child.[1] It left him where he was born, to the sole care of his family. As his sole protection and defense, there was the authority of the father, which is more or less a relic of that established by Roman Law over two thousand years ago. During so long a period of time, civilization evolved, changing its laws in favor and in the service of the adult, but it left the child without any social defense.[2] To him were reserved only the material, moral or intellectual resources of the family into which he was born. And if in his family there were no such resources, the child had to develop in material, moral and intellectual misery, without society's feeling the smallest responsibility for him. Society up till now has never claimed that the family should prepare itself in any way to receive and fittingly care for the children that might come to form part of it. The State, so rigorous in demanding official documents and meticulous preparations, and which so loves to regulate everything that bears the smallest trace of social responsibility, does not trouble to ascertain the capacity of future parents to give adequate protection to their children or to guard their development. It has provided no place of instruction or preparation for parents.[3] As far as the State is concerned, it is enough for anyone wishing to found a family to go through the marriage ceremony. In view of all this, we may well declare that society from earliest times has washed its hands of those little workers to whom nature has entrusted the task of building up humanity.[4] In the midst of a continual progress in favor of the adult they have remained as beings not belonging to human society, extra-social, without any means of communication that would allow society to become aware of their condition. They might be victims without society's being aware.

And, in truth, they were victims.

Victims indeed, as science recognized, when about half a century ago medicine began to interest itself in childhood. At that time childhood was still more abandoned than today, there were neither child specialists nor children's hospitals. Only when statistics revealed so high a mortality during the first year of life it caused a sensation. People began to reflect that though many children were born into families, few remained alive. The death of small children seemed so natural that families had accustomed themselves to it, comforting themselves with the thought that such little children went straight to heaven.[5] There had come to be a special spiritual preparation teaching resigned submission to this kind of recruitment of little angels, whom, it was said, God wished to have near Him. Such vast numbers of babies died through ignorance of lack of proper care that the phenomenon was termed the constant "slaughter of innocent."[6]

The facts were made public and at once an extensive propaganda was organized to awaken social conscience to a new sense of responsibility. It was not enough for families to give life to their children, but they must save that life. And science showed how this could be done: fathers and mothers must gain new knowledge and receive the instruction necessary for a proper care of the health of their babies.

But it was not only in families that children suffered.[7] Scientific investigations in the schools led to alarming revelations of torment.[8] And this was in the last decade of the XIX century—at a time when medicine was discovering and studying industrial diseases among workers, and showing the first steps to be taken for social hygiene in work. It was then acknowledged that besides infectious diseases resulting from unhygienic conditions children too has their "industrial" diseases—caused by their work.[9]

Their work lay in the schools. They were shut up there, exposed to the enforced torments of society. The narrow chest that brought an acquired predisposition to[10] tuberculosis, came from long hours spent bending over desks, learning to read and write. The spinal column was curved through the same enforced position; eyes were short-sighted through the prolonged effort of trying to see without sufficient light. The whole body was deformed and as it were asphyxiated, through long periods spent in small, overcrowded spaces.[11]

Yet their torment was not only physical; it extended to mental work. Studies were forced studies, and what with tedium and fear, the children's minds were tired, their nervous systems exhausted. They were lazy, prejudiced, discouraged, melancholic, vicious, with no faith in themselves, with none of the lovely gaiety of childhood.[12]

Unhappy children! Oppressed children.

Their families realized nothing of all this. What concerned them was that their children should pass their examinations and learn their lessons as quickly as possible, so as to save time and money.[13] It was not learning in itself, the attainment of a loftier culture that concerned the families, but the response to the summons of society, to the obligation imposed, an obligation which they found burdensome and which cost money.[14] What was therefore important was that their sons should acquire their passport into the life of society in the shortest time possible.

Enquiries and investigations then carried out among school-children brought to light other startling facts.[15] Many poor children when they came to school were already tired out by their morning's labors. Before going to school some of them had walked miles to distribute milk, or had gone running and shouting through the streets, selling newspapers, or had been working at home. They reached school hungry, sleepy, with the sole wish to rest. These poor little victims then received a larger share of punishments, for they could not pay attention to their teacher and so did not understand his explanations.[16] And the teacher, concerned for his responsibility and still more for his authority, tried by punishments to awaken the interest of these worn out children and to drive them to obedience by threats.[17] He would humiliate them before all their schoolfellows, for incapacity of obstinacy. Such unfortunate children spent their lives exploited at home and punished at school.

The injustice revealed by these first investigations and enquiries was such that it led to a genuine social reaction. The schools and the important branch of medicine was inaugurated, covering School Health and exercising a protective and regenerating influence on all the recognized schools of civilized countries.[18] Doctor and teacher were henceforth associated for the good of the pupils. This was, we may say, the first social sanction against an ancient unconscious error in the whole of humanity and it marked the first step towards the social redemption of the child.[19]

If we look back from this initial awakening and follow the course of history, we shall find no salient fact revealing a recognition of the rights of the child, or an intuitive awareness of his importance. Christ alone called them to Him pointing them out to adult man as his guides to the Kingdom of Heaven, and warning him of his blindness. He warned us: "Unless you convert and become like little children, you will never enter the kingdom of Heaven." But the adult continued to think only of converting the child, putting himself before him as an example of perfection. It seemed as if this terrible blindness was incurable. Mystery of the human soul! This blindness has remained a universal phenomenon and is perhaps as old as mankind.[20]

In fact in every educational ideal, in all pedagogy up to our own time, the word education has been almost always synonymous with the word punishment. The end was always to subject the child to the adult, who substituted himself for nature, and set his reasoning and his will in the place of the laws of life.[21] ent nations have different ways of punishing children. In private schools the punishments in use are often pointed out as they might point out their coat of arms. Some use humiliations, like tying placards to the children's backs, putting dunces' caps on their heads or putting them in a real pillory so that those who pass can laugh at them and mock them. Often the punishments used are physical tortures. Children are put to stand in a corner for several hours, tired, bored by idleness, seeing nothing, but condemned to hold their position by their own will.[22]

Other punishments are to make them kneel on the floor with bare knees, or whipping, or public caning. A modern refinement of cruelty comes from the theory of associating school and family in the work of education—a principle which resolves itself into organizing school and family in inflicting punishment and tormenting the child.[23] The child who is punished in school must consign his sentence to his father, so that the father may join with the teacher in punishing him and scolding him. He is then forced to take back to school a writing from his father, as a proof that he has accused himself to his other executioner, who associated himself, at least in principle, with the persecution of his own son.[24] Thus the child is condemned to carry his own cross.

There is no one to defend him. Where is the tribunal to whom the child can appeal, as condemned criminals appeal? It does not exist. Where is the love in which the child knows that he will find refuge and consolation? It is not there. School and family are agreed in punishing him, for if this were not so the punishment would be lessened and thus education would be abased.[25]

But the family does not need reminders from school to punish its children. Investigations recently carried out on the punishments in use in families (and one such enquiry was carried out on the initiative of the League of Nations) show that even in our own time there is no country great or small in the world where children are not punished in their families.[26] They are violently scolded, abused, beaten, slapped, kicked, driven out of sight, shut up in dark, frightening rooms, threatened with fantastic perils, or deprived of the little reliefs which are their refuge in their perpetual slavery or the solace of torments unconsciously endured, such as playing with their friends or eating sweets or fruit.[27] And finally there is the familiar punishment of fasting inflicted usually in the evening, to go to bed without supper, so that, all night through, sleep is disturbed by grief and hunger.[28]

4. The Secret of Childhood 童年的秘密

Although among educated families punishments have rapidly diminished, they are still in use, and rough manners, a harsh, severe and threatening voice, are usual forms of behaviour towards a child. It seems natural that the adults should have the right to chastise the child, that his mother should feel it her duty to slap him.

And yet arbitrary and public corporal punishment has been abolished for the adult, because it lowers his dignity and is a social disgrace.[29] And yet what greater baseness can be conceived than that of insulting and beating a child? It is evident that the conscience of humanity lies buried in a deep sleep.

The progress of civilization today does not depend on individual progress, it does not spring from the burning flame of the human soul, it is the advance of an insensible machine, driven by an external force.[30] The energy that moves it emanates from the outer world, like an immense impersonal power coming from society as a whole, and functioning inexorably. Forward! Ever forward!

注　释

1. Till yesterday, till the beginning of the present century, society showed not the smallest concern for the child. 直到昨天，直到本世纪的开始，社会对儿童毫不关心。
   show concern for：对……表示关心。比如：We all showed concern for her safety. 我们都关心她的安全。

2. During so long a period of time, civilization evolved, changing its laws in favor and in the service of the adult, but it left the child without any social defense. 在这样漫长的时期内，文明发展了，改变它的法律，使它有利于成人，并为成人服务，但是，儿童却丝毫没有社会的保障。
   changing its laws in favor and in the service of the adult 是分词短语作伴随状语。in favor of 是指"对……有利；赞成某人/某物；支持某人/某物"，比如：Was he in favor of the death penalty? 他赞成死刑吗？
   leave 指"使处于某种状态"，比如：Don't leave her waiting outside in the rain. 别让她在外边雨中等着。

3. The State, so rigorous in demanding official documents and meticulous preparations, and which so loves to regulate everything that bears the smallest trace of social responsibility, does not trouble to ascertain the capacity of future parents to give adequate protection to their children or to guard their development. 国家对官方的文件和繁琐的措施要求如此严格，热衷于把一切社会责任都规定好，哪怕只有一点点，而对于保证未来的父亲们能否给他们的子女以充分的保护并注意他们的成长等方面，却毫不关心。
   主语后面紧接形容词短语和 which 引导的定语从句来修饰，which 定语从句中又有一个 that 定语从句修饰 everything。
   bear responsibility 指"承担责任"，比如：He's a carefree fellow who bears his responsibilities lightly. 他是个满不在乎不大负责的人。

a trace of 是"极微的量",比如:He spoke without a trace of emotion. 她说话时毫不动感情。

4　In view of all this, we may well declare that society from earliest times has washed its hands of those little workers to whom nature has entrusted the task of building up humanity. 从这一切看来,我们可以说,从远古以来,社会对那些自然赋予了建设人类社会任务的幼小工作者就是撒手不管的。

　　wash one's hands of sb/sth:对……不负责;洗手不干。比如:I've washed my hands of the whole sordid business. 我已经彻底洗手不干那种肮脏的勾当了。

　　entrust A to B:委托某人负责某事物。比如:He entrusted the important task to his assistant. 他把这份重要的工作委托给他的助手负责。

5　The death of small children seemed so natural that families had accustomed themselves to it, comforting themselves with the thought that such little children went straight to heaven. 幼儿的死亡那么寻常,家庭似乎也习惯了,还以幼小儿童直接上升天国的思想来安慰自己。

　　accustom oneself to sth:使自己习惯于某事物。比如:She quickly accustomed himself to this new way of life. 她很快就习惯了这种新的生活方式。

6　Such vast numbers of babies died through ignorance or lack of proper care that the phenomenon was termed the constant "slaughter of innocent." 如此大量婴儿由于无知或缺乏正当的护理而死亡,这种现象可以把它说成"无辜者被不断屠杀"。

　　such…that 在这里是结果状语从句。term 在这被用作动词,表示"将……称作。"

7　But it was not only in families that children suffered. 但是不仅是在家里孩子们遭受折磨。

　　it is/was…that 句型,表示强调。

8　Scientific investigations in the schools led to alarming revelations of torment. 学校的科学研究对儿童遭受的痛苦作了惊人的揭露。

　　lead to:导致;带来。比如:His carelessness led to the accident. 他的粗心大意导致了这场事故。

9　It was then acknowledged that besides infectious diseases resulting from unhygienic conditions children too had their "industrial" diseases—caused by their work. 观察到了除不合格的卫生环境所引起的传染病以外,儿童也有着他们的"工业"病——他们学习的结果。儿童的疾病是指学校的学习和生活给他们带来的后果。

　　it 是形式主语,真正的主语是 that 从句。

10　predisposition to/towards sth:易患某病之身心素质。比如:The damp climate brings inhabitants a predisposition to rheumatism. 潮湿的天气容易使居民患上风湿病。

11　The whole body was deformed and as it were asphyxiated, through long periods spent in small, overcrowded spaces. 由于长时间关在狭小、闭塞的屋子里,整个身体被毁坏,好像被窒息了。

　　as 引导的是方式状语。spent 是过去分词短语作后置定语修饰 periods。

12　Studies were forced studies, and what with tedium and fear, the children's minds were tired, their nervous systems exhausted. They were lazy, prejudiced, discouraged, melancholic, vicious, with no faith in themselves, with none of the lovely gaiety of childhood. 学习是强制性的,充满了厌倦和恐惧,儿童的心智疲劳了,他们的神经系统倦竭了。他们变

4. The Secret of Childhood 童年的秘密

得懒散、沮丧、沉默、耽于恶习,对自己失却信心,毫无童年时期的快乐可爱的景象。
what with sth 用于列举各种原因,比如:What with the weather and my bad leg, I haven't been out for weeks. 由于天气不好,我的腿又不方便,我已经好几个星期没出门了。

13 What concerned them was that their children should pass their examinations and learn their lessons as quickly as possible, so as to save time and money. 家庭关心的是孩子们应该尽快地通过考试,尽快学好功课,以便节省时间和金钱。
what concerned them 是 what 引导的名词性从句作主语;so as to 表示目的。

14 It was not learning in itself, the attainment of a loftier culture that concerned the families, but the response to the summons of society, to the obligation imposed, an obligation which they found burdensome and which cost money. 家庭所关心的并不是学习本身,不是获得较高尚的教养,而是响应社会的召唤,完成交给的任务,他们感到这个义务负担沉重,耗费金钱。

15 Enquiries and investigations then carried out among school-children brought to light other startling facts. 当时对学校儿童所进行的许多调查和研究,发现了一些其他惊人的事实。
then carried out among school-children 是过去分词短语作后置定语修饰 enquiries and investigations。

16 These poor little victims then received a larger share of punishments, for they could not pay attention to their teacher and so did not understand his explanations. 这些可怜的小小牺牲品因而受到了更重的惩罚。因为他们不能集中注意听教师讲课,所以不懂得他的解释。

17 And the teacher, concerned for his responsibility and still more for his authority, tried by punishments to awaken the interest of these worn out children and to drive them to obedience by threats. 而教师呢,关心他的职责,尤其关心他的威信,企图用惩罚来唤起这些精疲力竭的儿童的兴趣,用恐吓来驱使他们听话。
wear out 指"精疲力竭",比如:They were worn out after a long day spent working in the fields. 他们在地里干了一整天的活儿,累得疲惫不堪。
drive 在这里是指"迫使某人行动",比如:A man driven by jealousy is capable of anything. 忌妒心可使人什么都做得出来。

18 A new and important branch of medicine was inaugurated, covering School Health and exercising a protective and regenerating influence on all recognized schools of civilized countries. 医学的一个新的重要分支建立了,这个分支经营学校卫生,对文明国家的所有公立学校施加保护性和具有再生作用的影响。
这句话中有三个分词短语作定语修饰 branch of medicine。
exercise 这里指"利用;使用;运用",比如:Teachers exercise authority over their pupils. 教师经常管束学生。

19 This was, we may say, the first social sanction against an ancient unconscious error in the whole of humanity and it marked the first step towards the social redemption of the child. 我们可以说,这是全人类的一个古代无意识的错误的第一次社会制裁,它标志着社会救赎儿童的第一步。

20 But the adult continued to think only of converting the child, putting himself before him as

an example of perfection. It seemed as if this terrible blindness was incurable. Mystery of the human soul! This blindness has remained a universal phenomenon and is perhaps as old as mankind. 但是,成年人依然只想转变儿童,把他自己当作完善的模范。似乎这种严重的蒙昧无知是不可救药的。奥秘的人类心灵! 这种蒙昧无知始终是一个普遍的现象,也许和人类同样古老。

21 In fact in every educational ideal, in all pedagogy up to our own time, the word education has been almost always synonymous with the word punishment. The end was always to subjects the child to the adult, who substituted himself for nature, and set his reasoning and his will in the place of the laws of life. 事实上,在每一个教育理想中,在迄今为止所有的教育理论中,教育这个词差不多总是和惩罚这个词是同义词,目的总是要儿童服从成人,成人替代了自然,并且用他的推理和目的取代了生活的法则。

subject...to...:使……臣服;征服;制伏。比如:Ancient Rome subjected most of Europe to its rule. 古罗马帝国征服了欧洲的大部分。

22 Children are put to stand in a corner for several hours, tired, bored by idleness, seeing nothing, but condemned to hold their position by their own will. 儿童一连几个小时罚站壁角,身体疲乏,闲得无聊,看不到一点东西,却责怪他们自愿那样站着。

"tired, bored by idleness, seeing...will"是分词短语表示方式或伴随情况,比如:Boys and girls came into the classroom, singing and laughing. 孩子们又唱又笑地走进教室。/The soldier sat there, surrounded by a lot of students. 战士坐在那里,周围坐着很多学生。

23 A modern refinement of cruelty comes from the theory of associating school and family in the work of education—a principle which resolves itself into organizing school and family in inflicting punishment and tormenting the child. 有一种新的巧妙的惩罚方法来自学校和家庭联合起来进行教育的理论,这个原则归结为把学校和家庭组织起来惩罚儿童,折磨儿童。

24 He is then forced to take back to school a writing from his father, as a proof that he has accused himself to his other executioner, who associated himself, at least in principle, with the persecution of his own son. 然后孩子被迫把他父亲的字条送回学校,证明他已经自己像另一个刽子手投案,这另一个刽子手至少在原则上参与了他对自己儿子的迫害。

that 从句作 proof 的同位语从句。

25 Where is the tribunal to whom the child can appeal, as condemned criminals appeal? It does not exist. Where is the love in which the child knows that he will find refuge and consolation? It is not there. School and family are agreed in punishing him, for if this were not so the punishment would be lessened and thus education would be abased. 儿童能像控告的犯人一样上诉的法庭在哪里? 这个法庭并不存在。孩子知道可以在其中避难和得到安慰的爱抚在哪里呢? 这爱抚也不存在。学校和家庭同意惩罚他,因为,如果不是这样,惩罚就要减轻,而教育就要贬低。

appeal...to:上诉。比如:She appealed to the high court against her sentence. 他不服判决而向高等法院上诉。

appeal to 还有"对某人有吸引力;使某人感兴趣"的意思,比如:The idea of camping has never appealed to me. 对露营这种想法我从来就不感兴趣。

26 Investigations recently carried out on the punishments in use in families(and one such enquiry was carried out on the initiative of the League of Nations) show that even in our own time there is no country great or small in the world where children are not punished in their families. 最近进行的关于家庭中所用惩罚的调查(由一个这样的研究是在国际联盟教育局的倡议下进行的)表明,甚至在我们这个时代,世界上国无大小,没有一个国家的儿童不在家庭受到惩罚。

在 that 宾语从句中是双重否定,表示肯定。

27 They are violently scolded, abused, beaten, slapped, kicked, driven out of sight, shut up in dark, frightening rooms, threatened with fantastic perils, or deprived of the little reliefs which are their refuge in their perpetual slavery or the solace of torments unconsciously endured, such as playing with their friends or eating sweets or fruit. 他们被痛斥、谩骂、殴打、扇耳光、脚踢、驱逐,关闭在又黑暗又恐怖的房间里,危言耸听地恐吓,或者不许他们和伙伴们玩游戏,不许他们吃糖果,他们被剥夺了那些他们在无休止的奴役下的小小慰藉或无意识地忍受痛苦的安慰。

be deprived of: 被剥夺。比如: Women were deprived of education rights in the old society. 在旧社会,妇女没有受教育的权利。

28 And finally there is the familiar punishment of fasting inflicted usually in the evening, to go to bed without supper, so that, all night through, sleep is disturbed by grief and hunger. 最后还有一种家庭惩罚,通常是在晚上使孩子断食,不给晚餐就要他睡觉,使他悲伤饥饿,彻夜不得安眠。

29 And yet arbitrary and public corporal punishment has been abolished for the adult, because it lowers his dignity and is a social disgrace. 但是,对成人来说,专横的当众体罚已经被废除了。现在再用体罚将有损他的威信,而且是一种社会耻辱。

corporal punishment: 体罚

30 The progress of civilization today does not depend on individual progress, it does not spring from the burning flame of the human soul, it is the advance of an insensible machine, driven by an external force. 今天,文明的进步并不依靠个人的进步,他并不来自人类心灵炽烈的火焰,他是一个被外力推动的没有知觉的机器的进步。

spring from: 发源于某事物;来自于某事物;出身于。比如: He sprang from peasant stock. 他是农民出身。

练　习

1. 回答问题

(1) How has society from earliest times treated children?
(2) How did families react to the death of their children in the past according to the author?
(3) What did science show to parents to do in order to save their children?
(4) Please take some examples of sufferings of children in the school.
(5) How are school and family associated in the work of education?

2. 判断正误

(1) According to the author, children all over the world are punished in their families.

(2) There is no punishment towards children among educated families.

(3) According to the author, teachers tried to awaken the interest of children by encouragement.

(4) Children were not only tormented physically, but also mentally.

(5) What concerned parents was that their children should have a good education to develop themselves and realize themselves.

3. 选词填空

as far as sth/sb be concerned, in the midst of, result from, carry out, subject…to, substitute for, appeal to, deprive of, entrust to, in one's place

(1) He had something urgent to do, so he _____ his child _____ me for the day.

(2) The car is fine _____ the engine _____ but the bodywork needs a lot of attention.

(3) The bankruptcy of the company _____ the leader's improper management.

(4) There is no wild animal _____ the forest because of pollution.

(5) Extensive tests have been _____ on the patients.

(6) Do these paintings _____ you?

(7) Honey can _____ sugar in this recipe.

(8) Some teachers tend to _____ their students _____ their authority by punishment.

(9) The trees _____ the house behind them _____ light.

(10) The chairmen was ill so his deputy spoke _____.

4. 句型模拟

(1) so as to

(2) what with

5. 英译汉

(1) In the midst of a continual progress in favour of the adult they have remained as being not belonging to human society, extra-social, isolated, without any means of communication that would allow society to become aware of their condition.

(2) They were shut up there, exposed to the enforced torments of society. The narrow chest that brought an acquired predisposition to tuberculosis, came from long hours spent bending over desks, learning to read and write.

(3) Before going to school some of them had walked miles to distribute milk, or had gone running. And shouting through the streets, selling newspapers, or had been working at home. They reached school hungry, sleepy, with the sole wish to rest.

(4) The child who is punished in school must consign his sentence to his father, so that the father may join with the teacher in punishing him and scolding him. He is then forced to

take back to school a writing from his father, as a proof that he has accused himself to his other executioner, who associated himself, at least in principle, with the persecution of his own son. Thus the child is condemned to carry his own cross.

(5) The energy that moves it emanates from the outer world, like an immense impersonal power coming from society as a whole, and functioning inexorably. Forward! Ever forward!

6. 汉译英

(1) 已经告诉过他,汽车这个样子开起来有危险。(warn...of)

(2) 我们一致谴责虐待儿童的行为。(condemn)

(1) 父母过世之后,这个小孩交给叔叔照料。(consign...to)

(2) 仇恨常常源于恐惧。(spring from)

(3) 他很快就习惯了当地的食物。(be accustomed to)

7. 写作指导

For this part, you are required to write a composition on the topic "The Things Which Shouldn't Happen to the Child". The following points taken from the text are useful expressions for your reference:

- leave the child without any social defence
- lack of proper care
- be forced to study
- tired out by morning's labour
- walk miles to distribute milk
- reach school hungry, sleepy
- receive a large share of punishments
- be humiliated before others
- stand in a corner for several hours

5. Education and Good Life[1]
教育与美好生活

Bertrand Russell
伯特兰·罗素

　　伯特兰·罗素(1872—1970)是二十世纪伟大的哲学家、数学家、逻辑学家以及社会思想家、活动家，是诺贝尔文学奖的获得者。他先后在剑桥大学、芝加哥大学、加利福尼亚大学任教。1920年到中国讲学，宣传他的唯心主义哲学，对旧中国学术界有一定影响。第一次世界大战时，他是和平主义者。晚年反对战争，同时却宣扬战争恐怖。主要教育著作有：《教育与美好生活》、《教育与社会秩序》。

　　罗素曾于1927—1934年开办一所私立学校，名皮肯希尔(Beaconhill)学校，试验他的教育理论，是当时英国资产阶级的"进步学校"之一。他一直鼓吹资产阶级的"自由教育"、"爱的教育"和更多地发展个人主义。他认为教育的基本目的是品格的发展，而"活力、勇气、敏感和智慧"是形成"理想品格"的基础；并深信通过对儿童的身体、感情和智力上的"恰当的处理"，可以使这些品质得到普遍的培养。

　　《教育和美好生活》是伯特兰·罗素在美国出版时书名，在英国出版时书名为《论教育，尤其是儿童早期教育》。本书出版后受到热烈欢迎，一版再版，成为二十世纪教育经典著作之一，罗素也因此跻身于二十世纪最杰出的教育家的行列。教育是一门复杂的科学，它的理论基础几乎涵盖与人类相关的所有学科，而罗素就是这样一位文理兼通的集大成学者。他以一个睿智的哲人眼光，从常人难以企及的深度和广度，对素质教育方方面面的问题都作了深入的理性的辩证的分析。自我牺牲精神一直被视为一种美德，罗素却强调，孩子真正需要的是公平的观念而不是自我牺牲的观念。每个人在世上都占有一席之地，维护自己应得的一切，不应被视为罪恶。基于这一认识，再对孩子进行公平公正的教育才具有说服力和真正收到效果。诚实被罗素认为是比财富和声望更重要的东西。他坦言，这个虚伪的世界对诚实的人是有些不利，但诚实所带来的整体的长远的优势要高于这种不利。对于一个优秀的人，内在的自重和正直是必不可少的。诸如让孩子尽情地玩；玩中学，学中玩；不管学什么，孩子没兴趣或厌烦了就不要勉强等论调目前正大行其道。罗素则认为，要使一种真正的教育完全不显枯燥是不可能的，关键是要激励孩子的好奇心和理想，让孩子体验克服困难取得成功的乐趣，明白学习枯燥部分的重要性，他就会为了实现某个雄心壮志自愿忍受单调乏味的训练。

5. Education and Good Life 教育与美好生活

The American public schools achieve successfully a task never before attempted on a large scale[2]: the task of transforming a heterogeneous selection of mankind into a homogeneous nation[3]. This is done so ably, and is on the whole such a beneficent work, that on the balance great praise is due to those who accomplish it.[4] But America, like Japan, is placed in a peculiar situation, and what the special circumstances justify is not necessarily an ideal to be followed everywhere and always. America has had certain advantages and certain difficulties. Among the advantages were: a higher standard of wealth; freedom from the danger of defeat in war; comparative absence of cramping traditions inherited from the Middle Ages[5]. Immigrants found in America a generally diffused sentiment of democracy and an advanced stage of industrial technique.[6] These, I think, are the two chief reasons why almost all of them came to admire America more than their native countries. But actual immigrants, as a rule, retain a dual patriotism[7]; in European struggles they continue to take passionately the side of the nation to which they originally belonged.[8] Their children, on the contrary, lose all loyalty to the country from which their parents have come, and become merely and simply Americans. The attitude of the parents is attributable to the general of America[9]; that of the children is very largely determined by their school education. It is only the contribution of the school that concerns us.

In so far as the school can rely upon the genuine merits of America, there is no need to associate the teaching of American patriotism with the inculcation of false standards.[10] But where the old world is superior to the new, it becomes necessary to instill a contempt for genuine excellences. The intellectual level in Western Europe and the artistic level in Eastern Europe are, on the whole, higher than in America[11]. Throughout Western Europe, except in Spain and Portugal, there is less theological superstition[12] than in America. In almost all European countries the individual is less subject to herd domination than in America[13]: his inner freedom is greater even where his political freedom is less. In these respects, the American public schools do harm. The harm is essential to the teaching of an exclusive American patriotism.[14] The harm, as with the Japanese and the Jesuits, comes from regarding the pupils as means to an end, not as ends in themselves.[15] The teacher should love his children better than his State or his church; otherwise he is not an ideal teacher.

When I say that pupils should be regarded as ends, not as means, I may be met by the retort that, after all, everybody is more important as a means than as an end. What s man is as an end perishes when he dies; what he reduces as a means continues to the end of time.[16] We cannot deny this, but we can deny the consequences deduced from it.[17] A man's importance as a means may be for good or for evil[18]; the remote effects of human actions are so uncertain that a wise man will tend to dismiss them from his calculations[19]. Broadly speaking, good men have good effects, and bad men bad effects. This, of course, is not an invariable law of nature[20]. A bad man may murder a tyrant, because he has committed crimes which the tyrant intends to punish; the effects of his act may be good, though he and his act are bad. Nevertheless, as a broad general rule, a community of men and women who are intrinsically excellent will have better effects than one composed of people who are ignorant and malevolent.[21] Apart from such considerations, children and young people feel instinctively the difference between those who genuinely wish them well and those who regard them merely as raw material for some scheme.[22] Neither character nor intelligence will develop as well or as freely where the teacher is deficient in love[23]; and love of this kind consists essentially in *feeling* the child as an end.[24] We all have this feeling about ourselves: we desire good things for ourselves without first demanding a proof that some purpose will be furthered by our obtaining them.[25] Every ordinarily affectionate parent feels the same sort of thing about his or her children. Parents want their children to grow, to be strong and healthy, to do well at school, and so on, in just the same way in which they want things for themselves[26]; no effort of self-denial and no abstract principle of justice is involved in taking trouble about such matters.[27] This is apparental instinct is not always strictly confined to one's own children.[28] Diffused form, it must exist in anyone who is to be a good teacher of little boys and girls.[29] As the pupils grow older, it grows less important. But only those who possess it can be trusted to draw up schemes of education. Those who regard it as one of the purposes of male education to produce men willing to kill and be killed for frivolous reasons are clearly deficient in diffused parental feeling[30]; yet they control education in all civilized countries except Denmark and China.

But it is not enough that the educator should love the young; it is necessary also that he should have a right conception of human excellence[31]. Cats teach their kittens to catch mice and play with them; militarists do likewise with the human young.[32] The cat loves the kitten, but not the mouse; the militarist may love his own son, but not the sons of his country's enemies. Even those who love all mankind may err through a wrong conception of the good life.[33] I shall try, therefore, before going any further, to give an idea of what I consider excellent in men and women, quite without regard to practicality, or to the educational methods by which it might be brought into being.[34] Such a picture will help us afterwards, when we come to consider the details of education; we shall know the direction in which we wish to move.

We must first make a distinction: some qualities are desirable in a certain proportion of mankind, others are desirable universally. We want artists, but we also want men of science. We want great administrators, but we also want ploughmen and millers and bakers. The qualities which produce a man of great eminence in some one direction are often such as might be undesirable if they were universal.[35] Shelley describes the day's work of a poet as follows:

> He will watch from dawn to gloom
> The lake-reflected sun illume
> The yellow-bees in the ivy bloom,
> Nor heed nor see what things they be.[36]

These habits are praiseworthy in a poet, but not—shall we say—in a postman.[37] We cannot therefore frame our education with a view to giving everyone the temperament of a poet.[38] But some characteristics are universally desirable, and it is these alone that I shall consider at this stage.

I make no distinction whatever between male and female excellence.[39]ain amount of occupational training is desirable for a woman who is to have the care of babies, but that only involves the same sort of difference as there is between a farmer and a miller. It is in no degree fundamental[40], and does not demand consideration at our present level.

I will take four characteristics which seem to me jointly to form the basis of an ideal character: vitality, courage, sensitiveness, and intelligence. I do not suggest that this list is complete, but I think it carries us a good way. Moreover, I firmly believe that, by proper physical, emotional, and intellectual care of the young, these qualities could all be made very common.[41]

注　释

1. 本文选自伯特兰·罗素的《教育与美好生活》。
2. a task never before attempted on a large scale：一个从未大规模尝试过的任务
   本句中 attempted 是过去分词作 a task 的定语。"on a large scale"是"大规模"的意思。
3. transforming a heterogeneous selection of mankind into a homogeneous nation：把一个不同种的人类集合体转化为一个同种的民族
   heterogeneous 是"各种各样的"的意思；homogeneous 是"同类的"的意思
   transform into sth 是"把……转化成……"的意思，比如：A year abroad has completely transformed a shy girl into a brave one. 一年的国外生活使一个腼腆的女孩变得大胆了。
4. This is done so ably, and is on the whole such a beneficent work, that on the balance great praise is due to those who accomplish it. 这项任务完成得如此出色，总的来说它又是如此有益，从各方面来考虑，应该大大表扬完成这项任务的人。
   本句是一个由 so...and such...that 引导的结果状语从句。
   "on the whole"和"on the balance"都是"总的来看，从各方面来说"的意思。
5. comparative absence of cramping traditions inherited from the Middle Ages：较少地继承中世纪的束缚人的传统
   本句中 absence of 是"缺少，较少"的意思，比如：After an absence of three months he returned to his hometown. 离开家乡三个月后，他又回来了。
6. Immigrants found in America a generally diffused sentiment of democracy and an advanced stage of industrial technique. 在美国的移民，发现了广泛传播的民主情操和先进的工业技术。
   diffused sentiment of democracy and an advanced stage of industrial technique 两个形容词短语共同作 found 的宾语。
7. retain a dual patriotism：保留着双重的爱国主义
   retain 是"保存，保留"的意思，比如：He managed to retain his dignity throughout the performance. 在整场演出中他都保持了自己的威严。
8. In European struggles they continue to take passionately the side of the nation to which they originally belonged. 在欧洲的斗争中，他们继续满腔热血地支持自己的本国。
   belonged to 中的介词 to 提到关系代词 which 前，和 which 共同引导定语从句，修饰先行词 the nation。
   take the side of 是"站在某一边"的意思，比如：To our surprise, he took side of his oppo-

nents at last meeting. 令我们吃惊的是,在上一次会议上他竟站在了对手的一边。

9　The attitude of the parents is attributable to the general of America. 父母的态度源于美国的大众

　　be attributable to 是"可归属于或归因于某人或某物"的意思,比如:Is this painting attributable to Michelangelo? 这幅画是米开朗琪罗画的吗?

10　In so far as the school can rely upon the genuine merits of America, there is no need to associate the teaching of American patriotism with the inculcation of false standards. 就学校还能依靠美国的自身优势这方面而言,无需把美国爱国主义的教学和错误标准的灌输联系起来。

　　in so far as 是"就……而言或在……范围之内"的意思,比如:In so far as we can believe these facts we will use them. 我们将在我们所相信的范围之内来利用这些事实。/He is a Russian in so far as he was born in Russia, but he became a French citizen in 1920. 就他出生于俄国而言,他是个俄国人,但他在1920年入了法国籍。

　　associate...with 是"把……和……联系起来"的意思,比如:Why do men associate enjoyment with drunkenness? 男人为什么把自得其乐与酩酊大醉联系在一起?

11　the intellectual level:学术水平。如:the artistic level 艺术水平

12　theological superstition:神学迷信

13　In almost all European countries the individual is less subject to herd domination than in America. 几乎在所有欧洲国家,个人对集团的支配不像美国人那么服从。

　　be subject to 是"从属于,受支配于,服从于"的意思,比如:Peasants used to be subject to the local landowner. 农民过去受地主的压迫。

14　The harm is essential to the teaching of an exclusive American patriotism. 教授一种绝对的美国的爱国主义,一定会带来危害。

　　be essential to 是"必要的,不可缺少的"意思,比如:A knowledge of French is essential to the Canadians. 会些法语对加拿大人很重要。

15　The harm, as with the Japanese and the Jesuits, comes from regarding the pupils as means to an end, not as ends in themselves. 就像日本人和耶稣会会员那样,这个危害来自于认为学生是达到目的的手段,而不是目的本身。

　　regard...as... 是"将某人/某物视为"的意思,比如:I regard your suggestion as worthy of consideration. 我觉得你的建议值得考虑。

16　What man is as an end perishes when he dies; what he produces as a means continues to the end of time. 一个人作为目的而存在,当他死亡时,什么都消逝了;而他所创造的东西,作为手段,却能继续存留下去。

　　what 从句作主句。

17　We cannot deny this, but we can deny the consequences deduced from it. 我们不能否认这一点,但是我们能否认由此推论出来的结果。

　　deduce from:推论,推断。比如:We cannot deduce very much from these figures. 我们无法从这些数据中做出多少推论。

18　A man's importance may be for good or for evil. 人既可以为善,也可以为恶。

5. Education and Good Life 教育与美好生活

be for good/evil 是"为了善或恶"的意思, 本结构中的"good"和"evil"是名词, 比如: Is religion always a force for good? 宗教一向是诲人从善的力量吗?

19 a wise man will tend to dismiss them from his calculations: 明智的人往往不会去考虑它们
dismiss from 是"决定忽略"意思。如: Just dismiss those thoughts from your mind, they're crazy and not worth thinking about. 就别理会你脑中的那些念头吧, 都是些疯狂的想法, 不值得考虑。

20 an invariable law of nature: 不可改变的自然法则

21 Nevertheless, as a broad general rule, a community of men and women who are intrinsically excellent will have *better* effects *than* one composed of people who are ignorant and malevolent. 虽然如此, 一般说来, 一个由本质优秀的男女所组成的社会, 它所产生的影响比由无知和心怀不轨的人所组成的社会要好得多。
a community of men and women 和 one composed of people 进行对比, 并且两者分别带一个由 who 引导的定语从句, one 指的是 a community。be composed of...是"组成"的意思, 比如: The committee is mainly composed of teachers and parents. 委员会主要由教师和学生家长组成。

22 Apart from such considerations, children and young people feel instinctively the difference between those who genuinely wish them well and those who regard them merely as raw material for some scheme. 除了考虑这些之外, 儿童和年轻人会本能地感觉到两种人之间的差别, 一种是那些真正希望他们好的人, 另一种是仅仅把他们看作实施某种计划的原料。
apart from 具有两种不同的含义: 一是"排除"或"例外"的意思; 二是"包括"的意思。此词组, 有时具有 except, except for 的含义, 有时具有 besides, in addition to, as well as 的含义。在此句中它表示"包括在内"的意思, 比如: Apart from the cost, it will take a lot of time. 除了价钱贵之外, 还要占用很多的时间。/Apart from that, all goes well. 除了这点之外, 一切都顺利。

23 Neither character nor intelligence will develop as well or as freely where the teacher is deficient in love. 凡是教师缺乏爱的地方, 不论是品格还是智慧都不能充分地或自由地发展。
be deficient in 意思是"缺乏, 不足", 比如: A diet deficient in vitamin D may cause the disease rickets. 缺少维生素 D 的饮食可能导致软骨病。

24 Love of this kind consists essentially in *feeling* the child as an end. 这种爱主要在于认为儿童是一种目的。
consist in 意思是"在于", 比如: The beauty of air travel consists in its speed and ease. 飞机旅行的好处在于快捷、舒适。

25 We desire good things for ourselves without first demanding a proof that some purpose will be furthered by our obtaining them. 我们自己希望一些好事情, 并不首先要求证明, 由于我们得到了它们, 将促进某个巨大的目的。
that some purpose will be furthered by our obtaining them 作 a proof 的同位于从句。We 是主语, desire 是谓语, good things 是宾语 without first demanding a proof 作伴随状语。

26 in just the same way in which they want things for themselves: 正如他们希望他们自己的事情一样。

in which they want things for themselves 句中的 in which 引导的是定语从句,修饰先行词 the way。

27 No effort of self-denial and no abstract principle of justice is involved in taking trouble about such matters. 在这些事情上所费的心思,用不着自我牺牲的努力和抽象的正义原则。
用 and 连接的两个单数名词作主语,若前面有 each, every, no 等修饰,谓语动词用单数形式,所以由 no...and no...结构作主语,谓语动词用 is。比如:No teacher and no student is admitted. 师生一律不得入内。

28 This parental instinct is not always strictly confined to one's own children. 这种父母的本能,并不总是严格地局限于一个人自己的子女。
be confined to 是"局限于"的意思,比如:It's an attitude which seems to be confined to the upper classes. 这种观点看来只存在于上层阶级中。

29 In its diffused form, it must exist in anyone who is to be a good teacher of little boys and girls. 每一个要成为幼年儿童的好教师的人,都必须具有弥漫四射的父母本能。
diffuse 是"散布、传播"的意思,比如:Television is a powerful means of diffusing knowledge. 电视是传播知识强有力的手段。

30 Those who regard it as one of the purposes of male education to produce men willing to kill and be killed for frivolous reasons are clearly deficient in diffused parental feeling. 那些把培养为了一些不重要的理由愿意去杀害人和被人杀害作为男子教育目的之一的人们,是明显地缺乏弥漫四射的父母之情。
Those...are clearly deficient in...feeling. 是主干部分,who 引导的定语从句修饰先行词 those。

31 have a right conception of human excellence:具有对人类优秀品质的正确理解

32 Cats teach their kittens to catch mice and play with them; militarists do likewise with the human young. 老猫教小猫捕捉老鼠并且玩弄它们;军国主义者对青年人做类似的事情。
likewise 意思是"同样地",比如:Watch how she does it and then do likewise. 看她是怎样做的,然后也这样做。

33 Even those who love all mankind may err through a wrong conception of the good life. 甚至那些爱全人类的人,也可能由于对美好生活的错误理解而犯错误。

34 I shall try, therefore, before going any further, to give an idea of what I consider excellent in men and women, quite without regard to practicality, or to the educational methods by which it might be brought into being. 因此,在我进一步论述之前,我将试图对我所认为的男子和女子的优秀品质提出一个看法,完全不考虑实际可行的问题,也不考虑用来培养这种优秀品质的教育方法。
without regard to 是"不考虑……"的意思,比如:He did everything at his own will without regard to the consequences. 他做事随心所欲,不考虑后果。

35 The qualities which produce a man of great eminence in some one direction are often such as might be undesirable if they were universal. 使一个人在某一方面非常突出的那些品质,如果普遍化了,往往可能成为不合乎需要的品质。
as 是关系代词在从句中作主语。

36 Shelley describes the day's work of a poet as follows：雪莱曾这样地描写一个诗人一天的工作：
   He will watch from dawn to gloom
   从拂晓到傍晚
   The lake-reflected sun illume
   他将守望那湖面映射的阳光
   The yellow-bees in the ivy bloom
   照亮着常青藤花丛中的蜜蜂
   Nor heed nor see what things they be.
   不理会也不理解它们是什么。

37 These habits are praiseworthy in a poet, but not— shall we say — in a postman. 这些习惯在一个诗人身上是值得称赞的，但是，譬如说，在一个邮递员身上就不值得称赞了。
   but not…shall we say…in a postman 完整的句子是：but we shall say these habits are not praiseworthy in a postman.

38 We cannot therefore frame our education with a view to giving everyone the temperament of a poet. 我们不能从使每个人具有诗人的气质的观点来制订我们的教育。
   frame 意思是"设计出，构思出"，比如：The peace proposals were framed by the five permanent members of the UN Security Council. 那个和平提案是由联合国安理会的五个常任理事国拟订的。

39 I make no distinction whatever between male and female excellence. 对男人和女人的优秀品质我不加以区别。
   make distinction between…and…：是"区分，区别开来"的意思，如：He made a quite artificial distinction between men and women readers. 他把男女读者硬是人为地区分开来。

40 no degree fundamental：绝不是根本的

41 Moreover, I firmly believe that, by proper physical, emotional, and intellectual care of the young, these qualities could all be made very common. 再者，我坚信，通过对儿童身体、感情和智力上恰当的爱护，可以使这些品质更加普遍。

练　习

1. 回答问题
   (1) What advantages does American education have?
   (2) Why did all immigrants admire America more than their native countries?
   (3) What kind of people can be trusted to draw up schemes of education?
   (4) To be an educator, what qualities should he have?

2. 判断正误
   (1) The teacher should love his State or his Church better than his students.
   (2) A man's importance as an end may be for good or for evil.

(3) A community of men and women who are intrinsically excellent will have worse effects than one composed of people who are ignorant and malevolent.

(4) It is enough that the educator only loves the young.

(5) The writer thinks four characteristics form the basis of an ideal character, they are: vitality, courage, sensitiveness, and intelligence.

3. 选词填空

on the whole, belong to, take one's side, be attributable to, deduce from, apart from, be confined to, likewise, make distinction between...and, retain

(1) It's important that the elderly should _____ a sense of dignity.

(2) This essay is good _____ a couple of spelling mistakes.

(3) _____ I prefer to listen to classical music.

(4) Death _____ gunshot wounds.

(5) Detectives _____ the clues who had committed the crime.

(6) After her operation, she _____ bed for a week.

(7) I'm going to bed and you would be well advised to do _____.

(8) You shouldn't take what doesn't _____ you.

(9) The politician said he would _____ terrorism and murder.

(10) My mother always _____ my brother's _____ when I argue with him.

4. 句型模拟

(1) in so far as

(2) no... and no...

5. 英译汉

(1) Their children, on the contrary, lose all loyalty to the country from which their parents have come, and become merely and simply Americans.

(2) But where the old world is superior to the new, it becomes necessary to instill a contempt for genuine excellences.

(3) Broadly speaking, good men have good effects, and bad men bad effects.

(4) Neither character nor intelligence will develop as well or as freely where the teacher is deficient in love.

(5) But only those who possess it can be trusted to draw up schemes of education.

6. 汉译英

(1) 我总是由他联想到高速汽车。(associate...with)

(2) 对她来说,幸福就是看电视和读杂志。(consist in)

(3) 你的饮食中缺少维生素 D,所以你很有可能得软骨病。(be deficient in)

(4) 他尽量不去想他,然而无济于事。(dismiss from)

(5) 我们必须遵守当地的法律。(be subject to)

7. 写作指导

For this part, you are required to write a composition on the topic "How to Be an Ideal Teacher". The following points taken from the text are useful expressions for your reference:
- love his children better than his State and his Church
- intrinsically excellent
- give his love to everyone
- feel the children as an end
- have parental instinct to all children
- not only love the young, but also have a right conception of human excellence
- know what qualities are useful to the children
- cultivate the young to have four characteristic: vitality, courage, sensitiveness, and intelligence.

6. The Aims of Education
教育的目的

Alfred North Whitehead
艾尔弗雷德·诺思·怀特海

艾尔弗雷德·诺思·怀特海（1861—1947）是现代著名的数学家、哲学家和教育理论家。他于1861年2月15日出生于英国东南部的拉姆斯盖特。他的祖父是当地一位有名望的教育家，曾任当地一所私立学校的校长。他的父亲先后从事教育、宗教工作，十分关心教育事业。受家庭的影响，怀特海对教育也很感兴趣。剑桥大学三一学院毕业，历任剑桥大学数学讲师，伦敦大学学院数学讲师，伦敦大学皇家科技学院教授。1924—1936年任哈佛大学哲学教授。主要教育著作：《教育的目的》(1929)和《科学与哲学论文集》(1948)。怀特海大声提出"两条教育的戒律"：一条"不要教过多的学科"，一条"凡是所教的东西，要教得透彻"，反对学校中传授死的知识或"无活力"的概念，即仅仅刻板地接受而不予运用，检验或重新组合的知识和概念，认为一切的教育中心是使知识保持活力和防止知识僵化，要求理论性的概念必须在学生课堂中经常得到应用，强调"规律是绝对的，凡是不重视智慧训练的民族是注定要失败的"。

怀特海在《教育的目的》(1929)中除了广泛接触和评析教育中的突出问题外，还深刻揭示了儿童成长的阶段和学习道路。他认为儿童的心灵是成长着的有机体，而成长和智慧发生在自由所给予的创造机会与学生学习知识之间达成平衡之际。他提出"教育韵律"——渲染（游戏）、精确（掌握）和概括化（抽象），认为这三者不断统合而非序列地排列。他提倡在小学和初中以观点的渲染和游戏为主，精确和掌握的发展始于高中，而抽象和概括则为大学时期的焦点，学校若脱离这一大致的计划，将违背学习的自然韵律。显然，这是夸美纽斯提出的自然适应性原则的延伸，它有益于教师认识不同时期的学生学习特点，从而采取有针对性的教学措施，值得我们深深体悟。

In the history of education, the most striking phenomenon is that schools of learning, which at one epoch are alive with a ferment of genius, in a succeeding generation, exhibit merely pedantry and routine.[1] The reason is, that they are over laden with inert ideas. Education with inert ideas is not only useless: it is, above all things, harmful—*corruptio optimi*, *pessima*.[2] Except at rare intervals of intellectual ferment, education in the past has been radically infected with inert ideas.[3] That is the reason why uneducated d clever women, who have seen much of the world, are in middle life so much the most cultured part of the community.[4] They have been saved from this horrible burden of inert ideas. Every intellectual revolution, which has never stirred humanity into greatness, has been a passionate protest against inert ideas.[5] Then, alas, with pathetic ignorance of human psychology, it has proceeded by some educational scheme to bind humanity afresh with inert ideas of its own fashioning.[6]

Let us now ask how in our system of education we are to guard against this mental dry rot.[7] We enunciate two educational commandments, "Do not teach too many subjects," and again, "what you teach, teach thoroughly."[8]

The result of teaching small parts of a large number of subjects is the passive reception of disconnected ideas, not illumined with any spark of vitality.[9] Let the main ideas, which are introduced into a child's education be few and important, and let them be thrown into every combination possible. The child should make them his own, and should understand their application here and now in the circumstances of his actual life.[10] From the very beginning of his education, the child should experience the joy of discovery. The discovery, which he has to make, is that general ideas give an understanding of that stream of events, which pours through his life, which is his life.[11] By understanding I mean more than a mere logical analysis, though that is included. I mean "understanding" in the sense in which it is used in the French proverb, "To understand all, is to forgive all." Pedants sneer at an education, which is useful.[12] But if education is not useful, what is it? Is it a talent, to be hidden away in a napkin? Of course, education should be useful, whatever your aim in life. It was useful to Saint Augustine and it was useful to Napoleon.[13] It is useful, because understanding is useful.

I pass lightly over that understanding which should be given by the literary side of education. Nor do I wish to be supposed to pronounce on the relative merits of a classical or a modern curriculum.[14] I would only remark that the understanding, which we want, is an understanding of an insistent present.[15] The only use of a knowledge of the past is to equip us for the present. No more deadly harm can be done to young minds than by depreciation of the present.[16] The present contains all that there is. It is holly ground; for it is the past, and it is the future. At the same time it must be observed that an age is no less past if it existed two hundreds years ago than if it existed two thousands years ago. Do not be deceived by the pedantry of dates. The ages of Shakespeare and of Moliere are no less past than are the ages of Sophocles and of Virgil.[17] The communion of saints is a great and inspiring assemblage, but it has only one possible hall of meeting, and that is, the present, and the mere lapse of time through which any particular group of saints must travel to reach that meeting—place, makes very little difference.[18]

Passing now to the scientific and logical side of education, we remember that here also ideas which are not utilized are positively harmful.[19] By utilizing an idea, I mean relating it to that stream, compounded of sense perceptions, feelings, hopes, desires, and of mental activities adjusting thought to thought, which forms our life.[20] I can imagine a set of beings, which might fortify their souls by passively reviewing disconnected ideas. Humanity is not built that way except perhaps some editors of newspapers.

In scientific training, the first thing to do with an idea is to prove it. But allow me for one moment to extend the meaning of "prove"; I mean—to prove its worth. Now an idea is not worth much unless the propositions in which it is embodied are true. Accordingly an essential part of the proof of a idea is the proof, either by experiment or by logic, of the truth of the propositions. But it is not essential that this proof of the truth should constitute the first introduction to the idea. After all, its assertion by the authority of respectable teachers is sufficient evidence to begin with. In our first contact with a set of propositions, we commence by appreciating their importance. That is what we all do in after—life. We do not attempt, in the strict sense, to prove or to disprove anything, unless its importance makes it worthy of that honor.[21] These two processes of proof, in the narrow sense, and of appreciation, do not require a rigid separation in time. Both can be proceeded with nearly concurrently. But in so far as either process must have the priority, it should be that of appreciation by use.

Furthermore, we should not endeavor to use propositions in isolation.[22] Practically I do not mean, a neat little set of experiments to illustrate Proposition I and then the proof of Proposition I, a neat little set of experiments to illustrate Proposition II and then the proof of Proposition II, and so on to the end of the book. Nothing could be more boring.[23] Interrelated truths are utilized *en bloc*, and the various propositions are employed in any order, and with any reiteration. Choose some important applications of your theoretical subject; and study them concurrently with the systematic theoretical exposition. Keep the theoretical exposition short and simple, but let it be strict and rigid so far as it goes. It should not be too long for it to be easily known with thoroughness and accuracy. The consequences of a plethora of half-digested theoretical knowledge are deplorable.[24] Also the theory should not be muddled up with the practice.[25] The child should have no doubt when it is proving and when it is utilizing. My point is that what is proved should be utilized, and that what is utilized should—so far, as is practicable—be proved. I am far from asserting that proof and utilization are the same thing.[26]

At this point of my discourse, I can most directly carry forward my argument in the outward form of a digression. We are only just realizing that the art and science of education require a genius and a study of their own; and that this genius and this science are more than a bare knowledge of some branch of science or of literature. This truth was partially perceived in the past generation; and headmasters, somewhat crudely, were apt to supersede learning in their colleagues by requiring left-hand bowling and a taste for football. But culture is more than cricket, and more than football, and more than extent of knowledge.

Education is the acquisition of the art of the utilization of knowledge. This is an art very difficult to impart.[27] Whenever a textbook is written of real educational worth, you may be quite certain that some reviewers will say that it will be difficult to teach from it. Of course it will be difficult to teach from it. If it were easy, the book ought to be burned; for it cannot be educational. In education, as elsewhere, the broad primrose path leads to a nasty place.[28] This evil path is represented by a book or a set of lectures, which will practically enable the student to learn by heart all the questions likely to be asked at the nest external examination. And I may say in passing that no educational system is possible unless every question directly asked of a pupil at any examination is either framed or modified by the actual teacher of that pupil in that subject. The external assessor may report on the curriculum or on the performance of the pupils, but never should be allowed to ask the pupil a question, which has not been strictly supervised by the actual teacher, or at least inspired by a long conference with him. There are a few exceptions to this rule, but they are exceptions, and could easily be allowed for under the general rule.[29]

We now return to my previous point, that theoretical ideas should always find important applications within the pupil's curriculum. This is not an easy doctrine to apply, but a very hard one.[30] It contains within itself the problem of keeping knowledge alive, of preventing it from becoming inert, which is the central problem of all education.

The best procedure will depend on several factors, none of which can be neglected, namely, the genius of the teacher, the intellectual type of the pupils, their prospects in life, the opportunities offered by the immediate surroundings of the school and allied factors of this sort. It is for this reason that the uniform external examination is so deadly. We do not denounce it because we are cranks, and like denouncing established things.[31] We are not so childish. Also, of course, such examinations have their use in testing slackness. Our reason of dislike is very definite and very practical. It kills the best part of culture. When you analyze in the light of experience the central task of education, you find that its successful accomplishment depends on a delicate adjustment of many variable factors.[32] The reason is that we are dealing with human minds, and not with dead matter. The evocation of curiosity, of judgment, of the power of mastering a complicated tangle of circumstances, the use of theory in giving foresight in special cases all these powers are not to be imparted by a set rule embodied in one schedule of examination subjects.

注　释

1　In the history of education, the most striking phenomenon is that schools of learning, which at one epoch are alive with a ferment of genius, in a succeeding generation, exhibit merely pedantry and routine. 在教育史上，最令人瞩目的现象是，学习流派在一个时代百家争鸣，而在后续的一个时代却墨守成规。
ferment是"蓬勃发展，激动，骚动，纷扰"的意思，比如：It is an age of the great period of creative ferment in literature. 这是个文学创作蓬勃发展的伟大时期。
pedantry是"迂腐，自炫博学，拘泥形式"的意思，比如：Pedantry proceeds from much reading and little understanding. 迂腐出自读得多而理解少。

2　The reason is, that they are over laden with inert ideas. Education with inert ideas is not only useless: it is, above all things, harmful—*corruptio optimi*, *pessima*. 原因是他们被固有的观念所累。这种教育不仅仅是没有用的，尤为重要的是，是有害的。
be laden with是"装载；装着"的意思，比如：He always comes back from France laden with presents for everyone. 他从法国回来总带了许多礼物给每个人。
inert是"无生命的、迟钝的"的意思，比如：A dull, lazy person is insert. 迟钝懒散的人士没有生气的。

corruptio optimi，*pessima* 腐蚀最好的东西是一种最坏的腐蚀。

3. Except at rare intervals of intellectual ferment, education in the past has been radically infected with inert ideas. 除了几次短暂的思想活跃的时期外，过去的教育深深地被这些固有的、无活力的思想影响着。

   at intervals 是"不时，到处，每隔……时间/距离"的意思，比如：They meet each other at intervals. 他们时不时地聚一次。

   be infected with 是"受影响，感染"的意思，比如：Whole societies were infected by these vices. 整个社会被这些恶习所腐蚀。

4. That is the reason why uneducated clever women, who have seen much of the world, are in middle life so much the most cultured part of the community. 这就是为什么一些没有受过教育的有才智的妇女她们饱经风霜到了中年却成为社会上最有教养的人。

   why 引导的是定语从句修饰 reason。在 why 引导的定语从句中，又有一个 who 引导的非限制性定语从句修饰 woman。

5. Every intellectual revolution, which has never stirred humanity into greatness, has been a passionate protest against inert ideas. 每一次曾经引起人类巨大震动的思想革命，就是对无活力的概念的一次激情的反抗。

6. Then, alas, with pathetic ignorance of human psychology, it has proceeded by some educational scheme to bind humanity afresh with inert ideas of its own fashioning. 啊，由于对人类心理的可悲的无知，有些教育制度就用它自己所造成的无活力的概念重新把人类束缚住了。

   with 介词短语作原因短语。ignorance of 是"不知，无知"的意思，比如：We are in complete ignorance of his plans. 我们完全不知道他的计划。

7. Let us now ask how in our system of education we are to guard against this mental dry rot. 现在我们要问：如何在教育系统中防止这种心理上的衰败。

   guard against 是"努力防止……使不要发生"的意思，比如：The best way to guard against financial problem is to avoid getting into debts. 防止发生财政问题的最好方法是避免负债。

   dryrot 是"干腐，腐败"的意思，比如：Lack of new people and new ideas often causes dryrot in an organization. 缺乏新人和新思想常使一个组织腐化。

8. We enunciate two educational commandments, "Do not teach too many subjects," and again, "what you teach, teach thoroughly." 我们要提出两条教育的戒律，"不要教过多的学科"，以及"要教，就要教得透彻"。

   enunciate 是"宣布，发表"的意思，比如：You must learn to enunciate your own ideas independently. 你必须学会独立地发表自己的观点。

9. The result of teaching small parts of a large number of subjects is the passive reception of disconnected ideas, not illumined with any spark of vitality. 教许多学科，而每门学科只教那么一少部分，其结果就是被动地接受一些互无联系的、毫无活力的概念。

   illumine 是"启明，照耀"的意思，比如：The room was poorly illuminated by one candle. 屋子被一支孤单的蜡烛照得半明不暗的。

a spark of:是"少量的,一点点"的意思,比如:There wasn't a spark of interest in the children's faces. 孩子们的脸上没有一丝感兴趣的表情。

10 The child should make them his own, and should understand their application here and now in the circumstances of his actual life. 儿童应该使这些概念成为他自己的概念,并且懂得这些概念此时此地在他实际生活环境中的应用。

11 The discovery, which he has to make, is that general ideas give an understanding of that stream of events, which pours through his life, which is his life. 他必须发现,普通概念使他理解那倾注在他生活中的川流不息的事件,这川流不息的事件也就是他们的生活。
第一个 which 引导的非限制性定语从句修饰 discovery, that 引导的是表语从句。第二个和第三个 which 引导的非限制性定语从句修饰 events。

12 Pedants sneer at an education, which is useful. 学究们藐视教育,但教育却是有益的。
sneer at 是"嘲笑,讥讽"的意思。比如:sneer at a girl's cheap clothes 嘲笑一个姑娘身穿的廉价衣服。

13 It was useful to Saint Augustine and it was useful to Napoleon. 对圣奥古斯丁来说,它是有用的,对拿破仑也是如此。
Saint Augustine:圣奥古斯丁,古代北非努米底亚国希波城(今突尼斯)主教。

14 Nor do I wish to be supposed to pronounce on the relative merits of a classical or a modern curriculum. 我也不想别人期待我在古典课程和现代课程价值比较的问题上发表意见。
由 nor 指代前面一句的内容,表示"也不"的意义时,通常位于句首,并引起倒装。比如:A: I disliked English when I was a student. B: Nor did I. 甲:我当学生时不喜欢英语。乙:我也不喜欢。

15 I would only remark that the understanding, which we want, is an understanding of an insistent present. 我只想指出,我们所要的领悟,是对当前的领悟。
insistent 是"坚持的,强求得,显著的,强烈的"意思,比如:He was insistent on going out last night. 昨晚他坚持出去。

16 No more deadly harm can be done to young minds than by depreciation of the present. 轻视对年轻人的心理危害极大。

17 The ages of Shakespeare and of Moliere are no less past than are the ages of Sophocles and of Virgil. 索福克勒斯和维吉尔的时代是过去,莎士比亚和莫里哀的时代也是过去。
Shakespeare 莎士比亚,英国戏剧家;Moliere 莫里哀,法国戏剧家;Sophocles 索福克勒斯,古希腊悲剧作家;Virgil 维吉尔,古罗马诗人。

18 The communion of saints is a great and inspiring assemblage, but it has only one possible hall of meeting, and that is, the present, and the mere lapse of time through which any particular group of saints must travel to reach that meeting—place, makes very little difference. 圣徒们的共同体是一个伟大并激发灵感的组合,但是这个团体只有一个可能的聚会地点,那就是现在;任何一批圣徒,最终到达这个地点所必需的时间本身并不重要。
lapse 是"堕落,终止,暂停"的意思,比如:He lapsed into bad habits since his parents got divorced. 自从他父母离婚后他就沾染了坏习气。
makes difference 是"区别对待,有关系,有影响,起作用"的意思,比如:Dollars make no dif-

ference to him. 钱对他不起作用。

19 Passing now to the scientific and logical side of education, we remember that here also ideas which are not utilized are positively harmful. 现在来谈谈科学的教育和逻辑的教育。我们记得这里也是这种情况，不加利用的概念是绝对有害的。

20 By utilizing an idea, I mean relating it to that stream, compounded of sense perceptions, feelings, hopes, desires, and of mental activities adjusting thought to thought, which forms our life. 所谓利用一个概念，我指的是把概念和由感性知觉、感情、希望、欲求以及调整思维与思维的关系的心理活动所组成的川流联系起来，这个川流就构成我们的生活。
by 介词短语作方式状语。compounded of... 是过去分词短语作后置定语修饰 steam。compounded of 是"混合，由……组成"的意思，比如：She looked at the burning house with a feeling compounded of curiosity and fear. 她带着一种好奇而有恐惧的表情看着熊熊燃烧的房屋。

21 We do not attempt, in the strict sense, to prove or to disprove anything, unless its importance makes it worthy of that honor. 我们并不试图在严格意义上去证明或者反证一件事，除非它很重要，值得这样做。
这是一个由 unless 引导的条件从句。be worthy of 是"值得的，应该的"意思，比如：That is very worthy of our attention. 那件事很值得我们注意。

22 Furthermore, we should not endeavor to use propositions in isolation. 而且我们不应该竭力去孤立地运用命题。
endeavor to do 是"努力，尽力，尝试"的意思，比如：He endeavored to control his disgust to her. 他尽力控制自己对她的厌恶情绪。
in isolation 是"孤立，分离，脱离"的意思，比如：look at something in isolation. 孤立地看某事。

23 Nothing could be more boring. 没有比这更令人厌烦的。
具有否定的词 + 比较级，相当于最高级，比如：Nobody could be worse than him. 没有比他更坏的人了。

24 The consequences of a plethora of half-digested theoretical knowledge are deplorable20. 过多的食而不化的理论知识的结果是可悲的。
plethora 是"太多，过剩"的意思，比如：There is a plethora of regulations in the government. 在政府中有很多泛滥的规章制度。
deplorable 是"可悲可叹的"意思，比如：The end of the hero is deplorable. 主人公的结局真是悲惨啊。

25 Also the theory should not be muddled up with the practice. 而且不应该混淆理论和实践。
be muddled up with 是"把……弄乱，混淆"的意思，比如：I am always muddling the twins up. 我老是分不清这一对孪生儿。

26 I am far from asserting that proof and utilization are the same thing. 我远不是主张证明和利用是一个东西。
far from 表示否定意义，比如：They were far from satisfied with situation. 我们对这种情况十分不满。

6. The Aims of Education 教育的目的

27 This is an art very difficult to impart. 这种艺术很难传授。
impart：传授，告知，揭发。如：You'd better never impart the secret to her, it's no good for both of you. 你最好永远不要告诉她那个秘密，这对你们两个都没有好处。

28 In education, as elsewhere, the broad primrose path leads to a nasty place. 在教育上，和在别处一样，华丽的大道是通向肮脏的地方的。
primrose 樱草花，这里作定语是指"华丽的"意思。

29 There are a few exceptions to this rule, but they are exceptions, and could easily be allowed for under the general rule. 这条规则也有少数例外，但毕竟是例外，大体上也是允许的。
exception 是"例外，异议，排除在外"的意思，比如：It has been cold this month, but today is an exception. 这个月一直很冷，但今天例外。

30 This is not an easy doctrine to apply, but a very hard one. 这个理论运用起来并不容易，而且很难。
apply to 是"应运，运用"的意思，比如：This rule applies to freshmen only. 这项规定仅限于一年级学生。

31 We do not denounce it because we are cranks, and like denouncing established things. 我们指责这件事，并不是因为我们是一些喜欢指责已有、规定的事情的古怪的人。
denounce 是"当众指责，告发，公然抨击"的意思，比如：She denounced his irresponsibility in the public meeting. 她在会议上公开指责他的不负责任。
crank 是"怪人，奇思妙想"的意思，比如：He is a crank with great ideas. 他是个总有奇思妙想的人。

32 When you analyze in the light of[28] experience the central task of education, you find that its successful accomplishment depends on a delicate adjustment of many variable factors. 当你借助经验来分析教育的中心任务时，你会发现它的成功取决于许多可变因素的细微调节。
in the light of 是"鉴于，由于；当作"的意思，比如：He reviewed his decision in the light of recent developments. 他根据最近的事态发展重新考虑自己的决定。

练　　习

1. 回答问题
   (1) How could the uneducated clever women become the most cultured part of the community?
   (2) What are the two educational commandments offered by the author?
   (3) What's the use of the knowledge of the past?
   (4) What's the central problem of all education?
   (5) Why does the author dislike the external examination?

2. 判断正误
   (1) All the education in the past has been radically infected with inert ideas.
   (2) No more deadly harm can be done to young minds than by depreciation of the present.

(3) Education is the acquisition of the art of the utilization of knowledge. This is an art easy to impart.

(4) If a textbook is easy to teach from it, it cannot be educational.

(5) Proof and utilization are the same thing.

3. 选词填空

in isolation, apply to, be worthy of, makes difference, sneer at, be infected with, at intervals, inert, ferment, exception

(1) The whole city was in a state of _____.

(2) You'd better consider it _____ from others.

(3) What I said does not _____ you.

(4) A stone is an/a _____ mass of matter.

(5) The noise would stop _____, then resume after a while.

(6) He is not _____ her.

(7) Anyone with a bad cold may _____ the people around him.

(8) I don't think it will _____.

(9) Don't _____ those who failed in the exam.

(10) All the students go there without any _____.

4. 句型模拟

(1) Nor (do)...

(2) No (more) than...

5. 英译汉

(1) That is the reason why uneducated clever women, who have seen much of the world, are in middle life so much the most cultured part of the community.

(2) The discovery, which he has to make, is that general ideas give an understanding of that stream of events, which pours through his life, which is his life.

(3) I pass lightly over that understanding which should be given by the literary side of education. Nor do I wish to be supposed to pronounce on the relative merits of a classical or a modern curriculum。

(4) No more deadly harm can be done to young minds than by depreciation of the present.

(5) Passing now to the scientific and logical side of education.

6. 汉译英

(1) 我和他的文件都弄混了。(be muddle up with)

(2) 你必须清晰地阐明你的意图。(enunciate)

(3) 不管他怎样努力,目标还是难以达到。(endeavor to do)

(4) 我一向把他当作自己的儿子看待。(in the light of)

(5) 理论应该被用于实践。(apply to)

7. 写作指导

For this part, you are required to write a composition on the topic "How to Be a Good Teacher". The following points taken from the text are useful expressions for your reference:
- "Do not teach too many subjects," and again, "what you teach, teach thoroughly."
- No more deadly harm can be done to young minds than by depreciation of the present.
- The consequences of a plethora of half-digested theoretical knowledge are deplorable.
- What is proved should be utilized, and that what is utilized should—so far, as is practicable—be proved.
- Education is the acquisition of the art of the utilization of knowledge. This is an art easy to impart.
- The theoretical ideas should always find important applications within the pupil's curriculum. This is not an easy doctrine to apply, but a very hard one. It contains within itself the problem of keeping knowledge alive, of preventing it from becoming inert, which is the central problem of all education.

Essentialism Education
要素主义教育

要素主义教育是当代美国影响较大的一个教育思想流派。它出现于二十世纪三十年代美国资本主义经济大危机时期。它在许多方面与"进步的"实用主义教育相对立。许多教育家根据它的特征将其归为新传统教育派。主要代表人物有巴格、科南特、里科弗莱等。

要素主义教育流派没有明显的哲学基础,也不像新行为主义教育或结构主义教育那样具备一定的心理学基础,它直接植根于美国的社会现实,为摆脱政治、经济的困境服务,有很强的现实感。二十世纪五十年代要素主义教育思潮开始在全美占统治地位,并且为六十年代后美国的中小学课程改革运动提供了理论武器。

要素主义教育认为人类文化遗产里有所谓永恒不变的、共同的要素,是一切人都应当学习的;强调经过历史考验的种族经验即社会遗产,比个人的知识和儿童的任何未经考验的经验更有意义;强调学校是传递文化的机构,应当把教育作为"社会生活再现的过程,通过教育,使社会遗产在每一个新生的一代中再现出来";强调教育过程要从一些最简单的、为儿童所理解和接受的"要素"开始,再逐步过渡到更为复杂的"要素",促进儿童天赋能力的全面和谐发展。它可以使儿童易于接受,任何人都容易掌握,且用起来方便。

因此,它主张把所谓"文化的共同要素"作为课程的核心,恢复传统课程。它极力反对实用主义的以儿童经验为中心,"从做中学"等。它强调学习的系统性,提出应严格按照逻辑系统编写教材。认为一些要求严格的科目,如拉丁文、代数和几何对心灵训练具有特殊价值,应在课程中占有重要地位,并作为中等学校的共同必修科目。强调对于学生的学业成绩要进行严格考核,作为升、留级的标准。

要素主义者一般很重视"天才教育"。主张提高所谓"智力标准",强调"智育的目的",认为一切教育的目标应该是发展人的"智慧力量"。由于特别强调系统的学习和智力的陶冶,它主张教育过程中的主动性在于教师而不在于学生,提出应该"把教师放在教育体系的中心",充分发挥教师的"权威"作用。1956年,以贝斯特为代表所组织的"基础教育协会"。六十年代,科南特、里科弗提出的一系列的教育"改革"方案。

　　要素主义教育虽然有值得肯定的部分,但也不可忽略它存在的一些严重不足:关于学习人类文化共同要素的思想缺乏科学依据和哲学基础;要素主义教育家们强调教师的权威,提出应该把"教师放在教育体系的中心"。这虽然有纠正实用主义造成的偏差的积极因素,但是他们又走了另一个极端,压抑了学生的积极性与创造性,有碍于教育、教学效率的提高。要素主义教育的这些弊端导致了教育与社会实践的脱离,因此,二十世纪六十年代末,在其他新兴教育思潮的挑战面前,要素主义教育黯然失色,退出了教育舞台。

7. The Wasteland of Education[1]
教育的荒地

Arthur Bestor
阿瑟·贝斯特

阿瑟·贝斯特(1908—?)是美国历史学家,教育家,耶鲁大学毕业。先后在耶鲁大学,哥伦比亚大学师范学院,斯坦福大学,牛津大学任教。1956年任美国基础教育协会会长。这个协会成立的目的在于促进中小学设置更多的基础课程。主要教育著作有:《教育的荒地》、《学术的复兴》和《科学时代的教育》。

贝斯特是要素主义教育的发言人之一。他尖锐地抨击美国的进步主义教育使中小学教学效果下降,坚持传统教育;认为经过训练的智慧才是力量的源泉,真正的教育就是智慧的训练;要求在中小学加强语文,历史,科学各门基础科目的教学,并按照严格标准测量学生的成绩;认为中学毕业生必须具备比以往更坚实的智慧基础与更高的技术和能力。

《教育的荒地》(1953)是贝斯特的主要代表作,他被认为是二十世纪五十年代对进步教育最尖锐、最彻底和最有影响的批评。《学术的复兴》一书根据教育界人士和社会界人士的评论,对《教育的荒地》作了增补和改编,1955年出版。贝斯特认为教育对国家的福利和民主制度的安全具有特别重要的意义。

在二十世纪中美国教育面临很多问题,公立学校没有经过认真选择,教学质量下降,美国学校成了一个巨大的收容所。其主要原因就是它没有目标。美国公众不要孩子懂得如何读写算,不关心孩子学习历史、科学和外语,把教育仅仅看作是生活的经验,对受教育者来说是愉快的,但对社会来说是没有价值的。美国教育的改革应表现在七个方面:科学家和学者的责任;改组教师训练;教育学习困难的学生;重建考试的标准;谨慎地使用教育资源;国家在天才方面的投资和文理学院的理想。

The Vanishing Sense of Purpose in Education

Americans have unbounded faith in schools, but they seem to distrust the results of schooling.[2] We send, at public expense, an ever-increasing proportion of the population to school and college, yet we are suspicious of the highly educated man who offers to make some return by devoting his special training to the public service.[3] At graduation we are proud to see our sons and daughters march forward in cap and gown, but in the morning newspaper we recognize the very same cap and gown as the cartoonist's accepted symbol for folly and ineffectiveness.

Universal, free, public education is part of the democratic creed, which Americans accept but which they would find it hard to explain in rational terms.[4] It doesn't appear that many of them seriously expect society to get its money's worth out of the process. We pay our school taxes, but we rarely conceive of ourselves as making thereby an investment in the intellectual advancement of the nation. Our motive seems to be little more than warm-hearted benevolence.[5] We hate to think that any child should be deprived of his fair share of anything so costly, so ornamental, and so well-regarded as education.[6] To put the matter bluntly, we regard schooling as a mere experience, delightful to the recipient but hardly valuable to society.[7] The school or college has become, to our minds, merely a branch of the luxury-purveying trade.[8] Like the club car on a passenger train, it dispenses the amenities of life to persons bound on serious errands elsewhere.

Now, public opinion is not so perverse as to adopt such a view without cause.[9] It is fully aware of the traditional claims of education. It is prepared to believe that knowledge is a good thing both in its own right and for the practical uses to which it can be put. It sees a connection between good citizenship and the ability to think. What it is skeptical about is the ability of our schools and colleges to impart these qualities of mind to their graduates. Responsibility for this disbelief rests squarely upon the men and women who are professionally engaged in education.[10] They have allowed themselves to become confused about the purposes of education, and they have transmitted that confusion to the public. They have sponsored school and college programs which make no substantial contribution to knowledge or to clear thinking, and which could not conceivably make such a contribution.[11] The public, seeing no point in much of what is done under the name of education, have developed a justifiable skepticism toward education itself.[12] They are willing to keep on playing the game, but they refuse to think of it as much more than a game.

The founders of our nation and of our school system betrayed no such confusion of purpose. "If a nation expects to be ignorant and free," wrote Thomas Jefferson, "...it expects what never was and never will be."[13] Jefferson intended his words to be taken literally. He knew, moreover, what he meant by education. It is, first of all, the opposite of ignorance. Its positive meaning is indicated by the synonyms, which Jefferson employs in his letters. The kind of schooling that is vital to a democratic society is the kind that results in "spread of information" and the "diffusion of knowledge"; the kind that regards "science...[as] more important in a republican than in any other government"; the kind that recognizes that "the general mind must be strengthened by education"; the kind that aims to make the people "enlightened" and to "inform their discretion."[14] These are the ends, which the schools must serve if a free people is to remain free. These, be it noted, are intellectual ends. Genuine education, in short, is intellectual training.

The founders of our public school system meant by education exactly what Jefferson meant by education and exactly what thoughtful men had always meant by it. They believed, quite simply, that ignorance is a handicap and disciplined intelligence a source of power.[15] A democracy, they argued, should make intellectual training available to every citizen, whether poor or rich. So great would be the benefit to the state from such a diffusion of knowledge and intelligence that it was legitimate to support the educational system by taxation, and even to use the coercive authority of law to compel every future citizen to secure an education by attending school for a substantial period of time.[16]

The American people, more than a century ago, committed themselves to this program, and they have invested heavily in the effort to bring it to full realization.[17] By every quantitative measure—time, effort, numbers, and money—we should be well on the way toward achievement of the noble ends in view. Enrollment has steadily increased until today four out of every five American children between the ages of five and seventeen, inclusive, are in school. We talk so much about overcrowding that we are apt to forget the significant fact[18] that the equipment and resources of the public schools have increased far more rapidly than attendance. Approximately four times as many children as in 1870 are now in school, but we spend more than ninety times as much on their education. The child of today enjoys a school year twice as long. The proportion of teachers to pupils is greater, and the teachers are required to have spent far more time in training. Compared with 1870 (after adjustments have been made for the changed value of the dollar), we find that nine times as much money is spent per year on the education of each child, and nearly thirteen times as much is invested in the buildings and equipment, which each one is privileged to use.[19] Inequalities and inadequacies persist, of course, and these must be eliminated. But the fact remains that the American people have generously and faithfully supported their schools. They have a right to ask whether the qualitative educational achievement of our public schools is commensurate with the money and effort that have been invested in them.[20] In effect this is to ask whether school administrators have been as faithful to the ideal of democratic education as have the American people.

Admittedly it is a complicated task to measure the effectiveness of a school system.[21] But on almost every count there is general dissatisfaction with the results of the twelve years of education currently provided by most of our public schools.[22] And it is an exceedingly important fact that the criticisms come with greatest intensity from those who believe most strongly in the value and importance of education, and who, by their professions, are best qualified to judge what sound education consists in.[23] Discontent with the training, which the public schools provide is all but unanimous, I discover, among members of the liberal arts and professional faculties of our universities and colleges.[24] It is almost equally widespread among doctors, engineers, clergymen, lawyers, and other professional men throughout the nation. Businessmen are dismayed at the deficiencies in reading, writing, arithmetic, and general knowledge displayed by the high school and college graduates they employ.[25] Parents are alarmed at the educational handicaps under which their children are obliged to labor as they enter upon the serious business of life.[26]

In every community, searching questions about present-day educational policy are being raised by intelligent, responsible, disinterested citizens. The criticism is not that of "reactionaries". Among my acquaintances and correspondents, the liberals in political and social matters are just as outspoken in their denunciation of current trends in the public schools as are the men and women whose views can be labeled conservative.[27] Upon college and university faculties the criticism does not come primarily from classicists in the order "traditional" branches of learning; it comes with perhaps greatest intensity from professors in the sciences, in mathematics, and in the other disciplines directly connected with the problems of a modern technological world.

The defense of their stewardship that is offered by public school administrators and by their allies in universities departments of education is so feeble as to amount to a confession of failure.[28] They quote criticisms of earlier date to show that discontent in the past was as great as it is today. The logic is that of Looking-Glass Land, where, the Red Queen explained to Alice, "it takes all the running you can do, to keep in the same place. If you want to get somewhere else, you must run at least twice as fast as that!" in every other area of American life progress is measured in terms of defects overcome[29]. Only the professional educationists take pride in the fact that, though they run several times as hard, they can always be found by their critics in pretty much the same spot.[30]

Some improvement, indeed, the professional educationalists do claim, but the evidence they adduce is exceedingly slight and scattered, and it never gives weight to the vastly increased time, effort, and money, which have gone into producing the results described.[31] Typical of the evidence which school administrator's offer is this: "Arithmetic tests given to ninth-grade pupils in Springfield, Massachusetts, in 1845, were administered to Minneapolis eighth-graders in 1926. The percent of correct answers in 1845 was 29.4 as compared to 67.1 in 1926." If these figures could be accepted as a valid statistical sample, they would merely prove that when the elementary schools stick to their traditional tasks they do a job appreciably better than the ill-equipped and financially impoverished schools of a century ago, with their short school terms and their inadequately trained teachers. In weighing this evidence let us remember (as a previous paragraph has pointed out) that by the time a pupil has finished a given grade today, he will have spent twice as many days in school as a comparable student would have spent eighty years ago.[32] He will have received a greater share of the personal attention of a better-trained teacher. Nine times as much money will have been expended in his education, and he will have used buildings and equipment at least thirteen times as good. A comparison with 1845, could it be made, would show an even greater increase in resources. If the achievement of a present-day student is only a little greater than that of his predecessor, instead of several times as great, there has been an alarming decline in the efficiency of public school instruction.

注　释

1　本文选自阿瑟·贝斯特的《教育的荒地》。
2　Americans have unbounded faith in schools, but they seem to distrust the results of schooling. 美国人对学校怀有无限的信仰，但是他们好像对教育成果表示怀疑。
　　have faith in 指"信任，信赖"，比如：My parents have great faith in me, and I can't disappoint them. 我的父母这样信赖我，我不能让他们失望。
3　We send, at public expense, an ever-increasing proportion of the population to school and college, yet we are suspicious of the highly educated man who offers to make some return by

7. The Wasteland of Education 教育的荒地

devoting his special training to the public service. 我们把人口中比例正在增长的人送到中小学和大学受公费教育,然而我们却对愿意把他的专项技能贡献给社会作为回报的受过高等教育的人才深感怀疑。

at expense 指"花……钱;以……为代价",比如:He bought the house at the expense of all his savings. 他把自己的所有的积蓄都用来买房子了。

be suspicious of 指"对某人或某事起疑心",比如:The public is suspicious of the government's intentions. 公众对政府的意图表示怀疑。

4 Universal, free, public education is part of the democratic creed, which Americans accept but which they would find it hard to explain in rational terms. 普及教育、提供免费教育和提供公共教育是美国人接受的民主信条的一部分,但又是他们感到难以用合理的词语进行解释的信条。

两个 Which 引导的是并列的同位语从句。creed 指"教条,信条,信念",比如:His creed is to be honest and just. 他的人生信条就是诚实正直。而 rational 则是"理智的,有理性的,合理的"之意,比如:Panic destroys rational thought. 惊恐使人不能做出理智的思考。

5 Our motive seems to be little more than warm-hearted benevolence. 我们的动机似乎不外是乐善好施。

benevolence 是指"善意,仁慈,善行",比如:He did it out of pure benevolence. 他做这件事完全是出于善意。

6 We hate to think that any child should be deprived of his fair share of anything so costly, so ornamental, and so well-regarded as education. 我们不愿考虑儿童被剥夺本属于他的那份东西,那贵重的、光彩的、受人尊敬的教育。

be deprived of 指"被剥夺,丧失",比如:He was deprived of his sight by the accident. 那次事故使他丧失了视力。

7 To put the matter bluntly, we regard schooling as a mere experience, delightful to the recipient but hardly valuable to society. 坦率地说,我们仅仅把教育看成是经验,它对受教育者来说是令人愉快的,但是对社会来说是毫无价值的。

To put the matter bluntly 坦率地说。比如:To put the matter bluntly, I don't think you are wiser than me. 坦率地说,我不认为你比我聪明。

Bluntly 指"迟钝的,率直的"。比如:to sharpen a blunt knife 磨钝刀/I am rather blunt in speech. 我说话很直率。

8 The school or college has become, to our minds, merely a branch of the luxury-purveying trade. 在我们的印象中,学校或大学仅仅成为奢侈供应行业的分支。

luxury-purveying trade:奢侈供应行业。purvey 指"供应,承办",比如:The media is to purvey information to the people. 媒体就是向大众传播信息的。

9 Now, public opinion is not so perverse as to adopt such a view without cause. 原来,公共舆论是不会那么荒谬到无故采取这一观点的。

perverse 指"任性的,荒谬的",比如:It would be perverse to refuse to support the plea. 不支持这种请愿是有悖常理的。

10 Responsibility for this disbelief rests squarely upon the men and women who are professional-

ly engaged in education. 之所以不信任，责任就在于专门从事教育的男男女女身上。

be engaged in 指"忙的，从事……的"，比如：Engaged in conversation, they did not see me. 他们正谈得来劲，没有看见我。

11 They have sponsored school and college programs which make no substantial contribution to11 knowledge or to clear thinking, and which could not conceivably make such a contribution. 他们赞助中小学和大学的课程，这些课程对知识或清晰的思维并没有实质性贡献，而且也不可能想像会做出这样的贡献。

make contribution to: 作贡献，促成。比如：make a notable contribution to public safety 为公共安全做出神圣的贡献

12 The public, seeing no point in much of what is done under the name of education, have developed a justifiable skepticism toward education itself. 公众由于看不出以教育的名义所作事情的意义，他们便产生了对教育本身无可非议的置疑。

seeing 引导的独立主格结构作状语修饰主语 the public。under the name of 是"用……的名字，以……的名义"的意思，比如：He lent 500 Yuan to him under the name of a friend. 他以朋友的名义借给他五百块钱。

skepticism 是"怀疑态度"的意思，比如：I regard his theory with skepticism. 我对他的理论持怀疑态度。

13 "If a nation expects to be ignorant and free...it expects what never was and never will be." 如果一个国家期望成为愚蠢和无拘无束的状态，……他所期望的便是过去从未有过的将来也不会再有的东西。

14 The kind of schooling that is vital to a democratic society is the kind that results in "spread of information" and the "diffusion of knowledge"; the kind that regards "science…[as] more important in a republican than in any other government"; the kind that recognizes that "the general mind must be strengthened by education"; the kind that aims to make the people "enlightened" and to "inform their discretion." 对一个民主社会极其重要的教育就是一种促进"知识传播"和"知识扩散"结果的、目的在于使人民"开明"和"激活他们的判断力"的教育。

be vital to 是"必不可少的，极其重要的"的意思。比如：These matters are vital to the national security. 这些问题对国家安全极其重要。

diffusion 是"散布，普及，传播"的意思，比如：Nowadays the diffusion of news is over radio, TV and internet quickly. 现在新闻通过无线电、电视及网络快速传播。

discretion 是"谨慎，明辨，自由选择或决定"的意思，比如：Discretion is the better part of valor. [谚语] 谨慎即大勇。

15 They believed, quite simply, that ignorance is a handicap and disciplined intelligence a source of power. 他们相信，过于单一地相信，愚昧是障碍，而经过磨炼的智慧乃是力量的源泉。

16 So great would be the benefit to the state from such a diffusion of knowledge and intelligence that it was legitimate to support the educational system by taxation, and even to use the coercive authority of law to compel every future citizen to secure an education by attending school for a substantial period of time. 这种知识和智慧的传播，给国家带来巨大利益，因此

7. The Wasteland of Education 教育的荒地

用赋税来支持教育制度,甚至用法律的强制作用迫使每一个未来的公民在相当长的时间内在学校获得教育,都是正当的。

本句中的 so…that 句型的前半部分 so 开头,句子用倒装。本句的正常语序为 the benefit to the state from such a diffusion of knowledge and intelligence would be so great that…。

legitimate 是"正当的,真实的,合理的"的意思,比如:The legitimate business practices will be protected by the laws. 正常的经营活动将得到法律的保护。

coercive 是"强迫的,抑制的,高压的"的意思,比如:His stealing behavior is coercive. 他的偷盗行为是被迫的。

compel…to 指"强迫,使不得不",比如:The big boy compelled his classmate to do the homework for him. 那个大孩子强迫他的同学为他做作业。

17 The American people, more than a century ago, committed themselves to this program, and they have invested heavily in the effort to bring it to full realization. 美国人在一个多世纪以前就致力于这个计划,而且他们投资了巨大人力使其全面实现。

commit…to:使承担义务,使作出保证,使卷入。比如:before committing themselves to marriage 在缔结婚姻之前

18 We talk so much about overcrowding that we are apt to forget the significant fact:我们对学校拥挤问题谈得很多,就容易忘记一个重要的事实。

be apt to 是"有……倾向的"意思,比如:A careless person is apt to make mistakes. 粗心的人易犯错误。

19 Compared with 1870 (after adjustments have been made for the changed value of the dollar), we find that nine times as much money is spent per year on the education of each child, and nearly thirteen times as much is invested in the buildings and equipment, which each one is privileged touse. 我们发现,同年相比,花在每个儿童教育上的经费增加到九倍(在对美元价值的变化进行调整之后),用于每个儿童特许使用的校舍和设备方面的资金将近十三倍。

be privileged to 是"享有或授予特权的,特许的"的意思,比如:We are privileged to live on a very precious planet. 我们庆幸自己生活在一个得天独厚的星球上。

20 They have a right to ask whether the qualitative educational achievement of our public schools is commensurate with the money and effort that have been invested in them. 他们有权质问我们公立学校的教育质量与我们投资在上面的经费和人力是否相称。

be commensurate with 是"相当的,相称的"的意思,比如:The salary is commensurate with the output. 工资与产量相称。

21 Admittedly it is a complicated task to measure the effectiveness of a school system. 不可否认,衡量一个学校制度的效果是一件复杂的工作。

22 But on almost every count there is general dissatisfaction with the results of the twelve years of education currently provided by most of our public schools. 但是目前我们公立学校十二年教育的结果几乎在每一方面普遍都令人不满意。

dissatisfaction with/at 是"对……不满"的意思,比如:Many teachers stated their dissatisfaction with existing methods of testing language skills. 许多教师说出了他们对现行的语言技

巧的测试方法的不满。

23 And it is an exceedingly important fact that the criticisms come with greatest intensity from those who believe most strongly in the value and importance of education, and who, by their professions, are best qualified to judge what sound education consists in. 一个非常重要的事实是,最严厉的批评来自那些最坚信教育的价值和重要性的人们,从他们的职业来说他们最有资格判断何为健全的教育。

本句是一个以 it 为形式主语,由 that 引导的从句为真正的主语的主语从句。exceedingly 是"非常,极端地,胜过地"的意思,比如:His rude behavior annoyed her pride exceedingly. 他粗鲁的行为令她极为恼怒。

consist in 是"在于,存在于"的意思,比如:Her charm does not only consist in her beauty. 她的魅力不仅在于她的美貌。

24 Discontent with the training, which the public schools provide is all but unanimous, I discover, among members of the liberal arts and professional faculties of our universities and colleges. 我发现,我们大学和学院的文理科和专业科系的同事,对公立学校提供的培训几乎一致地表示不满。

all but 是"几乎,差不多;除了……都;几乎完全的"的意思,比如:The shelf was all but empty. 架上几乎全空了。

25 Businessmen are dismayed at the deficiencies in reading, writing, arithmetic, and general knowledge displayed by the high school and college graduates they employ. 企业界人士对受雇于他们的大中学毕业生的读、写、算技能和贫乏的普通知识感到惊愕。

be dismayed at 是"使惊恐,使惊愕"的意思,比如:We were dismayed at the violence of his reaction. 他强烈的反映使我们惊愕。

26 Parents are alarmed at the educational handicaps under which their children are obliged to labor as they enter upon the serious business of life. 家长们对这种不利的教育感到震惊,因为他们的子女受其影响不得不在正式工作生活的开始时期加倍努力。

be obliged to 是"以道义,法律或体力强使,迫使"的意思,比如:I felt obliged to invite him into the parlor. 我只得把他让进客厅。

27 Among my acquaintances and correspondents, the liberals in political and social matters are just as outspoken in their denunciation of current trends in the public schools as are the men and women whose views can be labeled conservative. 我所熟悉的和与我通信的人士中,在政治和社会问题上持自由观点的人对公立学校目前趋势的指责,与那些被标榜在观点上保守的男男女女一样率直。

outspoken 是"直言无隐的,率直的,坦白的"的意思,比如:I like to make friends with those outspoken persons. 我愿意结交那些率直的人。

28 The defense of their stewardship that is offered by public school administrators and by their allies in universities departments of education is so feeble as to amount to a confession of failure. 公立学校行政人员和他们在大学教育系的同盟者为自己的管理职务作辩护,他们的辩护是如此软弱无力,就等于说他们在承认失败。

amount to 是"合计,共计,等同,接近"的意思,比如:This amounts to doing the thing over a-

7. The Wasteland of Education 教育的荒地

gain. 这就等于把这事再做一遍。

29 in every other area of American life progress is measured in terms of defects overcome：在美国生活的其他领域，衡量进步是以克服缺点为根据的。
in terms of 是"用……的话，用……的字眼；根据，按照；在……方面"的意思，比如：He condemned the protest in strong terms. 他用激烈的措辞谴责这场抗议。

30 Only the professional educationists take pride in the fact that, though they run several times as hard, they can always be found by their critics in pretty much the same spot. 只有职业的教育家确实对这一事实感到自豪，虽然他们跑得几倍那么快，但是评论家总是说他们还在原地。
take pride in 是"以……自豪，对……感到得意"的意思，比如：He takes great pride in his work. 他对自己的工作感到非常得意。

31 Some improvement, indeed, the professional educationists do claim, but the evidence they adduce is exceedingly slight and scattered, and it never gives weight to the vastly increased time, effort, and money, which have gone into producing the results described31. 职业的教育家确实声称有某些进步，但是他们引用的证据是非常不足而且零星的。而且这种证据对于为产生这样的结果而投入大量增加的时间、人力和资金来说是没有什么影响力的。
adduce 是"引证，举证"的意思，比如：More data may be adduced to reinforce the point. 可以引证更多的资料来近一步证实这一论点。
give weight to 是"给予重视"的意思，比如：We should give due weight to economic problems. 我们应对经济问题给予应有的重视。

32 In weighing this evidence let us remember that by the time a pupil has finished a given grade today, he will have spent twice as many days in school as a comparable student would have spent eighty years ago. 在衡量这个证据时，让我们记着，今天，当一个学生读完某一年级时，他在校花费的学习的时间是八十年前与他相似的学生的两倍。
本句中由 by the time 引出的将来时间状语，句子采用将来完成时态，表示将来某一时刻完成的动作。比如：By the time of this semester, I shall have finished four courses. 到这学期期末我将修完四门课程。

练　习

1. 回答问题
   (1) What are the attitudes of the Americans towards education?
   (2) How could public have such a so-called perverse opinion to the education?
   (3) Whether have school administrators been as faithful to the ideal of democratic education as the American people have?
   (4) What did Jefferson mean by education?
   (5) Why does the author say that there has been an alarming decline in the efficiency of public school instruction?

2. 判断正误

(1) The Americans have strong faith in schools and the results of schooling.

(2) It appears that many of Americans seriously expect society to get its money's worth out of the process of schooling.

(3) The public opinion is so perverse as to adopt such a view without cause.

(4) The founders of our public school system meant by education was totally different with what Jefferson meant by education.

(5) The American people, more than a century ago, committed themselves to this program, and they have invested heavily in the effort to bring it to full realization.

3. 选词填空

be suspicious of, conceive of, be engaged in, benevolence, be deprived of, be dismayed at, amount to, adduce, give weight to, be vital to

(1) We should _____ the students' oral skills.

(2) More data may be _____ to reinforce the point.

(3) We were _____ the violence of his reaction.

(4) This _____ doing the thing over again.

(5) He was _____ life by the accident.

(6) _____ his work, he did not look up to see me.

(7) These matters are _____ the national security.

(8) He did it out of pure _____.

(9) The public is _____ his intention.

(10) I can't _____ his writing skills.

4. 句型模拟

(1) by the time of

(2) all but

5. 英译汉

(1) Universal, free, public education is part of the democratic creed, which Americans accept but which they would find it hard to explain in rational terms.

(2) Now, public opinion is not so perverse as to adopt such a view without cause.

(3) Responsibility for this disbelief rests squarely upon the men and women who are professionally engaged in education.

(4) The defense of their stewardship that is offered by public school administrators and by their allies in universities departments of education is so feeble as to amount to a confession of failure.

(5) In weighing this evidence let us remember that by the time a pupil has finished a given grade today, he will have spent twice as many days in school as a comparable student

would have spent eighty years ago.

6. 汉译英

(1) 那个大孩子强迫他的同学给他钱。(compel...to)
(2) 在缔结婚姻之前他们并不认识。(commit...to)
(3) 粗心的人易犯错误。(be apt to)
(4) 我们庆幸自己生活在一个得天独厚的星球上。(be privileged to)
(5) 工资与劳动产量相称。(be commensurate with)

7. 写作指导

For this part, you are required to write a composition on the topic "How to Measure the Effectiveness of Education". The following points taken from the text are useful expressions for your reference:

- It is prepared to believe that knowledge is a good thing both in its own right and for the practical uses to which it can be put.
- It sees a connection between good citizenship and the ability to think.—Education is, first of all, the opposite of ignorance.
- Schooling is vital to a democratic society that results in spread of information and the diffusion of knowledge.
- Schooling regards science as more important in a republican than in any other government;
- Schooling recognizes that the general mind must be strengthened by education.
- Schooling aims to make the people enlightened and to inform their discretion.
- Genuine education, in short, is intellectual training.
- Ignorance is a handicap and disciplined intelligence a source of power.—A democracy, they argued, should make intellectual training available to every citizen, whether poor or rich.

8. Education and Freedom
教育与自由

H.G. Rickove
H.G.里科弗

里科弗(1900—1986),美国教育评论家、海军中将。美国海军学院毕业后,在哥伦比亚大学继续研究电机工程。曾任各种海军职务。第二次世界大战后,在田纳西州原子能委员会计划并监督制造了美国第一艘原子能潜艇。1959年获美国国会授予的"特殊金质奖章"。1980年获得美国总统颁发的"自由奖章"。在二十世纪六十年代,写了不少关于美国教育的评论。主要著作有:《美国教育:全国性的失败》、《教育与自由》、《瑞士教育与美国教育》。

里科弗反对杜威在芝加哥实验学校所运用的"从做中学"的教育理论,坚持欧洲的传统教育理论。他认为美国教育的主要缺陷在于对"优秀智力"和"心智训练"的漠不关心。为了使美国在科学技术领域中保持"世界领导权",极力主张必须学习欧洲的"教育经验",彻底"改造"教育制度,使儿童获得严格的学术性的教育,培养出大量的通晓数学、物理、化学、天文学等的科学家和工程师。他的思想和科南特一样,是美国六十年代"课程改革"、"天才教育"的理论依据。

《教育与自由》(1959)是由作者里科弗的一系列演讲稿汇集而成的,共十一章。此书在美国社会引起了巨大的反响,一年重印了五次。里科弗指出,教育对于美国发展起着十分重要的作用,社会的发展基于教育的发展,加强国防需要良好的教育,教育是解决人口增长与自然资源减少之间冲突的重要途径。发展教育远比追求眼前的物质利益更为重要,因此国家应为教育的发展投入大量的资金。青年人应该成为科学领域的主力军和开拓者,要加强对有天赋青年的教育。美国的教育与科研已经严重地落后,根本无法满足时代和社会的需求,也无法满足国际竞争的需要,理想的教育目的应该是学习基础知识和发展智力,美国必须改变教育落后的现状,迅速采取有力的教育改革措施:重视教育,尊重科学,增加教育投入,优化师资力量,建立全国统一的教育管理机构和教学评价标准。

The powerful thrust of Sputnik's launching device did more than penetrate outer space. It also pierced the thick armor encasing our complacent faith in America's present and future technological supremacy.[1] It blasted the comfortable conviction that only in an atmosphere of personal independence and political liberty can science and scientists flourish.[2] It shook the belief, long taken for granted, that a high standard of material well-being is both the outward manifestation and the necessary basis for technological progress.

It did greatest damage to our trust in the American educational system-up to now almost as sacrosanct as motherhood.[3] Harsh words are being said about its methods no less than about its aims. Sputnik has been seen as a triumph of Russian education, and rightly so. Reams of words and figures have filled the newspaper columns describing Russian education, comparing it with ours, and trying to pinpoint where we have failed in the vital educational task of motivating and training the skilled professionals needed by our country while Russia seems to have no trouble turning them out in vast numbers.[4]

We are asking searching questions about the aims of education in a modern technological society and how our schools can best achieve them. We are finally coming out of our traditional educational isolation and looking at the educational systems of other countries of Western civilization in order to compare them with ours. But we are still not ready to do this in a spirit of detachment, as I shall show later. The whole reappraisal has been painful but good for us.

Sputnik may well be the catalyst which brings about drastic and long-overdue reforms in utilizing the nation's intellectual resources.[5] It may thus do in matters of the intellect what Pearl Harbor did in matters industrial and military. Then, as now, a dramatic occurrence suddenly revealed that we had failed to develop our capacities to their maximum potential. As we found them that in a national emergency we could take prompt and vigorous action and perform industrial miracles, so I am convinced we can now take similar action and perform educational miracles.[6]

Let us not lose our heads and despair of American technological competence *as it is today*.[7] The real danger lies somewhat in the future and can be averted if we will act. At the moment, I for one am convinced that we have the men and the resources which, if properly directed and given priority, could have put a satellite in orbit ahead of the Russians.[8] This, of course, is no excuse for our mistake in letting Russia win a propaganda victory, damaging to our prestige among the uncommitted nations of the world and, it is to be feared, also among some of our friends.

The Sputnik was aloft first[9], and that is regrettable. What is particularly regrettable is that to many people it looks not like a military weapon but like pure, scientific adventure of a king which appeals to their imagination as no superior weapon could.[10] Russia indeed chose shrewdly where to concentrate for a blow to our scientific and technological prestige. It also fits nicely into the International Geophysical Year. In actual fact, Sputnik is of course great military significance[11] because of its relation to missile weaponry and because of the potential military advantages of outer-space control.

The successful Russian satellite program brings out two important facts which we would disregard at our peril[12]: First, it demonstrates conclusively that a modern totalitarian state can depress the standard of living of its people to the level of the most backward of countries while simultaneously raising a limited sector of the economy to a standard as high as, if not higher than, comparable sectors of the economy of the most highly developed country in the world.[13] Theoretically, the favored sector could be any one chosen as of greatest national importance by the rulers of a totalitarian state; in practice it will inevitably be the sector which significantly benefits the country's military and political power. Second, it proves that a modern despotism can devise an educational system shaped solely in the interest of the state and in complete disregard of[14] the needs of the individual child, and yet induce all children to stretch their intellectual capacities to the utmost[15]. These factors are worth examining in more detail.

In our country the major share of all our technical effort has gone into spreading ever higher standards of material well-being over ever larger segments of the population.[16] Perhaps too large an effort has gone into the things that make American life pleasant and comfortable and not enough into the things that insure continuous spiritual and material growth as well as military and political victory in any war, hot or cold.

In the long run, the more disturbing fact which is disclosed by the Russian satellite program is Russia's success in building in record time an educational system which produces exactly the sort of trained men and women her rulers need to achieve technological supremacy the day after tomorrow.[17] Russian education is, of course, deplorably utilitarian and authoritarian. However, it has virtually wiped out illiteracy[18]; today estimated to be only 2.5 to 5 per cent, which does not compare badly with our own rate—3.7 per cent in 1940 and about 2.5 per cent today. Russia has put a larger percentage of her smaller national income into public education than the United States. She has made the rewards of intellectual accomplishment so attractive that her children are working extremely hard to keep up with a tough curriculum.[19] Russia has as great a shortage as we in school buildings—she merely doubles up and so gets twice the benefit we do out of each classroom and school laboratory.[20] I feel sure she would use her schools on a three-shift basis if this were necessary. Russia has no teacher shortage, no substandard teachers—she has set their scholastic standards high and gives them a heavy work load, but she also honors them and pays them well. Russia evidently has no difficulty getting intelligent people with solid education in their chosen subjects to work devotedly and without worrying too much about lack of political freedom.[21] This has been a surprise to us-an unpleasant surprise.

Moreover, it is far easier to awaken in children a sense of personal achievement, of victory[22], in mastering the intellectual challenge of tough curricula, if there are no competing attractions such as those which claim the attention of our more fortunate children: no comfortable home, playrooms, and back yards to play in; no juke boxes; far fewer movies; hardly any distracting radio of TV programs; no senior proms, dating, long telephone conversations, and of course no hot rods. If they could have them, these pleasant things would greatly delight Russia's youngsters and probably cut into their study time; witness their avid interest in American jive and rock'n'roll records—to the dismay of the authorities[23]. Russia does have a problem with unruly so-called young hooligans who are—and this is significant—not the children of the poor, but the pampered offspring of Russia's elite[24]. Eventually there may be more of these disturbing youths, but for the moment they hardly make a dent in[25] the picture of an earnest, well-disciplined, polite, and studious school population.

Scientists also have needs of the kind common to all mortals, so Russia gives them attractive living quarters, country horses, vacations, maids, cars, and chauffeurs. Their pay is in the top-income bracket; in fact, the highest salary in Russia is paid to the president of the Soviet Academy of Sciences. Why should these men concern themselves about the lack of political freedom or the grim and dreary life of most of their compatriots?[26] They probably reason that these are temporary abuses and that their own scientific work will contribute to the wealth and power of their country and thus ultimately to a better life for everyone. Quite possibly, too, totalitarian states may have a built-in incentive for attracting gifted minds to science: the desire to escape from the grim reality of life to a safe and comfortable ivory tower.[27]

Faced with this formidable and ruthless adversary who has openly promised to "to bury" us and who grows daily in industrial and military might, what are we to do?[28]

First, I think, we must awaken American to the danger facing the nation-making public all the facts without soothing the impact of unpleasant truths. I have no doubt that as a people we have enough patriotism, let alone[29] enlightened self-interest, to recognize that we must put greater effort into the things which will make America strong, even if this may require a reappraisal of cherished convictions and ways of life; even at the cost of[30] some material sacrifices, which I doubt would be large.

Second, and equally important, I believe, we must reverse our treatment of scientists and trained professionals. It is easy to make a good living in this country without much serious education. Hence the temptation to do this is so great that it can be offset only by deliberate actions to elevate the status of professional people in terms both of prestige and of material reward. We had better stop calling scientists "long hairs" or "little men with beards". In the present mood of chastisement, scientists have been speaking up and telling us that such disparaging remarks hurt and may have discouraged many a young man from choosing the hard intellectual road to science rather than the easy and pleasant road to business success and country-club living.[31]

No educational reform is ever easy. It is more quickly put through where governments need not consult their people. This gives authoritarian countries such as Prussia an advantage over democratic countries such as England in the matter of keeping education in step with changing conditions. Similarly, it is giving totalitarian Russia an advantage over us which will take great effort on our part to overcome.[32]

注　释

1　It also pierced the thick armor encasing our complacent faith in America's present and future technological supremacy. 它也穿透了包着我们对美国现在和将来技术优势的自满信念的厚甲。
　　faith in 指"信任、信仰、信心"，比如：I haven't much faith in this medicine. 我对这种药没有多大信心。
　　encasing 是现在分词作后置定语修饰 armor。
2　It blasted the comfortable conviction that only in an atmosphere of personal independence and political liberty can science and scientists flourish. 它摧毁了认为只有在个人独立和政治自

由的气氛中科学和科学家才能繁荣昌盛的舒适信念。

句中的 that 从句是同位语从句，用来说明 conviction 的内容。在 that 从句中 only 放在句首，引起部分倒装，比如：Only later did he realize that it was his fault. 只有到后来他才意识到使自己的过错。

3. It did great damage to our trust in the American educational system—up to now almost as sacrosanct as motherhood. 它极大地损害了我们对于美国教育制度的信赖——直到现在我们几乎把美国教育制度看得像母性一样神圣不可侵犯。

    do damage to...指"对某人/某事造成伤害"，比如：The accident did a lot of damage to the car. 这一事故把汽车损坏得很厉害。

4. Reams of words and figures have filled the newspaper columns describing Russian education, comparing it with ours, and trying to pinpoint where we have failed in the vital educational task of motivating and training the skilled professionals needed by our country while Russia seems to have no trouble turning them out in vast numbers. 报纸充满了大量的文字和数字，描述俄国教育，并与我国教育作比较，试图精确地指出在激发和训练我国所需要的技术专家的教育工作上，有哪方面失败了，而俄国似乎没有任何困难地培养了大量技术专家。

    此句是由 while 并列连词引导的并列句，表示转折，相当于 but。在第一个分句中 where 引导的名词性从句作 pinpoint 的宾语。三个现在分词 describing, comparing 和 trying 并列作伴随状语。

    have no trouble doing sth：做某事没有难度

    turn out 指"培养出某人；生产或制造某物"，比如：The school has turned out some first-rate scholars. 这所学校培养出了一些第一流的学者。

5. Sputnik may well be the catalyst which brings about drastic and long-overdue reforms in utilizing the nation's intellectual resources. 人造卫星很可能是一帖催化剂，为利用国家智力资源带来了剧烈的和长期的改革。

    bring about 指"导致、带来"，比如：The Liberals wish to bring about changes in the electoral system. 自由党人想要改变选举制度。

    类似的表达法有：lead to; result in; cause。

6. As we found then that in a national emergency we could take prompt and vigorous action and perform industrial miracles, so I am convinced we can now take similar action and perform educational miracles：正如当时我们发现在全国紧急状态下，能采取迅速有力的行动创造工业奇迹一样，我相信，我们现在能采取类似的行动，创造出教育奇迹。

    句中 as 引导的是方式状语从句，与 so 连用时放在主句之前，常见于正式文体。比如：As a man sows, so he will reap. 种瓜得瓜，种豆得豆。

    take action 指"采取行动"，比如：Immediate action must be taken to stop the fire spreading. 必须立即采取行动阻止火势蔓延。

7. Let us not lose our heads and despair of American technological competence *as it is today*：我们不要惊慌失措，对今天美国的技术力量感到失望。

    lose one's head 指"昏了头；慌张失措。" despair of 指"绝望。"比如：We despair of him; he can't keep a job for more than six months. 我们对他已经绝望了,他做什么工作都不能超过半年。

8　At the moment, I for one am convinced that we have the men and the resources which, if properly directed and given priority, could have put a satellite in orbit ahead of the Russians. 当前,就我来看,我深信,如果对我们现有的人力和资源进行正确地引导,给予优先地位,我们是可以在俄国人之前把卫星推上轨道的。

本句 that 引导的是宾语从句,which 引导的是定语从句,由 if 引导的是与过去事实相反的虚拟条件从句的省略句,全句应为"If we had been properly directed and given priority"。ahead of 指"比……更早",比如:London is about five hours ahead of New York. 伦敦时间比纽约早五小时左右。

9　The Sputnik was aloft first: 苏联人造卫星先上天。

10　What is particularly regrettable is that to many people it looks not like a military weapon but like pure, scientific adventure of a kind which appeals to their imagination as no superior weapon could. 特别遗憾的是,在很多人看来,人造卫星不像是一件军事武器,而像是一次纯粹的科学探险,它比任何优越的器更能唤起人们的想像。

本句中 what 从句作主语, that 从句作表语, which 引导的是定语从句修饰 adventure, as 引导的是方式状语从句。

11　Sputnik is of great military significance: 苏联卫星具有巨大的军事意义。

12　The successful Russian satellite program brings out two important facts which we would disregard at our peril: 俄国人成功地发射人造卫星计划指出两个重要的事实,如果我们忽视这些事实,对我们是危险的。

bring out 指"清楚地显示出某失误;揭示出某事物",比如:The enlargement brings out the details in the photograph. 照片放大后细微之处都很清楚。

at one's peril 指"冒险",比如:The bicycle has no brakes—you ride it at your peril. 这辆自行车没有闸——你要骑可太危险了。/One ignores letters from the bank manager at one's peril. 忽视银行经理来函,后果堪虑。

13　First, it demonstrates conclusively that a modern totalitarian state can depress the standard of living of its people to the level of the most backward of countries while simultaneously raising a limited sector of the economy to a standard as high as, if not higher than, comparable sectors of the economy of the most highly developed country in the world. 第一,它明确地显示了,一个现代极权国家能够使人民的生活标准降低到最落后国家的水平,而同时能把经济的一个有限部门提高到世界上最发达国家相应的经济部门的标准的高度,即使不是更高的话。

本句 while 引导一个从句的省略形式。depress...to 是"把……降低到……"；而 raise...to 是"把……提高到……"。

14　disregard of/for: 是"忽视;漠视"的意思,比如:He shows a total disregard for other people and their feelings. 他显然丝毫也不顾及别人以及别人的感情。

15　stretch their intellectual capacities to the most: 使他们的智能发展到极限。

16　In our country the major share of all our technical effort has gone into spreading ever higher standards of material well-being over ever larger segments of the population 在我国,我们努力把技术的主要力量投入到使越来越多的人口享受越来越高的物质福利标准上。

17 In the long run, the more disturbing fact which is disclosed by the Russian satellite program is Russia's success in building in record time an educational system which produces exactly the sort of trained men and women her rulers need to achieve technological supremacy the day after tomorrow. 最后,俄国人造卫星计划所揭露的更加令人不安的事实是俄国成功地在最短时间内建立起一个教育制度,这个教育制度恰恰能培养出俄国统治者为将来达到技术优势所需要的那种训练有素的男男女女。

本句的主要结构为:The...fact...is Russia's success...。句中第二个 which 引导的是定语从句修饰 system。in the long run:指"从长远看;终究;最后",比如:In the long run prices are bound to rise. 从长远看,物价肯定要涨。

18 However, it has virtually wiped out illiteracy:但是,俄国教育确实已扫除了文盲。

wipe out 指"彻底消灭或摧毁某事物",比如:The government is trying to wipe out drug trafficking. 政府竭力清除毒品买卖活动。

19 She has made the rewards of intellectual accomplishment so attractive that her children are working extremely hard to keep up with a tough curriculum. 俄国对学术成就的奖励是那么吸引人,俄国儿童都非常努力学习,学好很深的课程。

so...that...结构此处表示"结果",比如:The problem is so complicated that it will take us much time to work it out. 这个问题这么复杂,结果我们用了很多时间才把它算出来。

so...that...结构也表示"目的",但句子中多数情况下有情态动词。比如:I'm going to the lecture early so that I'll get a good seat. 我想早点去听讲演,以便有个好座位。

20 Russia has as great a shortage as we in school buildings—she merely doubles up and so gets twice the benefit we do out of each classroom and school laboratory. 俄国和我们一样很缺乏校舍,他们采用二部制,所以对每一间教室和实验室的利用率都比我们高一倍。

这里是 as...as 与不定冠词 + 单数可属名词或不可属名词搭配构成的比较结构。比如:I don't want as expensive a car as this one. 此句可改为:I don't want a car as expensive as this one. 我不想买这么贵的车。

twice the benefit 是英语中倍数的表示法,即...times + 名词短语结构;比如:It is said that his new computer has so many times the speed of the old one. 据说他的新的计算机比那台旧的快很多倍。

英语中倍数的表示法还有:① ...times + 形容词/副词比较级 + than,比如:This house is about three times more expensive than that one. 这幢房子比那幢房子贵三倍。② ...times + as + 形容词/副词原级 + as,比如:The newly-opened road is four times as long as the old one. 这条新修的路是那条老路的四倍。③ ...times + what 从句 比如:He earns twice what he did ten years ago. 他现在挣的钱是十年前的二倍。

21 Russia evidently has no difficulty getting intelligent people with solid education in their chosen subjects to work devotedly and without worrying too much about lack of political freedom. 俄国显然不难找到对所学学科受到扎实教育的有才智的人,他们热心工作而不太忧

虑缺乏政治自由。

have no difficulty doing sth 指"做某事不费劲"，比如：We had no difficulty finding the house. 我们毫不费力地找到了那所房子。

22　awaken in children a sense of personal achievement, of victory：唤起儿童个人成就感，胜利感。

23　witness their avid interest in American jive and rock'n'roll records——to the dismay of the authorities：看到他们对美国的爵士乐和摇摆舞唱片有浓厚的兴趣，俄国当局感到惊愕。

24　but the pampered offspring of Russia's elite：而是俄国上层人物的纵容姑息的后代

25　make a dent in：指"减少；削减；削弱"，比如：The repairs made a dent in our funds. 这次修理用去了我们很多钱。

26　Why should these men concern themselves about the lack of political freedom or the grim and dreary life of most of their compatriots? 这些人何必要关心自己是否缺乏政治自由或者关心他们大多数同胞的可憎的惨淡生活呢？

concern about sth：指"担心；忧虑"，比如：There is growing concern about corruption. 人们越来越担心腐败现象。

27　Quite possibly, too, totalitarian states may have a built-in incentive for attracting gifted minds to science: the desire to escape from the grim reality of life to a safe and comfortable ivory tower. 极权国家很可能还有吸引天才人物从事科学研究的内在刺激：逃避严酷的生活现实，进入一个安全而舒适的象牙之塔的愿望。

ivory tower：象牙塔

28　Faced with this formidable and ruthless adversary who has openly promised "to bury" us and who grows daily in industrial and military might, what are we to do? 面对这样一个公开声称要"埋葬"我们而且逐日加强它的工业和军事力量的强大的和无情的对手，我们该怎么办？

might 这里用作名词，有"力量、威力、权利"的意思，比如：Might is right. 强权就是公理。

29　let alone 指"更不用说"，比如：There isn't enough room for us, let alone six dogs and a cat. 连我们的地方都不够，更不必说六条狗和一只猫了。

30　at the cost of 指"以牺牲某事物为代价"，比如：She saved him from drowning, but only at the cost of her own life. 他溺水时她把他救了，自己却牺牲了。

31　In the present mood of chastisement, scientists have been speaking up and telling us that such disparaging remarks hurt and may have discouraged many a young man from choosing the hard intellectual road to science rather than the easy and pleasant road to business success and country-club living. 在目前这种谴责的心情之下，科学家们大胆告诉我们说，这种侮辱性的称呼是伤人的，可能使很多年轻人宁愿选择走向实业成就和乡村俱乐部生活的轻松愉快的道路，而不选择走向科学的艰苦的学术工作的道路。

discourage sb from doing sth 指"使某人泄气；劝某人不要做某事"，比如：Parents should discourage their children from smoking. 做父母的应该劝子女不要吸烟。

32　Similarly, it is giving totalitarian Russia an advantage over us which will take great effort on our part to overcome. 同样，它使俄国极权主义比我们更处于有利的地位，我们要做极大的努力才能胜过它。

give advantage over 指"使……优越……",比如:Her French upbringing gives her certain advantages over other students in her class. 她有法国式的教养,使她比班上其他同学略胜一筹。

on one's part 指"由某人做出",比如:It was an error on my part. 那是我的过错。

练　习

1. 回答问题

   (1) What condition had been thought to be adequate for science and scientists to flourish in America before the launching of Sputnik?
   (2) Why does the author say Sputnik may well be the catalyst?
   (3) Why is Sputnik of great military significance?
   (4) What does the author think make Russians put a satellite in orbit ahead of Americans?
   (5) What suggestions has the author made to face with their adversary?

2. 判断正误

   (1) Americans had taken it for granted that high standard of material well-being was the necessary basis for technological progress.
   (2) The author owes the success of Sputnik to Russia's educational system.
   (3) According to the author, only by consulting their people can governments succeed in reforming education.
   (4) The author thinks that the needs of American children are completely disregarded by their educational system.
   (5) According to the author, Russian children have no interest in entertainment, such as, jive and rock'n-roll.

3. 选词填空

   take great effort to, on one's part, in terms of, at the cost of, concern about, let alone, keep up with, disregard of, do damage to, bring about

   (1) The flood _____ much _____ the crops.
   (2) Tom has been ill for a week, so he must work hard to _____ his classmates.
   (3) The fighters worked with a complete _____ their own safety.
   (4) Think of it _____ the interest of the customers.
   (5) I haven't decided on the menu yet, _____ bought the food.
   (6) We must _____ finish the project till the deadline.
   (7) I feel sure there will be no objections _____ to that.
   (8) She caught the robber, but _____ her own life.
   (9) The reform seems to _____ little change in people's life condition.
   (10) His wife _____ his safety, because he didn't come home so late.

4. 句型模拟

   (1) as...so

   (2) so...that

5. 英译汉

   (1) It shook the belief, long taken for granted, that a high standard of material well-being is both the outward manifestation and the necessary basis for technological progress.

   (2) Second, it proves that a modern despotism can devise an educational system shaped solely in the interest of the state and in complete disregard of the needs of the individual child, and yet induce all children to stretch their intellectual capacities to the utmost.

   (3) Perhaps too large an effort has gone into the things that make American life pleasant and comfortable and not enough into the things that insure continuous spiritual and material growth as well as military and political victory in any war, hot or cold.

   (4) Scientists also have needs of the kind common to all mortals, so Russia gives them attractive living quarters, country houses, vacations, maids, cars, and chauffeurs.

   (5) First, I think, we must awaken America to the danger facing the nation-making public all the facts without soothing the impact of unpleasant truths.

6. 汉译英

   (1) 我认为你一定读过这本书。(take......for granted)

   (2) 在紧急情况下,千万不要惊惶失措。(lose one's head)

   (3) 她的幽默感把他强烈地吸引住了。(appeal to)

   (4) 她在班上总是遥遥领先。(ahead of)

   (6) 让他感到惊愕的是他的小儿子经常逃学。(to one's dismay)

7. 写作指导

   For this part, you are required to write a composition on the topic "How can a country educate more skilled professionals?" The following points taken from the text are useful expressions for your reference:

   - an atmosphere of personal independence and political liberty
   - induce all children to stretch their intellectual capacities to the utmost
   - shape an educational system in the interest of the state
   - reward intellectual accomplishment
   - provide children with solid education
   - set high scholastic standards
   - awaken in children a sense of personal achievement
   - pay high salary to the scientists
   - to elevate the status of professional people in terms both of prestige and of material reward

IV

Perennialism Education
永恒主义教育

永恒主义教育于二十世纪三十年代在美国产生,属于西方现代教育理论中的新传统流派。它的主要代表人物有美国的赫钦斯、艾德勒,英国的利文斯通和法国的阿兰等。

它以实在论的哲学为依据,提倡古典主义的教育传统,是三十年代反对实用主义教育观和进步主义教育运动诸流派中的一支生力军。它在批判实用主义教育理论及其实践中发挥了十分重要的作用。永恒主义教育流派是以一种特定哲学观为理论基础,以演绎的方式对教育问题和教育观点进行阐述的一个教育哲学流派。它注重教育内容的永恒性,把文化遗产放在一个很重要的位置上,强调教育中较为长远的理论技能训练目标,主张教师和学校对学生的严格管理,以及为有能力的学生提供特别的教育机会,奖罚分明。它认为教育的性质是不变的,教育的基本原理也是不变的,永恒的。它强调"共同人性",主张加强"理智"训练,培养"民主公民",提高教育应集中与发展人的理性。在它看来,"教育就是理智的培养"。理智的培养对一切社会里的一切人都是同样适合的。永恒主义提出"永恒学科",认为"永恒学科"是"理智"训练的最好办法,要把永恒学科作为课程的核心,即:历代伟大思想家的伟大著作。在教学方法上,更强调让学生阅读和复述"伟大著作"的内容,熟记其中许多重要段落,并在自己心目中认定几个"伟大思想家"作为学习榜样,在各个方面模仿他们。

永恒主义教育除了对当时教育实践有直接指导作用外,它的某些观点也被后来证明是具有积极意义的。不过,尽管该教育流派有许多合理因素,但不可否认,这一理论的缺陷还很多,永恒主义教育提出的永恒教育目的、永恒课程、永恒人性等口号都是不足取的。他们在教育问题上所得出的结论和提出的主张,大多依赖于哲学思辨,缺乏较为坚实的心理学和社会学作为其实证依据。

9. General Education
普通教育

Robert Hutchins
罗伯特·赫钦斯

赫钦斯(1899—1977)美国教育家。耶鲁大学毕业。1929年,赫钦斯应聘担任芝加哥大学校长,推行"芝加哥计划",对这所大学进行改革。他又推行"名著教育计划",并专门设立了"西方名著编纂咨询委员会"。1937年,赫钦斯担任了马里兰州圣约翰学院的兼职董事,帮助该学院实施以名著教育为主的教育计划。

赫钦斯是永恒主义教育的代表人物。他认为杜威关于适应环境的全部理论都是错误的。他从唯心主义先验论出发,认为"真理在每个地方都是一样的","教育在每个地方也是一样的";还认为"人性是不变的,而且本质上是始终如一的,因此,教育的性质和基本原则也是不变的,永恒的"。他和艾德勒一样,是复古运动和读古书的鼓吹者、实行者。

赫钦斯主要教育著作有:《美国高等教育》,《为自由而教育》,《民主社会教育中的冲突》。

《普通教育》是赫钦斯的代表作之一。他提倡永恒主义教育哲学,强调人的理性发展,主张一种适用于任何时代的教育。赫钦斯认为,"普通教育"的核心任务是理智能力的训练。人的理智能力必须通过严格而又系统的训练才能形成。在赫钦斯看来,一个人是否受过教育,是否具有理智能力是其根本标志。因此,"普通教育"的目的是"促进人类思维的发展",掌握解决问题的方法。赫钦斯强调说:"理智的训练和发展就是教育。"赫钦斯又提出了"通才教育"的思想,试图克服教育过分专业化的弊病。他认为这种教育可以帮助学生养成阅读的习惯,掌握鉴赏和批评的标准,使他们在受完正式教育后能对当生活中的思想和运动明智地进行思考和行动,参与所处时代的理智活动。在赫钦斯那里,"普通教育"和"通才教育"实际上是一致的。前者是就教育任务而言的,后者是就教育途径而言的。它们"所关心的是引出我们共同的人性中种种因素;所关心的是属于民族的而不是属于个人的并非必需的东西"。在赫钦斯看来,"普通教育"和"通才教育"应该帮助每一个学生学会学习,学会自己思考,作出独立的判断,并作为一个负责的公民参加工作。

We can never get a university without general education. Unless students and professors (and particularly professors) have a common intellectual training, a university must remain a series of disparate schools and departments, united by nothing except the fact that they have the same president and board of trustees.[1] Professors cannot talk to one another, not at least about anything important. They cannot hope to understand one another.

We may take it for granted that we shall always have specialists; yet neither the world nor knowledge of it is arbitrarily divided up as universities are[2]. Everybody cannot be a specialist in every field. He must therefore be cut off from every field but his own unless he has the same basic education that other specialists have. This means more than having the same language and the same general interest in advancing knowledge. It means having a common stock of fundamental ideas. This becomes more important as empirical science advances and accumulates more and more data. The specialist in a narrow field has all he can do to keep up with the latest discoveries in it.[3] Other men, even in his own department, struggling to stay abreast of what is happening in their own segments of the subject, cannot hope to keep up with what is happening in his.[4] They may now expect to have some general understanding of what he is doing because they all have something in common; they are in the same department. But the day will shortly be upon us when even this degree of comprehension will be impossible, because of the infinite splitting of any ideas by our insistence on information as the content of education.[5]

Efforts to correct this tendency by administrative devices are mere palliatives. Roving professorships at Harvard, the divisional organization at Chicago, the Institute of Human Relations at Yale, noble and praiseworthy as they are, serve to mitigate and not to remove the disunity, discord, and disorder that have overtaken our educational system.[6] If professors and students had a common stock of fundamental ideas, it might be possible for those in physiology to communicate with those in physics, and even law and divinity might begin to find it worthwhile to associate with one another.

In this chapter I should like to talk about content, not about method. I concede the great difficulty of communicating the kind of education I favor to those who are unable or unwilling to get their education from books.[7] I insist, however, that the education I shall outline is the kind that everybody should have, that the answer to it is not that some people should not have it, but that we should find out how to give it to those whom we do not know how to teach at present. You cannot say my content is wrong because you do not know the method of transmitting it. Let us agree upon content if we can and have faith that the technological genius of America will solve the problem of communication.

Economic conditions require us to provide some kind of education for the young, and for all the young, up to about their twentieth year. Probably one-third of them cannot learn from books. This is no reason why we should not try to work out a better course of study for the other two-thirds. At the same time we should continue our efforts and experiments to find out how to give a general education to the hand-minded and the functionally illiterate.[8] Even these attempts may be somewhat simplified if we know what a general education is.

9. General Education 普通教育

Please do not tell me that the general education I propose should not be adopted because the great majority of those who pass through it will not go on to the university. The scheme that I advance is based on the notion that general education is education for everybody, whether he goes on to the university or not.[9] It will be useful to him in the university; it will be equally useful if he never goes there. I will admit that it will not be useful to him outside the university in the popular sense of utility[10]. It may not assist him to make money or to get ahead. It may not in any obvious fashion adjust him to his environment or fit him for the contemporary scene. It will, however, have a deeper, wider utility: it will cultivate the intellectual virtues.

The trouble with the popular notion of utility is that it confuses immediate and final ends.[11] Material prosperity and adjustment to the environment are good more or less, but they are not good in themselves and there are other goods beyond them. The intellectual virtues, however, are good in themselves and good as means to happiness[12]. By the intellectual virtues I mean good intellectual habits. The ancients distinguish five intellectual virtues: the three speculative virtues of intuitive knowledge, which is the habit of induction; of scientific knowledge, which is the habit of demonstration; and of philosophical wisdom, which is scientific knowledge, combined with intuitive reason, of things highest by nature, first principles and first causes.[13] To these they add the two virtues of the practical intellect: art, the capacity to make according to a true course of reasoning, and prudence, which is right reason with respect to action.[14]

In short, the intellectual virtues are habits resulting from the training of the intellectual power. An intellect properly disciplined, an intellect properly habituated, is an intellect able to operate well in all fields.[15] An education that consists of the cultivation of the intellectual virtues, therefore, is the most useful education, whether the student is destined for a life of contemplation or a life of action.[16] I would remind you of the words of Newman:

> If then the intellect is so excellent a portion of us, and its cultivation so excellent, it is not only beautiful, perfect, admirable, and noble in itself, but in a true and high sense it must be useful to the possessor and to all around him; not useful in any low, mechanical, mercantile sense, but as diffusing good, or as a blessing, or a gift, or power, or a treasure, first to the owner, then through him to the world.

I shall not be attentive when you tell me that the plan of general education I am about to present is remote from real life, that real life is in constant flux and change, and that education must be in constant flux and change as well.[17] I do not deny that all things are in change. They have a beginning, and a middle, and an end. Nor will I deny that the history of the race reveals tremendous technological advances and great increases in our scientific knowledge. But we are so impressed with scientific and technological progress that we assume similar progress in every field.[18] We renounce our intellectual heritage, read only the most recent books, discuss only current events, try to keep the schools abreast[19] or even ahead of the times, and write elaborate addresses on Education and Social Change.

Paul Shorey said:

If literature and history are a Heraclitean flux of facts, if one unit is as significant as another, one book, one idea, the equivalent of another..., we may for a time bravely tread the mill of scholastic routine, but in the end the soul will succumb to an immense lassitude and bafflement[20]. But if...the flux is not all, if the good, the true, and the beautiful are something real and ascertainable, if these eternal ideals re-embody themselves from age to age essentially the same in the imaginative visions of supreme genius and in the persistent rationality and sanity of the world's best books, then our reading and study are redeemed, both from the obsessions of the hour, and the tyranny of quantitative measures and mechanical methods.

Our erroneous notion of progress has thrown the classics and the liberal arts out of the curriculum, overemphasized the empirical sciences, and made education the servant of any contemporary movements in society, no matter how superficial.[21] In recent years this attitude has been accentuated by the world-wide depression and the highly advertised political, social, and economic changes resulting from it. We have been very much upset by all these things. We have felt that it was our duty to educate the young so that they would be prepared for further political, social, and economic changes. Some of us have thought we should try to figure out what the impending changes would be and frame a curriculum that embodied them. Others have even thought that we should decide what changes are desirable and then educate our students not merely to anticipate them, but also to take part in bringing them about.

One purpose of education is to draw out the elements of our common human nature. These elements are the same in any time or place. The notion of educating a man to live in any particular environment, is therefore foreign to a true conception of education.[22]

Education implies teaching. Teaching implies knowledge. Knowledge is truth. The truth is everywhere the same. Hence education should be everywhere the same. I don not overlook the possibilities of differences in organization, in administration, in local habits and customs. These are details. I suggest that the heart of any course of study designed for the whole people will be, if education is rightly understood, the same at any time, in any place, under any political, social, or economic conditions. Even the administrative details are likely to be similar because all societies have generic similarity.

If education is rightly understood, it will be understood as the cultivation of the intellect. The cultivation of the intellect is the same good for all men in all societies. It is, moreover, the good for which all other goods are only means. Material prosperity, peace and civil order, justice and the moral virtues are means to the cultivation of the intellect. So Aristotle says in the *Politics*: "Now, in men reason and mind are the end towards which nature strives, so that the generation and moral discipline of the citizens ought to be ordered with a view to them." An education which served the means rather than their end would be misguided.

If we are educators we must have a subject matter, and a rational, defensible one. If that subject matter is education, we cannot alter it to suit the whims of parents, students, or the public.[23] Whewell, Master of Trinity College, Cambridge, one hundred years ago, said:

Young person may be so employed and so treated, that their caprice, their self-will, their individual tastes and propensities, are educed and developed; but this is not Education. It is not the Education of a Man; for what is educed is not what belongs to man as man, and connects man with man. It is not the Education of a man's Humanity, but the Indulgence of his Individuality.

In general education we are interested in drawing out the elements of our common human nature; we are interested in the attributes of the race, not the accidents of individuals.[24]

注　释

1　Unless students and professors(and particularly professors)have a common intellectual training, a university must remain a series of disparate schools and departments, united by nothing except the fact that they have the same president and board of trustees. 如果学生和教授(特别是教授)没有共同的理智训练，一个大学必定仍旧是一系列毫不相关的学院和系科，除了有一个共同的校长和董事会外，没有什么东西会使他们统一在一起。
united by 是分词短语作后置短语修饰 schools and departments。
remain 表示"仍然是；保持不变"，比如：In spite of their quarrel, they remained the best of friends. 他们尽管吵过架，却仍不失为最好的朋友。

2　yet neither the world nor knowledge of it is arbitrarily divided up as universities are. 可是这个世界和世界上的知识，并不是像大学那样被任意地分割开来。
divide up 表示"分割开；分隔"，比如：The large house was divided up into flats. 这所大房子被分割成若干套间。

3　The specialist in a narrow field has all he can do to keep up with the latest discoveries in it: 一个狭隘领域里的专家，必须尽一切所能跟上这个领域中种种最新的发现。
keep up with 表示"跟上；赶上"，比如：She likes to keep up with the latest fashions. 她喜欢赶时髦。

4　Other man, even in his own department, struggling to stay abreast of what is happening in their own segments of the subject, cannot hope to keep up with what is happening in his. 其他的人，即使在他自己的系科里努力地密切注意科目本身在各个环节上所发生的一切，也不能期望跟上那个系科里正在发生的一切。
struggling to...the subject 是现在分词短语做状语表示条件。

5　But the day will shortly be upon us when even this degree of comprehension will be impossible, because of the infinite splitting of subject matters and the progressive submergence of any ideas by our insistence on information as the content of education. 但是，由于教材无限地分割，以及由于我们坚持以知识为教育的内容，将所有思想都淹没下去，即使那种理解程度还不可能达到的时候，这一天也会很快地到来。
when 引导的是定语从句，修饰 the day。由于定语太长，放在后面。
be upon sb 表示"迅速接近"，比如：Christmas is almost upon us again. 圣诞节又快到了。

6　Roving professorships at Harvard, the divisional organization at Chicago, the Institute of Human Relations at Yale, noble and praiseworthy as they are, serve to mitigate and not to remove the disunity, discord, and disorder that have overtaken our educational system. 哈佛轮换教授职位，芝加哥分设学院组织，耶鲁人类关系学院，尽管都是十分可贵而值得赞扬的，但它们只能缓解而不能消除我们教育体系的不统一、不协调和不正常的现象。

adj + as 放在句首引导让步状语从句，比如：Poor as he was, he was honest. 尽管他很穷，但他诚实。

7 I concede the great difficulty of communicating the kind of education I favor to those who are unable or unwilling to get their education from books. 我承认传授这种教育的极大困难，我对那些不能或不愿从书本中获得教育的人们，表示关切。

8 At the same time we should continue our efforts and experiments to find out how to give a general education to the hand-minded and the functionally illiterate. 同时，我们应当继续我们的努力和实验，找出怎样给予那些只用手操作和机能性文盲的人一种普通教育。

9 The scheme that I advance is based on the notion that general education is education for everybody, whether he goes on to the university or not. 我的计划是根据这个想法提出的，即普通教育是对每一个人的教育，不论他是上大学还是不上大学。

第一个 that 从句是定语从句修饰 the scheme，第二个 that 从句是 notion 的同位语从句。be based on 表示"以……为根据。"比如：This novel is based on historical facts. 这部小说是以历史事实为根据的。

10 in the popular sense of utility：按照流行的效用观点来看

11 The trouble with the popular notion of utility is that it confuses immediate and final ends. 流行的效用观点的问题在于它把直接的和终极的目的混淆起来。

confuse A and/with B：表示"混淆"。比如：Don't confuse Austria and/with Australia. 不要把奥地利跟澳大利亚弄混淆了。

12 a means to happiness：达到幸福的手段

13 The ancients distinguish five intellectual virtues: the three speculative virtues of intuitive knowledge, which is the habit of induction; of scientific knowledge, which is the habit of demonstration; and of philosophical wisdom, which is scientific knowledge, combined with intuitive reason, of things highest by nature, first principles and first causes. 古代人把理智的美德区分为五种：关于直觉知识的三种思辨美德，即归纳的习惯；关于科学知识，即论证的习惯；以及关于哲学智慧，即科学知识和直觉理性的结合，从性质上讲是最高级的东西，即第一原理和第一推动力。

三个 of 引导的短语修饰 virtues，每个 of 介词短语后又带一个 which 引导的非限制性定语从句，分别修饰 of 介词短语。

14 To these they add the two virtues of the practical intellect: art, the capacity to make according to a true course of reasoning, and prudence, which is right reason with respect to action. 他们还加上两种实践的理智美德：艺术，即按照正确的推理过程的创作能力；审慎，即关于行动的正确的理性。

with respect to sth：表示"涉及、提到或关于某事物"，比如：This is true with respect to English but not to French. 这一点在英语属实而在法语则不同。

15 An intellect properly disciplined, an intellect properly habituated, is an intellect able to oper-

ate well in all fields. 一种受过适当训练的理智是一切领域里都能够起着很好作用的理智,也是一种适当形成习惯的理智。

16. An education that consists of the cultivation of the intellectual virtues, therefore, is the most useful education, whether the student is destined for a life of contemplation or a life of action: 不论学生是否注定从事于沉思生活或实际生活,由理智美德培养所组成的教育是最有用的教育。

    consist of:意指"由……组成"。比如:The committee consists of ten members. 委员会由十人组成。

    be destined for/to do sth:表示"命中注定",比如:They were destined never to meet again. 他们命中注定再也无缘相遇了。

17. I shall not be attentive when you tell me that the plan of general education I am about to present is remote from real life, that real life is in constant flux and change, and that education must be in constant flux and change as well. 我将不介意你告诉我,我所建议的普通教育计划是远离现实生活的,而现实生活是经常不断变化的,教育也因此必须不断变化。

    在 when 引导的时间状语从句中,又有三个 that 引导的宾语从句。

    in constant flux and change:处于不断变化之中

18. We are so impressed with scientific and technologic progress that we assume similar progress in every field. 科学和技术的进步给我们深刻印象,使我们设想每个领域里类似的进步。

    be impressed with:表示"给……留下深刻的印象",比如:We were most impressed with your efficiency. 你的工作效率给我们留下了深刻的印象。

19. keep abreast of sth:跟上某事物。比如:You should read the newspapers to keep abreast of current affairs. 应该看报纸以便了解时事。

20. but in the end the soul will succumb to an immense lassitude and bafflement:但最后灵魂将屈服于极度的厌倦和困扰。

    succumb to:表示"不再抵抗(诱惑、疾病、攻击等);屈从",比如:Several children have measles, and the others are bound to succumb to it. 有几个孩子患了麻疹,其他孩子也必然传染上。

21. Our erroneous notion of progress has thrown the classics and the liberal arts out of the curriculum, overemphasized the empirical sciences, and made education the servant of any contemporary movements in society, no matter how superficial. 我们对于进步的错误观念已经把古典作品和自由艺术摒弃于课程之外,过分强调经验科学,并使教育成为社会上任何一种当代运动的附属品,不管它是如何体现在表面上的。

    no matter + 疑问词 引导的是让步状语从句。比如:No matter what you will say, I won't change my mind. 无论你要说什么,我都不会改变主意。

22. The notion of educating a man to live in any particular time or place, to adjust him to any particular environment, is therefore foreign to a true conception of education. 教育一个人在任何特殊时间或特殊地方生活,让他适应任何特殊的环境,这种意见同真正的教育是格格不入的。

be foreign to:表示"非某人所固有的;与某人的本性相异",比如:Dishonesty is foreign to his nature.他的本性与弄虚作假格格不入。

23 If we are educators we must have a subject matter, and a rational, defensible one. If that subject matter is education, we cannot alter it to suit the whims of parents, students, or the public. 如果我们是教育家,我们必须有一种教材,一种合理的和不可非议的教材。如果那种教材是起教育作用的,我们不能为迎合家长们、学生们、或公众的狂想而加以改变。

24 In general education we are interested in drawing out the elements of our common human nature; we are interested in the attributes of the race, not the accidents of individuals. 在普通教育中,我们所关心的是提出我们人性中共同的种种因素;我们所关心的是属于民族的而不是属于个人的不必需的东西。

练　习

1. 回答问题

（1）If students and professors have not a common intellectual training, what will a university be?

（2）In the sentence *This becomes more important as empirical science advances and accumulates more and more data*, what does 'this' refers to?

（3）What is the trouble with the popular notion of utility according to the author?

（4）What are five intellectual virtues?

（5）What is the most useful education according to the author?

2. 判断正误

（1）Among these five intellectual virtues, philosophical wisdom is the most important one.

（2）The training of the intellectual powers leads to the intellectual virtues.

（3）The author suggests that the heart of any course of study designed for the whole people shouldn't be the same because of different political, social, or economic conditions.

（4）The true conception of education is to educate a man to live in any particular time or place, to adjust him to any particular environment.

（5）Material prosperity, peace and civil order, justice and the moral virtues are means to the cultivation of the intellect, not the end of it.

3. 选词填空

be foreign to, bring about, succumb to, impress sb with sth, with respect to, remind sb of sth, favorable to, insist on, cut off, be divided up

（1）The class _____ into small groups.

（2）This song _____ me _____ France.

（3）The fence _____ our view of the sea.

(4) Is he _____ the proposal?

(5) Visiting a patient with pears _____ Chinese customs.

(6) The city _____ its enemy after only a short siege.

(7) The girl _____ her fiance's family _____ her liveliness and sense of humor.

(8) _____ your enquiry, I enclose an explanatory leaflet.

(9) The Liberals wish to _____ changes in the electoral system.

(10) I _____ your taking immediate action to put this right.

4. 句型模拟

(1) take it for granted that...

(2) no matter how(what, when, why...)

5. 英译汉

(1) Material prosperity and adjustment to the environment are good more or less, but they are not good in themselves and there are other goods beyond them.

(2) We renounce our intellectual heritage, read only the most recent books, discuss only current events, try to keep the schools abreast or even ahead of the times, and write elaborate addresses on Education and Social Change.

(3) Education implies teaching. Teaching implies knowledge. Knowledge is truth. The truth is everywhere the same. Hence education should be everywhere the same.

(4) In recent years this attitude has been accentuated by the world-wide depression and the highly advertised political, social, and economic changes resulting from it.

(5) In general education we are interested in drawing out the elements of our common human nature; we are interested in the attributes of the race, not the accidents of individuals.

6. 汉译英

(1) 他们简直宠着他随心所欲。(whim)

(2) 简和我毫无共同之处。(have...in common)

(3) 在我看来,他本身体现了教师应有的一切。(embody)

(4) 该词典的这一版本新增加了很多词。(add...to)

(5) 我生于戏剧工作者之家,注定了我的舞台生涯。(be destined for)

7. 写作指导

For this part, you are required to write a composition on the topic "What Is General Education?". The following points taken from the text are useful expressions for your reference:

- be education for everybody
- have a deeper, wider utility
- cultivate the intellectual virtues
- draw out the elements of our common human nature

- be everywhere the same
- not sacrificing the content of education to obsession of the hour or the caprices of the young
- have a rational and defensible subject matter
- the curriculum should be composed principally of the permanent studies

10. How to Read a Book[1]
怎样读一本书

Mortimer Adler
莫蒂默·艾德勒

莫蒂默·艾德勒(1912—2001)美国教育家。哥伦比亚大学毕业后,曾先后在芝加哥大学、马利兰州安纳利斯的圣约翰学院认教。1952 年,艾德勒在芝加哥开办哲学研究所并任该所所长。主要著作有:《怎样读一本书:获得自由教育的艺术》。

艾德勒是实用主义哲学的激烈反对者,哲学观点更接近于新柏拉图学说和托马斯主义。

艾德勒和赫钦斯一样,提倡复古主义,推行"百本名著计划",是读古书的最卖力的鼓吹者。他认为从古典著作中可以学到适应时代的永恒的东西,只有古典著作所提供的"自由教育",才能真正丰富生活,并使青年一代成为资本主义社会中"有理性和自由的人"。

《怎样读一本书》是一本教你怎么读书的工具书,前半部谈放诸四海皆准的通则,后半部依各种不同的文类做读书方法上的调整。主要的概念是从认出书的架构开始,从书的书名、目录、作者序开始看起,了解这本书是属于哪一种类型的书籍,并能以一两句话简洁地指出本书的主旨,拟出纲要,并找出作者的发问,了解书的架构后,透过找出书本的关键词、关键句以明白作者发问的目的,并找出作者以什么方式回答他所提出的问题,谈了些什么,哪些问题被解决了,而哪些仍未被解决。在完全了解一本书之后,读者才可以对一本书提出评论,包括赞同或反对作者的意见,为什么赞同或反对的理由,将这本书与自己产生关联。

As far back as I can remember, there have been complaints about the schools for not teaching the young to write and speak well. The complaints have focused mainly on the products of high school and college[2] An elementary-school diploma never was expected to certify great competence in these matters. But after four or eight more years in school, it seemed reasonable to hope for a disciplined ability to perform these basic acts. English courses were, and for the most part still are, a staple ingredient in the high-school curriculum.[3] Until recently, freshman English was required course in every college. These courses were supposed to develop skill in writing the mother tongue. Though less emphasized than writing, the ability to speak clearly, if not with eloquence, was also supposed to be one of the ends in view.[4]

The complaints came from all sources. Businessmen, who certainly did not expect too much, protested the incompetence of the youngsters who came their way after school. Newspaper editorials by the score echoed their protests and added a voice of their own, expressing the misery of the editor who had to blue-pencil the stuff college graduated passed across his desk.[5]

Teachers of freshman English in college have had to do over again what should have been completed in high school. Teachers of other college courses have complained about the impossibly sloppy and incoherent English which students hand in on term papers or examinations.[6] I have mentioned only writing and speaking, not reading. Until very recently, no one paid much attention to the even greater or more prevalent incompetence in reading, except, perhaps, the law professors who, ever since the introduction of the case of method of studying law, have realized that half the time in a law school must spent in teaching the student how to read the cases.[7] They thought, however, that this burden rested peculiarly on them, that there was something very special about reading cases. They did not realize that if college graduates had a decent skill in reading, the more specialized technique of reading cases could be acquired in much less than half the time now spent.[8]

It should be obvious at once that these skills are related. They are all arts of using language in the process of communication, whether initiating it or receiving it. We should not be surprised, therefore, if we find a positive correlation among defects in these several skills. Without the benefit of scientific research by means of educational measurements, I would be willing to predict that someone who cannot write well cannot read well either.[9] In fact, I would go further. I would wager that his inability to read is partly responsible for his defects in writing.

However difficult it may be to read, it is easier than writing and speaking well. To communicate well to others, one must know how communications are received, and be able, in addition, to master the medium to produce the desired effects.[10] Though the arts of teaching and being taught are correlative, the teacher, either as writer or speaker, must prevision the process of being taught in order to direct it.[11] He must, in short, be able to read what he writes, or listen to what he says, as if he were being taught by it. When teachers themselves do not possess the art of being taught, they cannot be very good teachers

Last year Professor James Mursell, of Columbia's Teachers of College, wrote an article in *The Atlantic Monthly*, entitled "The Defeat of Schools."[12] He based his allegation on "thousands of investigations" which comprise the "consistent testimony of thirty years of enormously varied research in education."[13] A large mass of evidence comes from a recent survey of the schools of Pennsylvania carried on by the Carnegie Foundation. Let me quote his own words:

What about English? Here, too, there is a record of failure and defeat. Do pupils in school learn to read their mother tongue effectively? Yes and no. Up to the fifth and sixth grade, reading, on the whole, is effectively taught and well learned. To that level we find a steady and general improvement, but beyond it the curves flatten out to a dead level.[14] This is not because a person arrives at his natural limit of efficiency when he reaches the sixth grade, for it has been shown again and again that with special tuition much older children, and also adults, can make enormous

10. How to Read a Book 怎样读一本书

improvement. Nor does it mean that most sixth-graders read well enough for all practical purposes.[15] A great many pupils do poorly in high school because of sheer ineptitude in getting meaning from the printed page.[16] They can improve; they need to improve; but they don't.

The Regents' Inquiry investigated the kind of learning which high-school students do by themselves, apart from school and courses.[17] This, they rightly thought, could be determined by their out-of-school reading. And they tell us, from their results, "that once out of school, most boys and girls read solely for recreation, chiefly in magazines of mediocre or inferior fiction and in daily newspapers." The range of their reading, in school and out, is woefully slight and of the simplest and poorest sort.[18] Nonfiction is out of the question. They are not even acquainted with the best novels published during their years in school.[19] They know the names only of the most obvious bestsellers. Worse than that, "once out of school, they tend to let books alone.[20] Fewer than 40 per cent. of the boys and girls interviewed had read any book or any part of a book in the two weeks preceding the interviews. Only one in ten had read nonfiction books."[21] For the most part, they read magazines, if anything. And even here the level of their reading is low: "fewer than two young people in a hundred read magazines of the type of *Harper's*, *Scribner's*, or *The Atlantic Monthly*."[22]

I want to repeat, because I want to remember, that however distressing these findings may seem, they are not half as bad as they would if the tests were themselves more severe.[23] The tests measure a relatively simple grasp of relatively simple passages. The questions the students being measured must answer after they have read a short paragraph call for very little more than a precise knowledge of what the writer said.[24] They do not demand much in the way of interpretation, and almost nothing of critical judgment.

I say that the tests are not severe enough, but the standard I would set is certainly not too stringent. Is it too much to ask that a student be able to read a whole book, not merely a paragraph, and report not only what was said therein but show an increased understanding of the subject matter being discussed?[25] Is it too much to expect from the schools that they train their students not only to interpret but to criticize; that is, to discriminate what is sound from error and falsehood, to suspend judgment if they are not convinced, or to judge with reason if they agree or disagree?[26] I hardly think that such demands would be exorbitant to make of high school or college, yet if such requirements were incorporated into tests, and a satisfactory performance were the condition of graduation, not one in a hundred students now getting their diplomas each June would wear the cap and gown.[27]

Let me suppose this last statement by one other citation.[28] In June, 1939, the University of Chicago held a four-day conference on reading for teachers attending the summer session. At one of the meetings, Professor Diederich, of the department of education, reported the results of a test given at Chicago to top-notch high-school seniors who came there from all parts of the country to complete for scholarships.[29] Among other things, these candidates were examined in reading. The results, Professor Diederich told the thousand teachers assembled, showed that most of these very "able" students simply could not understand what they read.

Moreover, he went on to say, "our pupils are not getting very much direct help in understanding what they read or hear, or in knowing what they mean by what they say or write."[30] Nor is the situation limited to high schools. It applied equally to colleges in this country, and even in England concerning the linguistic skill of undergraduates in Cambridge University.[31]

Why are the students not getting any help? It cannot be because the professional educators are unaware of the situation. That conference at Chicago ran for four days—with many papers presented at morning, afternoon, and evening sessions—all on the problem of reading.[32] It must be because the educators simply do not know what to do about it; in addition, perhaps, because they do not realize how much time and effort must expected to teach students how to read, write, and speak well. Too many other things, of much less importance, have come to clutter up the curriculum.[33]

Some years ago I had an experience which is illuminating in this connection. Mr. Hutchins and I had undertaken to read the great books with a group of high-school juniors and seniors in the experimental school which the university runs. This was thought to be a novel "experiment" or worse, a wild idea.[34] Many of these books were not being read by college juniors and seniors. They were reserved for the delectation of graduate students. And we were going to read them with high-school boys and girls!

At the end of the first year, I went to the principal of the high school to report on our progress. I said that these younger students were clearly interested in reading the books. The questions they asked showed that. The acuteness and vitality of their discussion of matters raised in class shoed that they were better than older students who had been dulled by years of listening to lectures, taking notes, and passing examinations.[35] They had much more edge than college seniors or graduate students.[36] But, I said, it was perfectly obvious that they did not know how to read a book. Mr. Hutchins and I, in the few hours a week we had with them, could not discuss the books and also teach them how to read. It was a shame that their native talents were not being trained to perform a function that was plainly of the highest educational importance.[37]

注 释

1 本文选自莫蒂默·艾德勒的《怎样读一本书》。
2 The complaints have focused mainly on the products of high school and college. An elementary-school diploma never was expected to certify great competence in these matters. 这种怨言主要集中在中学和大学的教育效果上。一纸小学文凭从来没有被指望证明有很好的写作和说话能力。
  focus on 是"集中"的意思,比如:Tonight's programme focuses on the way that homelessness affects the young. 今晚的节目集中讨论无家可归现象如何影响年轻一代。
3 English courses were, and for the most part still are, a staple ingredient in the high-school curriculum. 英语课过去是,现在大多数仍然是中学课程的主要组成部分。
  for the most part 是"大部分,主要地"的意思,比如:We spent the day for the most partlook-

ing round the museum. 我们这一天大部分都在逛博物馆。

本句主要部分是：English courses... were, and are... a staple ingredient... 主语是 English courses, 而谓语有两个：were 和 are。

4 Though less emphasized than writing, the ability to speak clearly, if not with eloquence, was also supposed to be one of the ends in view. 虽然不像对写作那样强调，也是作为培养的目标之一的。

Though less emphasized than writing 是独立主格结构，作让步状语，the ability to speak clearly 是句子的主语，was supposed to be 是谓语，one of the ends 是宾语，if not with eloquence 作条件状语。

in view 是"考虑在内"的意思，比如：Keep your career aims constantly in view. 要时刻牢记自己在事业上的奋斗目标。

5 Newspaper editorials by the score echoed their protests and added a voice of their own, expressing the misery of the editor who had to blue-pencil the stuff college graduated passed across his desk. 新闻编辑响应他们的抗议，连同他们自己的呼声一起，表达了教育者的悲哀，他们对自己办公桌上的大学毕业生的作品，不得不大加修改。

句子的主语是 Newspaper editorials, echoed 和 added 作并列谓语，protests 和 a voice 共同作宾语，expressing the misery of... 作伴随状语，who 引导的从句作 editor 的定语。

6 Teachers of other college courses have complained about the impossibly sloppy and incoherent English which students hand in on term papers or examinations. 担任其他大学课程的教师，抱怨学生交来的学期论文或试卷，文理不通，草率得令人无法忍受。

complain about/of 意思是"抱怨"，比如：He complains about anything—his job, his wife, his back... 他什么都要抱怨——工作，妻子，背痛……。

sloppy 意思是"草率的"，比如：Spelling mistakes always look sloppy in a formal letter. 在正式的信件中，拼写错误总让人觉得草率马虎。

incoherent 意思是"无条理的，语无伦次的"，比如：He was confused and incoherent and I didn't get much sense out of him. 他很慌乱说话语无伦次，我听不太懂他在说什么。

7 Until very recently, no one paid much attention to the even greater or more prevalent incompetence in reading, except, perhaps, the law professors who, ever since the introduction of the case of method of studying law. 也许，除了那些法学教授从一开始采用判例法研究法律就已经认识到在法学院有一半时间是用来教学生阅读判例外，直到最近才有人注意这种更为严重的普遍缺乏阅读能力的情况。

本句是由 until 引导的时间状语，except 介词后接名词词组，the law professors, 是主语 no one 中的例外，who 引导的从句是 the law professors 的定语，ever since... 短语作时间状语。incompetence in doing sth., "做某事不胜任"，比如：local politicians have accused the government of incompetence in failing to restore public services after the earthquake. 地方的政客们指责政府在震后的公共事业恢复方面无能。

8 They thought, however, that this burden rested peculiarly on them. 但是，他们认为这个任务特别落在他们身上。

rest on "由……来决定"，比如：It rests on her to decide whether to press charges against

111

him. 由她来决定是否对他起诉。

9　Without the benefit of scientific research by means of educational measurements, I would be willing to predict that someone who cannot write well cannot read well either. 不必借助于以教育测验为工具的科学研究,我就能预测,一个写作能力差的人,阅读能力也不会好。

Without...介词短语作状语,I 是主语,would be willing to predict 是谓语,that 引导的是宾语从句,在宾语从句中主语是 someone,谓语是 cannot read,who 引导的从句作 someone 的定语。

With/without the benefit of..."有/没有……的帮助",比如:With the benefit of hindsight, it is easy for us to see where we went wrong in the past. 通过事后认识,我们比较容易认清自己所犯的错误。

by means of "通过……途径,方法",比如:She tried to explain by means of sign language. 她试图通过手语来解释。

10　To communicate well to others, one must know how communications are received, and be able, in addition, to master the medium to produce the desired effects. 一个人要和别人交流思想,就必须懂得怎样接受,还要掌握交流工具以达到预期的效果。

communicate sth. to sb. 是"传达,表达"的意思,比如:Without meaning to, she communicated her anxiety to her child. 没什么特别的意思,她只是对她的孩子表达她的担忧。

11　Though the arts of teaching and being taught are correlative, the teacher, either as writer or speaker, must prevision the process of being taught in order to direct it. 虽然教和受教的艺术是相关的,一个教师,不管作为作家还是作为演说家,为了知道受教的过程,他必须先懂得这个过程。

correlative 是."相关联的"意思,correlate 是"使…相关联"的 意思,比如:In some societies a poor diet often correlates with poverty. 在一些社会里营养不良往往和贫穷有关。

either...or 是"或者…或者"的意思;如果 either...or 连接的两个部分在句子中作主语,谓语动词的数要与后一个主语保持一致。比如:Either your brakes or your eyesight is at fault. 或者你的刹车有毛病,或者你的视力有毛病。

12　Last year Professor James Mursell, of Columbia's Teachers of College, wrote an article in *The Atlantic Monthly*, entitled "The Defeat of Schools." 去年,哥伦比亚师范大学的詹姆斯·默盖尔教授在《大西洋月刊》上发表一篇题为《学校的失败》的文章。

13　He based his allegation on "thousands of investigations" which comprise the "consistent testimony of thirty years of enormously varied research in education." 文章根据"成千次调查研究",包括"三十年来大量的多方面教育研究的一贯的证据"。

base on/upon 是"以……为根据"的意思,比如:I based my hopes upon the news we had yesterday. 我的希望是以我的昨天所得的消息为根据。

14　To that level we find a steady and general improvement, but beyond it the curves flatten out to a dead level. 我们发现,阅读能力达到这个水平才能稳步地、普遍地提高,但是,超过这个水平,曲线就趋于平坦,停滞不前了。

本句的主语是 we,谓语是 find,宾语是 a steady and general improvement 和 the curves,而 flatten out...分词短语作 the curves 的宾语补足语。flatten out "把……弄平",比如:I need to get the dents in my car flattened out. 我需要将我车上撞瘪的地方弄平。

15. Nor does it mean that most sixth-graders read well enough for all practical purposes. 这并不意味大多数六年级学生的阅读能力能满足一切实际的需要。

nor 是否定词，位于句首，句子要用倒装结构。比如：She will not leave, nor will she allow him to continue treating her badly. 她不会离开，也不许他继续虐待她。

16. A great many pupils do poorly in high school because of sheer ineptitude in getting meaning from the printed page. 很多中学生阅读能力成绩差，仅仅由于他们不懂文字的意义。

ineptitude in doing sth. 是"不适于做某事"的意思，比如：The newspaper editorial correctly pointed out the government's ineptitude in dealing with the ozone crisis. 报纸社论正确地指出了政府在处理臭氧危机中的无能。

17. The Regents' Inquiry investigated the kind of learning which high-school students do by themselves, apart from school and courses. 纽约州立大学评议会的调查，还研究了中学生在学校课程以外自己进行的那类学习。

apart from "除了"，比如：Apart from you and me, I don't think there was anyone there under thirty. 除了你我二人，我想那儿当时没有谁是不到三十岁的。

18. The range of their reading, in school and out, is woefully slight and of the simplest and poorest sort. 他们在校内校外阅读的范围，少得令人遗憾，而且所阅读的东西是最简单的、质量最差的。

woefully 是"悲哀地"的意思，woeful 是"悲哀的"，比如：When I saw her woeful face, I knew she had bad news. 看到她悲伤的面孔时，我就知道她有坏消息了。

19. Nonfiction is out of the question. They are not even acquainted with the best novels published during their years in school. 小说以外的书是不必谈了。他们甚至对在自己学生时代所出版的最优秀的小说都毫无所知。

out of the question 是"不可能的"的意思，比如：A trip to New Zealand is out of the question this year. 今年去趟新西兰是不可能的。

out of question 是"毫无疑问"的意思，比如：He is out of question the greatest authority on this subject row living. 他无疑是现在在世的，这方面最伟大的权威。

be acquainted with 是"熟悉，了解"的意思，比如：The police said the thieves were obviously well acquainted with the alarm system at the department store. 警方说窃贼显然对百货大楼的报警系统非常了解。

20. "once out of school, they tend to let books alone". 他们一旦离开学校，往往就不再接触书本了。

let sb./sth. alone 是"不管，不干涉"的意思，比如：let it alone. 不要管它。

let alone "更不用说"，比如：some people never even read a newspaper, let alone a book. 有些人从未读过报纸，更不用说书了。

21. Only one in ten had read nonfiction books. 读过非小说一类的书的，十人中只有一人。

22. "fewer than two young people in a hundred read magazines of the type of *Harper's, Scribner's,* or *The Atlantic Monthly.*" 看《哈珀》《斯克里布纳》或《大西洋月刊》这一类杂志的人，百人中不到二人。

23. however distressing these findings may seem, they are not half as bad as they would if the tests were themselves more severe. 尽管这些研究结果似乎令人感到苦恼，要是所用的测验本身更难些，结果将更坏。

not half as bad/good as 是"远非，差得远，绝不是"的意思，比如：It wasn't half as bad as that restaurant we went to. 它比我们去的那家餐馆差远了。

24. The questions the students being measured must answer after they have read a short paragraph call for very little more than a precise knowledge of what the writer said. 学生在读了一段短文以后回答几个问题，只要求他们掌握作者所写的知识内容就够了。

little more than 是"只仅仅"的意思，比如：It's worth little more than a shilling. 这只不过值一先令。/ In the beginning he was little more than a slave. 起初他们只不过是奴隶而已。

25. Is it too much to ask that a student be able to read a whole book, not merely a paragraph, and report not only what was said therein but show an increased understanding of the subject matter being discussed? 要求一个学生不仅能读一段文章而且能读整本书，要求他不仅报告其中的内容而且表明对讨论的题材有进一步的理解，难道这个要求过高吗？

therein 是"在那里"的意思，比如；Susan opened the box to find a key and a faded, dusty map therein. 苏珊打开盒子在里面发现把钥匙和一张褪了色满是灰尘的地图。

26. Is it too much to expect from the schools that they train their students not only to interpret but to criticize; that is, to discriminate what is sound from error and falsehood, to suspend judgment if they are not convinced, or to judge with reason if they agree or disagree? 希望学校不仅训练学生能解释而且能批评；就是说，训练他们辨别正确与谬误，假如他们还不信服就不作判断，或者对他们同意或不同意作出合理的判断，难道这是过高的期望吗？

that 引导的从句作 expect 的宾语从句，在宾语从句中动词不定式短语 to interpret..., to discriminate,... to suspend,... to judge 作目的状语。

27. I hardly think that such demands would be exorbitant to make of high school or college, yet if such requirements were incorporated into tests, and a satisfactory performance were the condition of graduation, not one in a hundred students now getting their diplomas each June would wear the cap and gown. 我不认为这种要求对中学或大学有什么成分，但是，假如这种要求体现在测验里，并且把合格的成绩定为毕业条件之一，那么，现在每年六月得到他们文凭的学生，百人中没有一个人能戴上学士帽，穿上学士衣。

be incorporated into sth 是"包含，加上"的意思，比如：Hanover was incorporated into Prussia in 1886. 汉诺威于1886年被并入普鲁士。

28. In June, 1939, the University of Chicago held a four-day conference on reading for teachers attending the summer session. 1939年6月，芝加哥大学为参加夏季学期教学的教师举行了四天有关阅读的研讨会。

session 是"学期，上课时间"的意思，比如：Access to these buildings is restricted when school is in session. 学校上课时间，这些大楼是不能随便进入的。

session 还有另一个意思"（议会的）会议，（法庭的）开庭"，比如：The UN Security Council met in emergency session to discuss the crisis. 联合国安全理事会举行紧急会议讨论危机问题。

29. reported the results of a test given at Chicago to top-notch high-school seniors who came there from all parts of the country to complete for scholarships. Among other things, these candidates were examined in reading. The results, Professor Diederich told the thousand teachers assembled, showed that most of these very "able" students simply could not understand what they read. 在一次会议上,芝加哥大学教育系迪德里希教授报告了一个测试的结果,这个测试是为从全国各地到芝加哥参加奖学金竞争考试的最优秀的中学高年级生举行的。

本句主语是 Professor Diederich,谓语是 reported,宾语是 the results of a test, given at Chicago to top-notch high-school... 作 test 的定语,而 who 引导的从句作 seniors 的定语。

30. Moreover, he went on to say, "our pupils are not getting very much direct help in understanding what they read or hear, or in knowing what they mean by what they say or write." 然而,他继续说,"我们的学生无论在理解他们所阅读的或听到的,或者在懂得他们所讲的或写的东西的含义方面,并没有很多直接的帮助"。

本句的组要成分是:our pupils...are not getting help in understanding...in knowing...what...in knowing what...。句中两个 what 从句作 understanding 和 knowing 的宾语。moreover 是"而且,此外"的意思,比如:It was good car, and it was moreover, a fair price they were asking for it. 这是辆好车,而且他们开出了一个好价钱。

31. It applied equally to colleges in this country, and even in England concerning the linguistic skill of undergraduates in Cambridge University. 它对美国大学同样适用,甚至对英国大学,从理查兹最近关于剑桥大学本科生的语言能力的研究来看,同样也是适用的。

apply to "适用",比如:That bit of the form is for UK citizens—it doesn't apply to you. 表格上的那一项是针对英国公民的,并不适用于你的情况。

concerning 是"关于"的意思,比如:He refused to answer questions concerning his private life. 他拒绝回答关于他私生活的问题。

32. That conference at Chicago ran for four days—with many papers presented at morning, afternoon, and evening sessions—all on the problem of reading. 芝加哥会议进行了四天,在上午、下午和晚间的会议上提交了很多关于阅读问题论文。

本句主语是 that conference,谓语是 ran, with many papers...作伴随状语, presented...过去分词短语作 papers 的后置定语。

33. Too many other things, of much less importance, have come to clutter up the curriculum. 很多次要的东西塞满了课程。

clutter up:堆满,乱堆。比如:She says she deliberately tries not to clutter up her mind with useless information. 她说她刻意不使脑子里堆满无用的东西。

34. This was thought to be a novel "experiment" or worse, a wild idea. 这被认为是一个新颖的"实验",或者更坏一些,被认为是一个狂妄的设想。

35. The acuteness and vitality of their discussion of matters raised in class showed that they were better than older students who had been dulled by years of listening to lectures, taking notes, and passing examinations. 他们在课堂上讨论问题时的敏锐和活跃,表明他们具有足够的智力阅读名著。在很多方面,他们比年长的学生强得多,这些年长的学生几年来听讲课、

记笔记、应付考试,已被搞得迟钝了。

本句的主要成分是:The acuteness and vitality... showed that 从句,在从句中 who 引导的从句修饰先行词 students,作它的定语。

36 They had much more edge than college seniors or graduate students. 他们比大学四年级学生或研究生更有锋芒。

edge 是"锋芒,优越之处"的意思,比如:Because of her experience she had the edge over the other people that we interviewed. 她有经验,因此比我们面试过的其他人有优势。

37 It was a shame that their native talents were not being trained to perform a function that was plainly of the highest educational importance. 他们的天赋才能没有得到训练,去行使一个在教育上明显地具有头等重要性的职能,这是一个耻辱。

第一个 that 引导的是宾语从句,第二个 that 引导从句的是定语从句,修饰先行词 function。

练 习

1. 回答问题

    (1) What did people from all source complain about?

    (2) How many students read magazines of the type of Harper's, or The Atlantic Monthly?

    (3) What demands does the writer think are not exorbitant to make of high school or college?

    (4) What does the results of a test given by Professor Diederich at Chicago top-notch high-school seniors illustrate?

    (5) Why are the students not getting any help from the professional educators?

2. 判断正误

    (1) When students are on the fifth and sixth grade, their reading is taught effectively, and then there is a steady and general improvement, beyond the level, it is also improved for a long time.

    (2) Out of school, many students read a lot of books, ranging over many aspects.

    (3) Students are acquainted with the best novels published during their years in school.

    (4) The more difficult questions the students are measured, the better results they get.

    (5) It is too much to ask that a student be able to read a whole book, and report not only what was said but also show an increased understanding of the subject matter being discussed.

3. 选词填空

    by means of, moreover, clutter up, nor, complain of, rest on, for the most part, apply to, incompetence in, incorporated into

    (1) Japanese TV sets are, _____, of excellent quality.

    (2) Dan's been _____ severe headaches recently.

    (3) Management have demonstrated an almost unbelievable _____ their handling of the

dispute.

(4) Success in management ultimately _____ good judgment.

(5) Thoughts are expressed _____ words.

(6) She never laughed, _____ did she ever lose her temper.

(7) Suggestions from the survey have been _____ the final design.

(8) The rent is reasonable and, _____, the location is perfect.

(9) The questions on this part of the form only _____ married men.

(10) The front room was _____ with antique furniture.

4. 句型模拟

(1) either...or...

(2) not half as bad/good as

5. 英译汉

(1) Until recently, freshman English was required course in every college.

(2) Teachers of freshman English in college have had to do over again what should have been completed in high school.

(3) However difficult it may to read, it is easier than writing and speaking well.

(4) It cannot be because the professional educators are unaware of the situation.

(5) At the end of the first year, I went to the principal of the high school to report on our progress.

6. 汉译英

(1) 这部电影是根据马克·吐温的短篇小说改编的。(base on)

(2) 小路到了山顶就变平坦了。(flatten out)

(3) 孩子们没有钱,因此他们不可能看电影。(out of the question)

(4) 已学会一门外语的学生会发现再学一门外语更容易些。(be acquainted with)

(5) 要是你了解有关最近车站所发生事情的情况,请与警方联系。(concerning)

7. 写作指导

For this part, you are required to write a composition on the topic "The importance of Reading". The following points taken from the text are useful expressions for your reference:

- realize that half the time in a law school must spent in teaching the student how to read the cases
- realize that if college graduates had a decent skill in reading, the more specialized technique of reading cases could be acquired in much less than half the time now spent
- wager that his inability to read is partly responsible for his defects in writing
- able to read what he writes
- cannot read well enough for all practical purposes even though they are sixth graders

- do poorly in high school because of sheer ineptitude in getting meaning from the printed page
- the range of reading is woefully slight and of the simplest and poorest sort
- not acquainted with the best novels published during their years in school
- ask that a student be able to read a whole book, not merely a paragraph, and report not only what was said therein but show an increased understanding of the subject matter being discussed
- train their students not only to interpret but to criticize

Existialism Education
存在主义教育

　　存在主义教育是现代西方教育思想的一个流派,产生于二十世纪五十年代,美国教育家尼勒、莫里斯等把存在主义应用于教育理论,形成了一个教育思想流派。其他主要代表人物还有德国的海德格尔、雅斯贝斯、法国的萨特尔和奥地利的布贝尔等。

　　存在主义以"主观性"为"第一原理",认为人的存在或者纯粹的自我意识"先于本质",鼓吹周围世界和"自我"是对立的,因而每个人都是孤立的,充满着"死亡的恐惧"。由此出发,存在主义教育认为教育应以个人的"自我完成"为目标,否认"外界因素"对个性形成的作用,而把个人作为"教育的主体",鼓吹把"在发现自我的境遇中进行个人的自由发展"作为教育的基本目标。主张实行"天才教育",反对普及教育。

　　在道德教育上,主张让学生"自由选择"道德标准,鼓吹以"自由选择"道德标准为原则的品格教育。强调"名副其实的教育实质上就是品格教育",认为只有这样,才能培养出"一个品格崇高的人"。

　　它还认为知识的真实性要看他对个人主观的价值,教学应把个人的"主观性"作为出发点。因此,在教学内容上,它提出"课程的全部重点必须从事物世界转移到人格世界",特别强调人文学科,要使所有的儿童,除《圣经》以外还要熟悉古代历史和古典著作。在教学方法上,推崇古希腊哲学家苏格拉底的教育方法,认为这才是"理想的教育方法",因为学生用这种方法学到的是他自己肯定的东西"。在教学组织形式上,则强调"个别对待"。

11. The Education of Character
品格教育

Martin Buber
马丁·贝布尔

马丁·贝布尔(1876—1965),犹太神学家、哲学家、存在主义者。生于奥地利维也纳。先后在维也纳、莱比锡、柏林和苏黎世等大学学习,专攻犹太教神秘的教义。曾从事犹太复国主义运动。当过德国法兰克福大学、耶路撒冷希伯来大学哲学教授。主要著作有:《我和你》、《人与人之间》、《生存的对话:哲学和教育学全集》。

《品格教育》中贝布尔从人性论出发,认为人与人之间是一种相互的"对话"、"我和你"的关系,而不是彼此把对方看作一件东西那样"我和它"的关系。他提出的所谓"品格教育",认为教育的关系就是"一种纯粹的(师生之间)对话的关系",要求一个人应当在行动和态度上乐于"承担责任",在师生之间必须建立一种"信任感"。主张教育必须通过这种师生关系,才能帮助学生按照个人的意志自由选择道路,并激发他们去发现关于上帝和永恒性价值。

Education worthy of the name is essentially education of character.[1] For the genuine educator does not merely consider individual functions of his pupil, as one intending to teach him only to know or be capable of certain definite things; but his concern is always the person as a whole, both in the actuality in which he lives before you now and in his possibilities, what he can become. But in this way, as a whole in reality and potentiality, a man can be conceived either as personality, that is, as a unique spiritual-physical form with all the forces dormant in it, or as character, that is, as the link between what this individual is and the sequence of his actions and attitudes.[2] Between these two modes of conceiving the pupil in his wholeness there is a fundamental difference. Personality is something which its growth remains essentially outside the influence of the educator; but to assist in the moulding of character is his greatest task. Personality is a completion, only character is a task. One may cultivate and enhance personality, but in education one can and one must aim at character.

However—as I would like to point out straightaway—it is advisable not to over-estimate what the educator can even at best[3] do to develop character. In this more than in any other branch of the science of teaching it is important to realize, at the very beginning of the discussion, the fundamental limits to conscious influence, even before asking what character is and how it is to be brought about.[4]

If I have to teach algebra I can expect to succeed in giving my pupils an idea of quadratic equations with two unknown quantities. Even the slowest-witted child[5] will understand it so well that he will amuse himself by solving equations at night when he cannot fall asleep. And even one with the most sluggish memory will not forget, in his old age, how to play with x and y. But if I am concerned with the education of character, everything becomes problematic. I try to explain to my pupils that envy is despicable, and at once I feel the secret resistance of those who are poorer than their comrades. I try to explain that it is wicked to bully the weak, and at once I see a suppressed smile on the lips of the strong. I try to explain that lying destroys life, and something frightful happens: the worst habitual liar of the class produces a brilliant essay on the destructive power of lying[6]. I have made the fatal mistake of *giving instruction* in ethics, and what I said is accepted as current coin of knowledge[7]; nothing of it is transformed into character-building substance.

But the difficulty lies still deeper. In all teaching of a subject I can announce my intention of teaching as openly as I please, and this does not interfere with the results. After all, pupils do want, for the most part, to learn something, even if not overmuch, so that a tacit agreement becomes possible. But as soon as my pupils notice that I want to educate their characters I am resisted precisely by those who show most signs of genuine independent character: they will not let themselves be educated, or rather, they do not like the idea that somebody wants to educate them.[8] And those, too, who are seriously labouring over the question of good and evil, rebel when one dictates to them, as though it were some long established truth, what is good and what is bad; and they rebel just because they have experienced over and over again how hard it is to find the right way. Does it follow that one should keep silent about one's intention of educating character, and act by ruse and subterfuge?[9] No; I have just said that the difficulty lies deeper. It is not enough to see that education of character is not introduced into a lesson in class; neither may one conceal it in cleverly arranged intervals.[10] Education cannot tolerate such politic action. Even if the pupil does not notice the hidden motive it will have its negative effect on the actions of the teacher himself by depriving him of the directness which is his strength. Only in his whole being, in all his spontaneity can the educator truly affect the whole being of his pupil.[11] For educating characters you do not need a moral genius, but you do need a man who is wholly alive and able to communicate himself directly to his fellow beings. His aliveness streams out to them and affects them most strongly and purely when he has no thought of affecting them.[12]

The Greek word *character* means impression. The special link between man's being and his appearance, the special connection between the unity of what he is and the sequence of his actions and attitudes is impressed on his still plastic substance. Who does the impressing? Everything does: nature and the social context, the house and the street, language and custom, the world of history and the world of daily news in the form of rumour, of broadcast and newspaper, music and technical science, play and dream—everything together. Many of these factors exert their influence by stimulating agreement, imitation, desire, effort; others by arousing questions, doubts, dislike, resistance. Character is formed by the interpenetration of all those multifarious,

11. The Education of Character 品格教育

opposing influences.[13] And yet, among this infinity of form-giving forces the educator is only one element among innumerable others, but distinct from them all by his *will* to take part in the stamping of character and by his *consciousness* that he represents in the eyes of the growing person a certain *selection* of what is, the selection of what is "right," of what *should* be. It is in this will and this consciousness that his vocation as an educator finds its fundamental expression. From this the genuine educator gains two things: first, humility, the feeling of being only one element amidst the fullness of life, only one single existence in the midst of all the tremendous inrush of reality on the pupil[14]; but secondly, self-awareness, the feeling of being therein the only existence that *wants* to affect the whole person, and thus the feeling of responsibility for the selection of reality which he represents to the pupil[15]. And a third thing emerges from all this, the recognition that in this realm of the education of character, of wholeness, there is only *one* access to the pupil: his *confidence*. For the adolescent who is frightened and disappointed by an unreliable world, confidence means the liberating insight that there is human truth, the truth of human existence. When the pupil's confidence has been won, his resistance against being educated gives way to[16] a singular happening: he accepts the educator as a person. He feels he may trust this man, that this man is not making a business out of him, but is taking part in his life, accepting him before desiring to influence him. And so he learns to *ask*.

The teacher who is for the first time approached by a boy with somewhat defiant bearing, but with trembling hands, visibly opened-up and fired by a daring hope, who asks him what is the right thing in a certain situation—for instance, whether in learning that a friend has betrayed a secret entrusted to[17] him one should call him to account or be content with entrusting no more secrets to him—the teacher to whom this happens realizes that this is the moment to make the first conscious step towards education of character; he has to answer, to answer under a responsibility, to give an answer which will probably lead beyond the alternatives of the question by showing a third possibility which is the right one. To dictate what is good and evil in general is not his business. His business is to answer a concrete question, to answer what is right and wrong in a given situation. This, as I have said, can only won by the strenuous endeavour to win it, but by direct and ingenuous participation in the life of the people on is dealing with—in this case in the life of one's pupils—and by assuming the responsibility which arises from such participation.[18] It is not the educational intention but it is the meeting which is educationally fruitful. A soul suffering from the contradictions of the world of human society, and of its own physical existence, approaches me with a question. By trying to answer it to the best of my knowledge[19] and conscience I help it to become a character that actively overcomes the contradictions.

If this is the teacher's standpoint towards his pupil, taking part in his life and conscious of responsibility, then everything that passes between them can, without any deliberate or politic intention, open a way to the education of character: lessons and games, a conversation about quarrels in the class, or about the problems of a world-war. Only, the teacher must not forget the limits of education; even when he enjoys confidence he cannot always expect agreement. Confidence implies a break-through from reserve, the bursting of the bonds which imprison an unquiet heart.[20] But it does not imply unconditional agreement. The teacher must never forget that conflicts too, if only they are decided in a healthy atmosphere, have an educational value. A conflict with a pupil is the supreme test for the educator. He must use his own insight wholeheartedly; he must not blunt the piercing impact of his knowledge, but he must at the same time have in readiness the healing ointment for the heart pierced by it[21]. Not for a moment may he conduct a dialectical manoeuvre instead of the real battle for truth.[22] But if he is the victor he has to help the vanquished to endure defeat; and if he cannot conquer the self-willed soul that faces him(for victories over souls are not so easily won), then he has to find the word of love which alone can help to overcome so difficult a situation.

I have already said that the test of the educator lies in conflict with his pupil. He has to face this conflict and, whatever turn it may take, he has to find the way through it into life, into a life, I must add, where confidence continues unshaken—more, is even mysteriously strengthened. But the example I have just given shows the extreme difficult of this task, which seems at times to have reached an impassable frontier[23]. This is no longer merely a conflict between two generations, but between a world which for several millennia has believed in a truth superior to man, and an age which does not believe in it any longer—will not or cannot believe in it any longer.

But if we now ask, "How in this situation can there be any education of character?" something negative is immediately obvious: it is senseless to want to prove by any kind of argument that nevertheless the denied absoluteness of norms exists. That would be to assume that the denial is the result of reflection, and is open to argument, that is, to material for renewed reflection. But the denial is due to the disposition of a dominant human type of our age. We are justified in regarding this disposition as a sickness of the human race. But we must not deceive ourselves by believing that the disease can be cured by formulae which assert that nothing is really as the sick person imagines. It is an idle undertaking to call out, to a mankind that has grow blind to eternity: "Look! The eternal values!" Today host upon host of men have everywhere sunk into the slavery of collective is the supreme authority for its own slaves; there is no longer, superior to the collectives, any universal sovereignty in idea, faith, or spirit. Against the values, decrees and decisions of the collective no appeal is possible. This is true, not only for the totalitarian countries, but also for the parties and party-like groups in the so-called democracies. Men who have so lost themselves to the collective Moloch cannot be rescued from it by any reference, however eloquent, to the absolute whose kingdom the Moloch has usurped. One has to begin by pointing to that sphere where man himself, in the hours of utter solitude, occasionally becomes aware of the disease through sudden pain: by pointing to the relation of the individual to his own self. In order to enter into a personal relation with the absolute, it is first necessary to be a person again, to rescue one's real personal self from the fiery jaws of collectivism which devours all self-hood. The desire to do this is latent in the pain the individual suffers through his distorted relation to his own self. Again and again he dulls the pain awake, to waken the desire—that is the first task of everyone who regrets the obscuring of eternity. It is also the first task of the genuine educator in our time.

11. The Education of Character 品格教育

The educator's task can certainly not consist in educating great characters. He cannot select his pupils, but year by year the world, such as it is, is sent in the form of a school class to meet him on his life's way as his destiny; and in this destiny lies the very meaning of his life's work.[24] He has to introduce discipline and order, he has to establish a law, and he can only strive and hope for the result that discipline and order will become more and more inward and autonomous, and that at last the law will be written in the heart of his pupils. But his real goal which, once he has well recognized it and well remembers it, will influence all his work, is the great character.

A section of the young is beginning to feel today that, because of their absorption by the collective, something important and irreplaceable is lost to them—personal responsibility for life and the world. These young people, it is true, do not yet realize that their blind devotion to the collective, *eg* to a party, was not a genuine act of their personal life[25]; they do not realize that it spring, rather, from the fear of being left, in this age of confusion, to rely on themselves, on a self which no longer receives its direction from eternal values. Thus they do not yet realize that their devotion was fed on the unconscious desire to have responsibility removed from them by an authority in which they believe or want to believe.[26] They do not yet realize that this devotion was an escape. I repeat, the young people I am speaking of do not yet realize this. But they are beginning to notice that he who no longer, with his whole being, decides what he does or does not, and assumes responsibility for it, becomes sterile in soul. And a sterile soul soon ceases to be a soul.[27]

This is where the educator can begin and should begin. He can help the feeling that something is lacking to grow into the clarity of consciousness and into the force of desire. He can awaken in young people the courage to shoulder life again. He can bring before his pupils the image of a great character who denies no answer to life and the world, but accepts responsibility for everything essential that he meets. He can show his pupils this image without the fear that those among them who most of all need discipline and order will drift into a craving for aimless freedom[28]: on the contrary, he can teach them in this way to recognize that discipline and order too are starting-points on the way towards self-responsibility. He can show that even the great character is not born perfect, that the unity of his being has first to mature before expressing itself in the sequence of his actions and attitudes. But unity itself, unity of the person, unity of the lived life, has to be emphasized again and again. The confusing contradictions cannot be remedied by the collectives, not one of which knows the taste of genuine unity and which if left to themselves would end up, like the scorpions imprisoned in a box, in the witty fable, by devouring one another. This mass of contradictions can be met and conquered only by the rebirth of personal unity, unity of being, unity of life, unity of action—unity of being, life and action together. This does not mean a static unity of the uniform, but the great dynamic unity of the multiform in which multiformity is formed into unity of character.[29] Today the great characters are still "enemies of the people," they who love their society, yet wish not only to preserve it but to raise it to a higher level. Tomorrow they will be the architects of a new unity of mankind. It is the longing for personal unity, from which must be born a unity of mankind. It is the longing for personal unity, from which must be born a unity of mankind, which the educator should lay hold of and strengthen in his pupils. Faith in this unity and the will to achieve it is not a "return" to individualism, but a step beyond all the dividedness of individualism and collectivism. A great and full relation between man and man can only exist between unified and responsible persons. That is why it is much more rarely found in the totalitarian collective than in any historically earlier form of society; much more rarely also in the authoritarian party than in any earlier form of free association. Genuine education of character is genuine education for community.[30]

注　释

1　Education worthy of the name is essentially education of character. 名副其实的教育,本质上是品格教育。
worthy of the name 是"名副其实"。worthy of sth 指"应得某事物",比如：a statement worthy of contempt 应该摒弃的说法。

2　But in this way, as a whole in reality and potentiality, a man can be conceived either as personality, that is, as a unique spiritual-physical form with all the forces dormant in it, or as character, that is, as the link between what this individual is and the sequence of his actions and attitudes. 只有像这样把一个人看作一个现实的并有潜在可能性的整体,才算能把他看作个性,即其中潜伏着各种力量的一个独特的精神——物质结构,或把他看作品格,即介于这个人的为人与他的一连串行动和态度之间的纽带。

3　at best：充其量。如：We can't arrive before Friday at best. 我们无论如何星期五以前也到不了。

4　In this more than in any other branch of the science of teaching it is important to realize, at the very beginning of the discussion, the fundamental limits to conscious influence, even before asking what character is and how it is to be brought about. 在讨论的最初,甚至在探讨什么是品格以及怎样加以培养这个问题之前,在这一点上,不是教学科学的任何其他分支,认识到要从根本上限制有意识的影响是很重要的。
bring about：使(某事物)发生；导致

5　slowest-witted child：智力发展最迟缓的儿童

6　the worst habitual liar of the class produces a brilliant essay on the destructive power of lying. 班上的一个最恶劣的撒谎老手竟能对说谎的破坏力写出了一篇绝妙的短文。

7　current coin of knowledge：老生常谈

8　But as soon as my pupils notice that I want to educate their characters I am resisted precisely by those who show most signs of genuine independent character: they will not let themselves be educated, or rather, they do not like the idea that somebody wants to educate them. 可是,一旦我的学生觉察到我想要培养他们的品格时,我恰恰就会受到那些最明显表示出真正独立品格学生的对抗：他们不愿听任自己被人教育,更确切地说,他们不喜欢别人有教育他们的意图。

9　Does it follow that one should keep silent about one's intention of educating character, and act by ruse and subterfuge? 那么，是否可由此断定人们应该闭口不谈培养品格的意图，而应采取诡秘和圆滑些的行动呢？

10 It is not enough to see that education of character is not introduced into a lesson in class; neither may one conceal it in cleverly arranged intervals. 只看到品格教育不能纳入课堂教学里，这还不够；也不能把品格教育隐藏在巧妙安排的课间休息时间内。

11 Only in his whole being, in all his spontaneity can the educator truly affect the whole being of his pupil. 教师只能以他一个完整的人形象，以他全部的自发性本能才足以对学生的整个人起着真实的影响。

only 短语放在句首，句子部分倒装，表示强调。

12 His aliveness streams out to them and affects them most strongly and purely when he has no thought of affecting them. 当他无意影响他们时，他向他们倾注着自己的蓬勃生气，对他们有着极其有力而彻底地影响。

13 Character is formed by the interpenetration of all those multifarious, opposing influences. 品格就是由所有这些各种各样的矛盾影响交织在一起形成的。

14 first, humility, the feeling of being only one element amidst the fullness of life, only one single existence in the midst of all the tremendous inrush of reality on the pupil: 第一是谦逊感，既感到自己只是丰富多彩的生活中的一分子，只是一个对学生施行一切猛烈的现实冲击中的单一的实体。

in the midst of:在……中间

15 but secondly, self-awareness, the feeling of being therein the only existence that wants to affect the whole person, and thus the feeling of responsibility for the selection of reality which he represents to the pupil: 而第二却是自觉感，即意识到自己是一切事物中想要影响整个人的惟一实体，并从而产生提示学生对现实应作抉择的责任感。

两个 the feeling of... 是 self-awareness 的同位语。

16 give way to:"让步，妥协"。比如:We must not give way to their demands.我们绝不能对他们的要求让步。

17 entrust...to...:委托某人负责某事物。比如:entrust the task to an assistant 把一项工作交给助手。

18 Confidence, of course, is not won by the strenuous endeavour to win it, but by direct and ingenuous participation in the life of the people one is dealing with—in this case in the life of one's pupils—and by assuming the responsibility which arises from such participation. 当然，信任不是强求得来的，只有坦率而真诚地参与所要交往的人的生活(在这里是指自己的学生的生活)，并担负起因这样地参与生活所引起的责任，这样才能赢得他的信任。

19 to the best of one's knowledge:尽其所知

类似的表达:to the best of one's ability:尽其所能

20 Confidence implies a break-through from reserve, the bursting of the bonds which imprison an unquiet heart. 信任意味着打破限制、摧毁那种禁锢一个不平静心灵的枷锁。

21 but he must at the same time have in readiness the healing ointment for the heart pierced by it:但他必须同时做好准备对于被他刺伤的心灵敷以刀伤药膏。

have in readiness：做好准备

22　Not for a moment may he conduct a dialectical manoeuvre instead of the real battle for truth. 他一刻也不会用诡辩技巧为真理进行真正的争辩。
本句把否定词 not 放在句首,句子是部分倒装。

23　to have reached an impassable frontier：达到了难以逾越的极限

24　He cannot select his pupils, but year by year the world, such as it is, is sent in the form of a school class to meet him on his life's way as his destiny; and in this destiny lies the very meaning of his life's work. 他不能选择学生,在他的生活道路上年复一年所接触到的那种世界,就是按学校班级形式派给他的各批学生,这是他命中注定的遭遇;他一生工作的真正意义就存在于这种遭遇中。

25　These young people, it is true, do not yet realize that their blind devotion to the collective, *eg* to a party, was not a genuine act of their personal life. 的确,这些青年人还未认识到,他们对集体,例如对一个党的盲目信仰,不是他们个人生活中的一种真正行为。
devotion to:献身,忠心,比如:devotion to duty 忠于职守

26　Thus they do not yet realize that their devotion was fed on the unconscious desire to have responsibility removed from them by an authority in which they believe or want to believe. 因此,他们还未认识到,他们的这种信仰之所以滋长,是由于一种不知不觉的愿望,即甘心让他们所深信的或想要深信的一个权威解除他们责任的那种愿望。

27　And a sterile soul soon ceases to be a soul. 而一个心灵空虚的人立刻就不称其为人了。

28　He can show his pupils this image without the fear that those among them who most of all need discipline and order will drift into a craving for aimless freedom：他能把这种形象显示给学生,而不必担心他们中最需要纪律和秩序的那些学生倾向于追求毫无目的的自由。
that 从句是同位语从句补充说明 fear。crave for：是"渴望,渴求某事物"的意思,比如：She is craving for their admiration. 她渴望得到他们的赞赏。

29　This does not mean a static unity of the uniform, but the great dynamic unity of the multiform in which multiformity is formed into unity of character. 这不意味着同样的东西是静止的统一,却意味着形形色色的东西是高度动态的统一,在这种高度动态的统一中的多样性形成了品格的统一。

30　Genuine education of character is genuine education for community. 真正的品格教育就是真正的共同相处的教育。

练　习

1. 回答问题
   (1) According to the author, what difference is there between personality and character?
   (2) Why do the pupils resist me when they notice that I want to educate their characters?
   (3) How can the educator truly affect the whole being of his pupil?
   (4) How can confidence be won according to the author?
   (5) What is the supreme test for the educator?

2. 判断正误

(1) The pupil's character can be educated in cleverly arranged intervals.

(2) Character is formed only by the influence of the educator.

(3) If conflicts are solved in a healthy atmosphere, they also have an educational value.

(4) Only a moral genius can educate characters.

(5) Genuine education is essentially education of character; and genuine education of character is genuine education for community.

3. 选词填空

spring from, feed on, cease, crave for, lay hold of, deprive...of..., in the midst of, give way to, superior to, devote to

(1) He _____ all his efforts _____ this difficult task.

(2) Hatred often _____ fear.

(3) He was born in a noble family, so he always thinks _____ others.

(4) Fighting between the two sides _____ at midnight.

(5) I managed to _____ the jug before it fell.

(6) The storm _____ bright sunshine.

(7) There are wild animals _____ forest.

(8) Women _____ the rights for education in the old society.

(9) The cows are _____ hay in the barn.

(10) He is very thirsty. So he _____ a drink.

4. 句型模拟

(1) it is... that

(2) would like to do

5. 英译汉

(1) I try to explain to my pupils that envy is despicable, and at once I feel the secret resistance of those who are poorer than their comrades.

(2) And yet, among this infinity of form-giving forces the educator is only one element among innumerable others, but distinct from them all by his will to take part in the stamping of character and by his consciousness that he represents in the eyes of the growing person a certain selection of what is, the selection of what is "right", of what should be.

(3) This is no longer merely a conflict between two generations, but between a world which for several millennia has believed in a truth superior to man, and an age which does not believe in it any longer—will not or cannot believe in it any longer.

(4) This mass of contradictions can be met and conquered only by the rebirth of personal unity, unity of being, unity of life, unity of action—unity of being, life and action together.

(5) Faith in this unity and the will to achieve it is not a "return" to individualism, but a step

beyond all the dividedness of individualism and collectivism.

6. 汉译英

(1) 他的成就值得给予最高赞赏。(worthy of)
(2) 不要让娱乐妨碍了职责。(interfere with)
(3) 他托我照看一天孩子。(entrust...to)
(4) 要到那农舍去只有穿过田地。(access to)
(5) 最初他拒不承认有任何责任,到头来还是道了歉。(end up)

7. 写作指导

For this part, you are required to write a composition on the topic "How to educate the pupil's character." The following points taken from the text are useful expressions for your reference:

- consider the pupil as a whole
- educator should be wholly alive and able to communicate himself directly t his fellow beings
- educate the pupil to be confident
- to answer what is right and wrong in a given situation
- to rescue one's real personal self from the fiery jaws of collectivism
- to keep the pain awake
- to waken the desire
- to encourage the pupil to be responsible

VI

New Behavorism Education
新行为主义教育

行为主义教育开始于二十世纪初，主要代表人物是华生。行为主义者反对"内省法"，强调"客观法"，认为心理学是行为的科学。认为采用"刺激"和"反应"公式就能预测和控制行为的发生和变化。新行为主义教育是十九世纪五十年代形成于美国，六十年代波及众多国家的国际性教育流派。它的程序教学理论以 J.B. 华生，更主要是 B.F. 斯金纳的行为主义心理学为理论基础，遵循"操作性条件作用"和"积极强化"的原理，通过倡导操作主义学习理论和推行程序教学而对当时的教育理论和实践产生了巨大的影响。主要代表人物有陶尔曼、赫尔、普莱西、斯金纳、提客瑞艾等。其中对教育改革影响较大的是斯金纳。

斯金纳认为人类必须用行为来解释思维，而且一切行为都是由外界所引起，受外界控制的。他认为"操作性条件作用"和"积极强化"在教育上起着重要的意义，"人性"具有很强的可塑性，"正如一个雕刻师塑造一块烂泥一样"任何行为都能通过环境的"操作"和某些行为的"积极强化"随意地创造、设计、塑造和改变。

新行为主义教育流派继承发展了实验主义教育流派的使教育理论与实践走向客观化、科学化的思想，同时努力避免了进步主义教育流派凭"简单的哲学信条"进行改革的不足。它向人们展示了教育的科学化必须以科学的心理学为支柱这样一个已为大家所接受的信念。

作为一种教育思潮的新行为主义程序教学已完成了它的历史使命，它所倡导的"学习是一门科学，教学是一种艺术"的命题将不断激励人们去上下求索。

12. The Science of Learning and the Art of Teaching
学习的科学和教学的艺术

B.F. Skinner
B.F. 斯金纳

斯金纳(1904—?)美国当代著名的心理学家、教育学家,新行为主义心理学及新行为主义教育流派的主要代表人物。斯金纳出生在美国宾夕法尼亚州的一个小城镇中。1931年获哈佛大学哲学博士学位。1936至1945年间,斯金纳执教于明尼苏达大学。五十年代以后,斯金纳在继续从事实验心理学研究的同时,开始把兴趣转向了教育方面,领导了一场新行为主义的程序教学运动。他以自己的学习理论为依据,积极倡导和推动发展程序教育。1966年,斯金纳对自己程序教学的理论和实践活动进行了总结,写成了《教学技术学》一书。他对程序教学理论所作出的杰出贡献,使得西方学者把他誉为"程序教学之父"。

主要著作有:《有机体的行为》,《言语行为》,《强化程式.》以及《科学与人类行为》等。

《学习的科学和教学的艺术》是美国杰出心理学家、"新行为主义"的主要代表斯金纳在1954年发表的一篇论文。该论文迅速掀起了一个关于程序教学和教学机器开发的运动。斯金纳在文章中提出了"小步子、循序渐进、序列化、学习者参与、强化、自定步调"等六个教学设计原则,从而确立了行为主义教学设计的基础。北美教学设计理论早期发展中的几个主要人物如加涅、格拉泽、帕期科无不受斯金纳的影响。程序教学的浪潮也不可避免地波及欧洲,在欧洲引起广泛讨论。但是,由于欧洲大陆的教育教学研究受"理性主义"哲学支配。其教育学更多表现为"人文科学取向"。因此,当北美的教育科学和程序教学传到欧洲以后,除一些热心的支持者从教学技术的角度对之赞同以外,许多教育学者则从人文科学的角度对之批评。当程序教学运动衰微以后,更强化了许多欧洲教育学者和教师反对教学技术的偏见,这种状况持续至今。

Some promising advances have recently been made in the field of learning.[2] Special techniques have been designed to arrange what are called "contingencies of reinforcement"—the relations which prevail between behavior on the one hand and the consequences of that behavior on the other—with the result that a much more effective control of behavior has been achieved. It has long been argued that an organism learns mainly by producing changes in its environment, but it is only recently that these changes have been carefully manipulated. In traditional devices for the study of learning—in the serial maze, for example, or in the T-maze, the problem box, or the familiar discrimination apparatus—the effects produced by the organism's behavior are left to many fluctuating circumstances.[3] There is many a slip between the turn-to-the-right and the food-cup at the end of the alley.[4] It is not surprising that techniques of this sort have yielded only very rough data from which the uniformities demanded by an experimental science can be extracted only by averaging many cases.[5] In none of this work has the behavior of the individual organism been predicted in more than a statistical sense.[6] The learning processes, which are the presumed object of such research, are reached only through a series of inferences. Current preoccupation with deductive systems reflects this state of the science.

Recent improvements in the conditions, which control behavior in the field of learning, are of two principal sorts. The Law of Effect has been taken seriously; we have made sure that effects do occur and that they occur under conditions, which are optimal for producing the changes, called learning.[7] Once we have arranged the particular type of consequence called reinforcement, our techniques permit us to shape up the behavior of an organism almost at will.[8] It has become a routine exercise to demonstrate this in classes in elementary psychology by conditioning such an organism as a pigeon. Simply by presenting food to a hungry pigeon at the right time, it is possible to shape up three or four well-defined responses in a single demonstration period—such responses as turning around, pacing the floor in the pattern of a figure-8, standing still in a corner of the demonstration apparatus, stretching the neck, or stamping the foot. Extremely complex performances may be reached through successive stages in the shaping process, the contingencies of reinforcement being changed progressively in the direction of the required behavior.[9] The results are often quite dramatic. In such a demonstration one van see learning take place. A significant change in behavior is often obvious as the result of a single reinforcement.

One of the most dramatic applications of these techniques has recently been made in the Harvard Psychological Laboratories by Floyd Ratliff and Donald S. Blough, who have skillfully used multiple and serial schedules of reinforcement to study complex perceptual processes in the infrahuman organism.[10] They have achieved a sort of psychophysics without verbal instruction. In a recent experiment by Blough, for example, a pigeon draws a detailed dark-adaptation curve showing the characteristic breaks of rod and cone vision.[11] The curve is recorded continuously in a single experimental period and is quite comparable with the curves of human subjects. The pigeon behaves in a way, which, in the human case, we would not hesitate to describe by saying that it adjusts a very faint patch of light until it can just be seen.[12]

In all this work, the species of the organism has made surprisingly little difference. It is true that the organisms studied have all been vertebrates, but they still cover a wide range. Comparable results have been obtained with pigeons, rats, dogs, monkeys, human children, and most recently, by the author in collaboration with Ogden R. Lindsley, human psychotic subjects.[13] In spite of great phylogenetic differences, all these organisms show amazingly similar properties of the learning process.[14] It should be emphasized that this has been achieved by analyzing the effects of reinforcement and by designing techniques, which manipulate reinforcement with considerable precision. Only in this way can the behavior of the individual organism be brought under such precise control.[15] It is also important to note that through a gradual advance to complex interrelations among responses, the same degree of rigor is being extended to behavior, which would usually be assigned to such fields as perception, thinking, and personality dynamics.

From this exciting prospect of an advancing science of learning, it is a great shock to turn to that branch of technology, which is most directly concerned with the learning process—education.[16] Let us consider, for example, the teaching of arithmetic in the lower grades. The school is concerned with imparting to the child a large number of responses of a special sort. The responses are all verbal. They consist of speaking and writing certain words, figures, and signs, which, to put it roughly, refer to numbers and to arithmetic operations.[17] The first task is to shape up these responses—to get the child to pronounce and to write responses correctly, but the principal task is to bring this behavior under many sorts of stimulus control.[18] This is what happens when the child learns to count, to recite tables, to count while ticking off the items in an assemblage of objects, to respond to spoken or written numbers by saying "odd", "even", "prime", and so on.[19] Over and above this elaborate repertoire of numerical behavior, most of which is often dismissed as the product of rote learning, the teaching of arithmetic looks forward to those complex serial arrangements of responses involved in original mathematical thinking.[20] The child must acquire responses of transposing, clearing fractions, and so on, which modify the order or pattern of the original material so that the response called a solution is eventually made possible.

Now, how is this extremely complicated verbal repertoire set up? In the first place, what reinforcements are used? Fifty years ago the answer would have been clear. At that time educational control was still frankly aversive. The child read numbers, copied numbers, memorized tables, and performed operations upon numbers to escape the threat of the birch rod or cane. Some positive reinforcements were perhaps eventually derived from the increased efficiency of the child in the field of arithmetic and in rare cases some automatic reinforcement may have resulted from the sheer manipulation of the medium—from the solution of problems or the discovery of the intricacies of the number system.[21] But for the immediate purposes of the education the child acted to avoid or escape punishment.[22] It was part of the reform movement known as progressive education to make the positive consequences more immediately effective, but any one who visits the lower grades of the average school today will observe that a change has been made, not from aversive to positive control, but from one form of aversive stimulation to another.[23] The child at his desk, filling in his workbook, is behaving primarily to escape from the threat of a series of minor aversive events—the teacher's displeasure, the criticism or ridicule of his classmates, an ignominious showing in a competition, low marks, a trip to the office "to be talked to" by the principal, or a word to the parent who may still resort to the birch rod.[24] In this welter of aversive consequences, getting the right answer is in itself an insignificant event, any effect of which is lost amid the anxieties, the boredom, and the aggressions, which are the inevitable by-products of aversive control.

Secondly, we have to ask how the contingencies of reinforcement are arranged. When is a numerical operation reinforced as "right"? Eventually, of course, the pupil may be able to check his own answer and achieve some sort of automatic reinforcement, but in the early stages the reinforcement of being right is usually accorded by the teacher. The contingencies she provides are far from optimal.[25] It can easily be demonstrated that, unless explicit mediating behavior has been set up, the lapse of only a few seconds between response and reinforcement destroys most of the effect.[26] In atypical classroom, nevertheless, long periods of time customarily elapse. The teacher may walk up and down the aisle, for example, while the class is working on a sheet of problems, pausing here and there to say right or wrong. Many seconds or minutes intervene between the child's response and the teacher's reinforcement. In many cases—for example, when papers are taken home to be corrected—as much as 24 hours may intervene. It is surprising that this system has any effect whatsoever.

A third notable shortcoming is the lack of a skilful program, which moves forward through a series of progressive approximations to the final complex behavior desired. A long series of contingencies is necessary to bring the organism into the possession of mathematical behavior most efficiently. But the teacher is seldom able to reinforce at each step in such a series because she cannot deal with the pupil's responses one at a time. It is usually necessary to reinforce the behavior in blocks of responses—as in correcting a work sheet or page from a workbook. The responses within such a block must not be interrelated. The answer to one problem must not depend upon the answer to another. The number of stages through which one may progressively approach a complex pattern of behavior is therefore small, and the task so much the more difficult. Even the most modern workbook in beginning arithmetic is far from exemplifying an efficient program for shaping up mathematical behavior.[27]

Perhaps the most serious criticism of the current classroom is the relative infrequency of reinforcement. Since the pupil is usually dependent upon the teacher for being right, and since many pupils are usually dependent upon the same teacher, the total number of contingencies, which may be arranged during, say, the first four years, is of the order of only a few thousand. But a very rough estimate suggests that efficient mathematical behavior at this level requires something of the order of 25,000 contingencies. We may suppose that even in the brighter student a given contingency must be arranged several times to place the behavior well ion hand. The responses to be set up are not simply the various items in tables of addition, subtraction, multiplication, and division; we have also considered the alternative forms in which each item may be stated. To the learning of such material we should add hundreds of responses concerned with factoring, identifying primes, memorizing series, using short-cut techniques of calculation, constructing and using geometric representations or number forms, and so on. Over and above all this, the whole mathematical repertoire must be brought under the control of concrete problems of considerable variety.[28] Perhaps 50,000 contingencies are a more conservative estimate. In this frame of reference the daily assignment in arithmetic seems pitifully meager.

The result of all this is, of course, well known. Even our best schools are under criticism for their inefficiency in the teaching of drill subjects such as arithmetic.[29] The condition in the average school is a matter of widespread national concern. Modern children simply do not learn arithmetic quickly or well. Nor is the result simply incompetence. The very subjects in which modern techniques are weakest are those in which failure is most conspicuous, and in the wake of an ever-growing incompetence come the anxieties, uncertainties, and aggressions, which in their turn present other problems to the school.[30] Most pupils soon claim the asylum of not being "ready" for arithmetic at a given level for, eventually, of not having a mathematical mind. Such explanations are readily seized upon by defensive teachers and parents.[31] Few pupils ever reach the stage at which automatic reinforcements follow as the natural consequences of mathematical behavior. On the contrary, the figures and the symbols of mathematics have become standard emotional stimuli.[32] The glimpse of a column of figures, not to say an algebraic symbol or an integral sign, is likely to set off—not mathematical behavior—but a reaction of anxiety, guilt, or fear.[33]

注　释

1　本文选自 B.F. 斯金纳的《学习的科学和教学的艺术》。

2　Some promising advances have recently been made in the field of learning. 近来在学习领域中已经做出一些有希望的进展。
　　promising 是"有前途的,大有可为的,有希望的"的意思,比如:The weather is promising. 天气可望好转。

3　In traditional devices for the study of learning—in the serial maze, for example, or in the T-maze, the problem box, or the familiar discrimination apparatus—the effects produced by the organism's behavior are left to many fluctuating circumstances. 在研究学习的传统装置(例如,连串迷宫,或 T 型迷宫,问题箱,或大家熟悉的识别仪器)中,有机体的行为所产生的效果受许多情况变动的影响。
　　此句中 the effects 为主语,此前的三个 in 短语为并列状语,此后的 produced 为过去分词作定语修饰主语。
　　discrimination 是"辨别,识别,辨别力"的意思,比如:He shows fine discrimination in choosing wines. 他在挑选酒时显示出敏锐的辨别力。

4　There is many a slip between the turn-to-the-right and the food-cup at the end of the alley. 在向右转弯与小路终点的食物杯之间,存在着许多错误。
　　many a 是"许多的,多的,一个又一个的"的意思,后接单数名词,比如:Many a man would welcome such a chance. 许多人会欢迎有这样的机会。

5　It is not surprising that techniques of this sort have yielded only very rough data from which the uniformities demanded by an experimental science can be extracted only by averaging many cases. 这种技巧仅仅会产生一些大概的数据,从这些数据中可以整理出试验性科学所需要的一致性。这些数据只能通过许多案例的平均数才能取得,这是不足为奇的。
　　yield 是"出产,屈服,放弃"的意思,比如:The cow yields milk twice a day. 这头母牛每天产

两次奶。/He never yields up himself to a rival easily.他从不轻易向对手屈服。/He will not yield even a limited measure of editorial control.他连有限的一点点编辑权都不肯放弃。

6 In none of this work has the behavior of the individual organism been predicted in more than a statistical sense. 在这种研究中,对于有机体行为的预测没有超出统计学的意义。

in none of 置于句首作为句首状语时,一般必须采用部分倒装语序,比如:In none of the bottles is there any sugar.在任何一个瓶子里都没有糖。

7 The Law of Effect has been taken seriously; we have made sure that effects do occur and that they occur under conditions, which are optimal for producing the changes, called learning. 认真对待了效果定律;我们已经证实效果的确产生了,而且它们是在那种称为学习的变化的最适宜条件下产生的。

此句子为并列句,which 引导的分句为定语从句修饰后一个并列成分。make sure 是"查明,弄清楚,确保"的意思,比如:You'd better make sure of the time and place.你最好把时间和地点弄清楚。

optimal 是"最佳的,最理想的"的意思,比如:Here is the optimal place for the growth of the flower.这里是最适合这种花生长的地方。

8 Once we have arranged the particular type of consequence called reinforcement, our techniques permit us to shape up the behavior of an organism almost at will. 只要我们考虑好了称为强化的特殊形式后果,我们的技术就容许我们完全随意地塑造一个有机体的行为。

permit somebody to do something 是"容许,准许"的意思,比如:Please permit me to see him again.请允许我再见他一面。

at will 是"任意,随意"的意思,比如:With an air conditioner, you can enjoy comfortable temperature at will.有了空调机就可以随意享受使人舒适的温度。

9 Extremely complex performances may be reached through successive stages in the shaping process, the contingencies of reinforcement being changed progressively in the direction of the required behavior. 如果把出现的强化朝所需要的行为方向循序渐进地变动,就可以通过塑造过程中的一系列阶段得到极其复杂的行为。

本句中 being changed 是非谓语动词,此句是独立主格结构,表示条件。

10 One of the most dramatic applications of these techniques has recently been made in the Harvard Psychological Laboratories by Floyd Ratliff and Donald S. Blough, who have skillfully used multiple and serial schedules of reinforcement to study complex perceptual processes in the infrahuman organism. 弗洛伊德·拉特立夫和唐纳德·S.布劳,新近在哈佛心理学实验室对这些技术做了一次最富戏剧性的运用,他们巧妙地运用了多重的和连串的强化程式,研究动物的复杂知觉过程。

11 In a recent experiment by Blough, for example, a pigeon draws a detailed dark-adaptation curve showing the characteristic breaks of rod and cone vision. 例如,在布劳最近的一个实验中,一只鸽子画出一条详细的对黑暗的适应曲线,这是条曲线表明特有的棒体视觉和锥体视觉的转折点。

showing 引导的分词短语作定语,修饰 curve。

12 The pigeon behaves in a way, which, in the human case, we would not hesitate to describe

12. The Science of Learning and the Art of Teaching 学习的科学和教学的艺术

by saying that it adjusts a very faint patch of light until it can just be seen. 鸽子的这种行为方式,如果是人的话,将会毫不迟疑地将它以下面方式描述,即把一束很微弱的光线调节到恰好能看见程度。

adjust 是"调节,对准,调整,适应的意思,比如:To put it in a simple way, his job is to adjust the errors. 简单地说,他的工作就是调整误差。/He adjusted well to Washington. 他很能适应华盛顿的生活。

13　Comparable results have been obtained with pigeons, rats, dogs, monkeys, human children, and most recently, by the author in collaboration with Ogden R. Lindsley, human psychotic subjects. 可供比较的结果已经获得通过鸽子、白鼠、狗、猴和儿童的试验。最近,通过作者与奥格登·R.林斯利的合作,用精神病患者作受试者。

in collaboration with 意思是"与……合作,与……勾结",比如:He is in collaboration with me in writing the play. 我和他合作写剧本。

14　In spite of great phylogenetic differences, all these organisms show amazingly similar properties of the learning process. 虽然所有这些有机体的种族发展存在巨大差异,但它们的学习过程显示出惊人的相似之处。

in spite of 是"不顾,不管"的意思,比如:In spite of what you say, I still believe he is honest. 不管你说什么,我还是相信他是诚实的。

15　Only in this way can the behavior of the individual organism be brought under such precise control. 只有这样,才能精密的控制各个有机体的行为。

当句首状语由 only 修饰时,需要采用部分倒装,比如:Only then did I realize the importance of English. 只有那时我才意识到英语的重要性。

16　From this exciting prospect of an advancing science of learning, it is a great shock to turn to that branch of technology, which is most directly concerned with the learning process—education. 从不断前进的学习科学那令人振奋的前景,回到与学习过程密切相关的技术分支——教育,就会产生极大的震惊。

be concerned with 是"有关的,有牵连的"的意思,比如:His new work is concerned with Africa. 他的新作是关于非洲的。

17　They consist of speaking and writing certain words, figures, and signs, which, to put it roughly, refer to numbers and to arithmetic operations. 他们包含说和写一些词、数字和符号,简单地说,是指数字和数学运算。

to put it roughly 是"大体说来"的意思,比如:To put it roughly, the work is ok. 大体说来:大体说来这份工作做得还可以。

18　The first task is to shape up these responses—to get the child to pronounce and to write responses correctly, but the principal task is to bring this behavior under many sorts of stimulus control. 使儿童正确地读出和写出这些反应,即形成这些反应,这是第一个任务。但是主要任务是使这种行为处于各种刺激控制之下。

under control 是"处于控制之下"的意思,比如:keep one's temper under control 克制着不发脾气。

19　This is what happens when the child learns to count, to recite tables, to count while ticking off the items in an assemblage of objects, to respond to spoken or written numbers by saying "odd", "even", "prime", and so on. 当儿童学习数数,背计算表,用手点着数一堆物体,对说出或写出的数目用回答"基数"、"偶数"、"质数"方式进行反应的时候,所发生的情况正是如此。

这是一个由 when 引导的时间状语从句,从句中 learn 后面接四个动词不定式短语,作 learn 的宾语。

tick off 是"给……标记号"的意思,比如:Tick off each item on the list as you complete it. 在你已经完成的项目上做上记号。

respond to 是"作出反应"的意思,比如:How did she respond to the news? 她对这消息的反应如何?

20 Over and above this elaborate repertoire of numerical behavior, most of which is often dismissed as the product of rote learning, the teaching of arithmetic looks forward to those complex serial arrangements of responses involved in original mathematical thinking. 大多数详尽的用数字表示的行为,常常被当作机械学习的产物而被扔掉。除此之外,算术数字期待创造性数字思维所包含的那些复杂的反应序列。

over and above 是"除……之外;多于;过于,太"的意思,比如:She earns a large amount over and above her salary. 她除了薪金之外,还有很大一笔收入。

21 Some positive reinforcements were perhaps eventually derived from the increased efficiency of the child in the field of arithmetic and in rare cases some automatic reinforcement may have resulted from the sheer manipulation of the medium—from the solution of problems or the discovery of the intricacies of the number system. 在少数情况下,某些自动的强化来自于方法操作的本身,即解决问题或发现数系的复杂关系。

derive from 是"追溯……的起源,说明……的起源"的意思,比如:The custom derived from an old story. 这项风俗起源于一个古老的故事。

22 But for the immediate purposes of the education the child acted to avoid or escape punishment. 如果不是因为教育的直接目的,儿童就是为了避免惩罚。

But for 是"要不是因为……;如果没有……"的意思,经常与虚拟语气连用,比如:But for the rain we would have had a picnic. 要不是因为下雨,我们就去野餐。

23 It was part of the reform movement known as progressive education to make the positive consequences more immediately effective, but any one who visits the lower grades of the average school today will observe that a change has been made, not from aversive to positive control, but from one form of aversive stimulation to another. 进步教育改革运动的一部分,即是使积极的后果更加直接有效。但凡参观过今天普通学校低年级的人都会注意到这样一种变化,这个变化不是从消极的、令人厌恶的控制变为积极的控制,而是从一种消极的刺激变为另一种消极的刺激。

aversive 是"厌恶的,促使退避的"的意思,比如:She is aversive to flattery. 她不喜欢听奉承话。

24 The child at his desk, filling in his workbook, is behaving primarily to escape from the threat of a series of minor aversive events—the teacher's displeasure, the criticism or ridicule

12. The Science of Learning and the Art of Teaching 学习的科学和教学的艺术

of his classmates, an ignominious showing in a competition, low marks, a trip to the office "to be talked to" by the principal, or a word to the parent who may still resort to the birch rod. 在桌旁做练习册的儿童,其活动主要是逃离一系列令人讨厌的小事情的威胁——老师的不满,同学的批评或嘲笑,竞争中不光彩的表现,低的分数,被校长叫到办公室谈话的经历或招致家长棍棒的报告。

ridicule 是"讥笑,嘲弄"的意思,比如:Why did you ridicule his proposal? 你为什么嘲笑他的建议?

ignominious 是"可耻的,没面子的"的意思,比如:He deserved his ignominious end. 他罪有应得。

resort to 是"求助,凭借,采用"的意思,比如:resort to stealing when in poverty. 在贫困中靠行窃度日。

25 The contingencies she provides are far from optimal. 她所提供的强化远不是最佳的。
far from 是"远远不,完全不",比如:The struggle is far from over. 这场斗争远远没有结束。

26 It can easily be demonstrated that, unless explicit mediating behavior has been set up, the lapse of only a few seconds between response and reinforcement destroys most of the effect. 下列事实很容易证明这点:除非建立了明显的中介行为,在反映和强化之间只要相隔几秒钟就会破坏大部分的效果。

27 Even the most modern workbook in beginning arithmetic is far from exemplifying an efficient program for shaping up mathematical behavior. 甚至最初的初学算术的作业本,也远不是一种塑造数学行为的有效程序。

28 Over and above all this, the whole mathematical repertoire must be brought under the control of concrete problems of considerable variety. 除此以外,全部数学行为必须置于多样的具体问题的控制之外。
over and above "除……之外(包含在内)",比如:Mothers with young children receive an extra allowance over and above the usual welfare payments. 有小孩子的母亲在平常的福利费之外还收到一笔额外的补助。

29 Even our best schools are under criticism for their inefficiency in the teaching of drill subjects such as arithmetic. 甚至我们最好的学校也因为诸如算术之类的技能性科目教学效率低而受到批评。
under criticism for 是"因……而遭受指责,受到批评"的意思,比如:The mayor is under criticism for corruption in the government. 市长因腐败问题而遭受指责。

30 The very subjects in which modern techniques are weakest are those in which failure is most conspicuous, and in the wake of an ever-growing incompetence come the anxieties, uncertainties, and aggressions, which in their turn present other problems to the school. 那些失败的、最引人注目的科目正是现代技术水平最低的那些科目,儿童不及格情况日益发展,随之而来的是焦虑、怀疑和攻击性行为,这些情况反过来又给学校带来了许多其他的问题。
in the wake of 是"紧紧跟随……,随着……而来"的意思,比如:hunger and disease in the wake of war 战争带来的饥饿与疾病

31 Such explanations are readily seized upon by defensive teachers and parents. 这样的解释是很容易被处于防御地位的教师和家长抓住的。

seize upon 是"大加利用"的意思,比如:The loopholes in the law have already been sized upon by unscrupulous car dealers. 法律的漏洞早已被肆无忌惮的汽车商大加利用。

32 On the contrary, the figures and the symbols of mathematics have become standard emotional stimuli. 相反,数字和数学的符号已成为了标准的情绪刺激物。

on the contrary 是"正相反"的意思,比如:My view is just on the contrary with yours. 我的观点与你的正相反。

33 The glimpse of a column of figures, not to say an algebraic symbol or an integral sign, is likely to set off—not mathematical behavior—but a reaction of anxiety, guilt, or fear. 只要看一眼一行数字就容易引起反应,更不用说一个代替符号或一个积分符号了,这不是数学行为,而是一种焦虑、罪过或恐惧的反应。

not to say "即使不……,也是",比如:It would be unwise, not to say stupid to leave your first job after six months. 你只干了六个月就放弃了第一份工作,即使不算愚蠢,也是不明智的。

练 习

1. 回答问题
   (1) What are the traditional devices for the study of learning?
   (2) How could the behavior of the individual organism be brought under precise control?
   (3) Is the consequence of the progressive education really as effective as expected?
   (4) How many shortcomings of reinforcement in the classroom teaching have been mentioned?
   (5) Why is it hard for the teacher to reinforce at each step of teaching?

2. 判断正误
   (1) It has long been argued that an organism learns mainly by producing changes in its environment, but it is only recently that these changes have been carefully manipulated.
   (2) The experiments show that the animals and the human children show similar properties of the learning.
   (3) In the past, the immediate purposes of education the child acted to avoid or escape punishment.
   (4) Maybe the most serious criticism of the current classroom is the relative infrequency of reinforcement.
   (5) Modern children learn arithmetic quickly and well.

3. 选词填空
   promising, many a, make sure, optimal, at will, in collaboration with, in spite of, under control, over and above, resort to

12. The Science of Learning and the Art of Teaching   学习的科学和教学的艺术

(1) He _____ begging when in poverty。
(2) He is trying to keep his temper _____.
(3) _____ what you say, I won't go with you.
(4) He is always _____ me in work.
(5) You are doomed to have a _____ future.
(6) Summer is the _____ season for traveling.
(7) I just want to _____ who will take responsibility of the accident.
(8) _____ girl would love such a handsome man.
(9) She has a lot of friends _____ her classmates.
(10) With a computer in hand, you can enjoy comfortable life _____.

4. 句型模拟

(1) in none of
(2) on the contrary

5. 英译汉

(1) Special techniques have been designed to arrange what are called "contingencies of reinforcement"—the relations which prevail between behavior on the one hand and the consequences of that behavior on the other—with the result that a much more effective control of behavior has been achieved.

(2) Simply by presenting food to a hungry pigeon at the right time, it is possible to shape up three or four well-defined responses in a single demonstration period—such responses as turning around, pacing the floor in the pattern of a figure-8, standing still in a corner of the demonstration apparatus, stretching the neck, or stamping the foot.

(3) This is what happens when the child learns to count, to recite tables, to count while ticking off the items in an assemblage of objects, to respond to spoken or written numbers by saying "odd", "even", "prime", and so on.

(4) A third notable shortcoming is the lack of a skilful program, which moves forward through a series of progressive approximations to the final complex behavior desired.

(5) A long series of contingencies is necessary to bring the organism into the possession of mathematical behavior most efficiently. But the teacher is seldom able to reinforce at each step in such a series because she cannot deal with the pupil's responses one at a time.

6. 汉译英

(1) 学习永无止境。(far from)
(2) 灾难带来饥饿与恐惧(in the wake of)
(3) 你应该懂得辨别是非。(discrimination)
(4) 这个农场出产梨和苹果。(yield)
(5) 老师允许他们午后进行足球比赛。(permit somebody to do something)

7. 写作指导

For this part, you are required to write a composition on the topic "How to improve the students' motivations in the classroom teaching". The following points taken from the text are useful expressions for your reference:

- The child at his desk, filling in his workbook, is behaving primarily to escape from the threat of a series of minor aversive events—the teacher's displeasure, the criticism or ridicule of his classmates, an ignominious showing in a competition, low marks, a trip to the office "to be talked to" by the principal, or a word to the parent who may still resort to the birch rod.
- In this welter of aversive consequences, getting the right answer is in itself an insignificant event, any effect of which is lost amid the anxieties, the boredom, and the aggressions, which are the inevitable by-products of aversive control.
- But the teacher is seldom able to reinforce at each step in such a series because she cannot deal with the pupil's responses one at a time.
- The very subjects in which modern techniques are weakest are those in which failure is most conspicuous, and in the wake of an ever-growing incompetence come the anxieties, uncertainties, and aggressions, which in their turn present other problems to the school.

VII

Structualism Education
结构主义教育

  结构主义教育流派是当代西方的一个重要流派。结构主义也叫作建构主义(constructivism)，它是人们对儿童智力结构的发生和发展以及知识结构规律的探讨与教育变革的需要相结合的产物。从这个角度看，结构主义教育流派的最初萌芽可以追溯到二十世纪三十年代瑞士心理学家、教育家皮亚杰的工作。然而，作为一个与教育的实际有着更为紧密关系的教育思潮，它的出现和兴盛的标志则是五十年代末六十年代初，以布鲁纳为首的一大批认知心理学家、科学家在美国推动的一场结构主义课程改革运动。主要代表人物有让·皮亚杰(J. Piaget)、科恩伯格(O. Kernberg)、斯滕伯格(R.J. Sternberg)、卡茨(D. Katz)、维果斯基(Vogotsgy)、布鲁纳等。

  在结构主义旗帜下教育理论研究的深入，结构主义教育思想很快就波及到了包括中国在内的世界许多国家和地区。一时间，智力结构发生发展的理论、知识和学科结构理论成了不少国家的教育家、教师和教育行政人员改革教育制度、教学方式及课程的主要理论依据；成为他们对那种把儿童和成人一样对待，忽视儿童的年龄特征，不了解儿童认识活动内部过程特征的传统教育进行批判、评价的有力武器。

  结构主义教育的基本思想是：强调在科技革命和知识激增的条件下，必须按结构主义原理进行课程改革，让学生掌握科学知识的基本结构，即基本原理或基本概念体系；强调得到的概念越基本，概念对新问题的适用面就越广；断言在结构主义课程前提下，任何学科都能够有效地教给任何发展阶段的任何儿童；强调不仅要教出成绩良好的学生，而且还要帮助每个学生获得智力上的发展，为此就要抛弃传统的复现法，代之以有利于开发智力的发现法。

> 结构主义理论的内容很丰富,但其核心只用一句话就可以概括:以学生为中心,强调学生对知识的主动探索、主动发现和对所学知识意义的主动建构(而不是像传统教学那样,只是把知识从教师头脑中传送到学生的笔记本上)。以学生为中心,强调的是"学";以教师为中心,强调的是"教"。这正是两种教育思想、教学观念最根本的分歧点,由此而发展出两种对立的学习理论、教学理论和教学设计理论。由于建构主义所要求的学习环境得到了当代最新信息技术成果的强有力支持,这就使建构主义理论日益与广大教师的教学实践普遍地结合起来,从而成为世界各国学校深化教学改革的指导思想。

13. Educational Principles and Psychological Data
教育的原则与心理学的论据

Jean Piaget
让·皮亚杰

让·皮亚杰(1896—1980),瑞士心理学家,发生认识论创始人。自 1918 年获得博士学位后,1921 年开始任日内瓦卢梭研究所研究主任。1929 年任日内瓦大学教授兼卢梭学院副院长。1924—1954 年一直任日内瓦大学教授。1954 年任国际心理学会主席。1955 年任日内瓦"发生认识论研究中心"主任。先后当选为瑞士心理学会、法语国家心理科学联合会主席,1954 年任第 14 届国际心理科学联合会主席。为了致力于研究发生认识论,皮亚杰于 1955 年在日内瓦创建了"国际发生认识论中心"并任主任,集合各国著名哲学家、心理学家、教育家、逻辑学家、数学家、语言学家和控制论学者研究发生认识论,对于儿童各类概念以及知识形成的过程和发展进行多学科的深入研究。1972 年退休。此外,皮亚杰还长期担任联合国教科文组织领导下的国际教育局局长和联合国教科文组织总干事之职。皮亚杰还是多国著名大学的名誉博士或名誉教授。

主要著作有:《儿童的语言与思维》、《智慧心理学》、《结构主义》等。他和同事英海尔德等人组成以他为代表的:"日内瓦学派",研究儿童心理学,对西方心理学和教育学有较广泛的影响。

《教育的原则与心理学的论据》选自皮亚杰的《教育科学与儿童心理学》(1970)一书。

皮亚杰认为教育的主要目的是促进儿童智力的发展,培养儿童的思维能力和创造性,智慧训练的目的是形成智慧而不是贮存记忆,是培养出智慧的探索者而不仅仅是博学之才;真正的学习是儿童主动的、自发的学习从儿童认知发展理论和儿童发展阶段理论出发,儿童所获得的这些巨大成就主要不是由教师传授,而是出自儿童本身,是儿童主动发现、自发学习的结果;皮亚杰提出了一个适度新颖的原则,认为给儿童学习的材料必须和儿童的己有经验有一定的联系,同时又要足够新颖,这样才产生认知上的不协调和冲突,引起儿童的兴趣,促进他们主动、自发地学习;儿童必须通过动作进行学习,在教学过程中,应该放手让儿童去动手、动脑探索外部世界,不断建构自己的知识经验系统;教育应该按儿童的年龄特点进行,儿童的认知和成人有着质的不同,有着独自的特点和发展规律,因此,教师在教育中必须根据儿童心理发展的年龄和阶段特征来安排教材和选用教法；注重儿童的社会交往，这种交往是在"合作"的意义上的交往，也就是，学习中交往的重点应放在儿童之间的合作而不是竞争之上，在与同伴共同合作和相互学习中，相互影响，他们能集思广益，使学习效果更佳。这就是皮亚杰提倡的同伴影响法，积极鼓励儿童的互教和互相影响，以此促进儿童的学习和发展。

To educate means to adapt the individual to the surrounding social environment.[1] The new methods, however, seek to encourage this adaptation by making use of the impulses inherent in childhood itself, allied with the spontaneous activity that is inseparable from mental development.[2] And they do so, moreover, with the idea that society itself will also thereby be enriched. The new education, therefore, cannot be understood in its methods and its applications unless one takes care to analyze its principles in detail and to check their psychological value on at least four points: the significance of childhood, the structure of the child's thought, the laws of development, and the mechanism of infantile social life.

The traditional school imposes his work on the student: it "makes him work". And it is doubtless true that the child is free to put a greater or lesser degree of interest and personal effort into that work, so that insofar as the teacher is a good one the collaboration that takes place between his students and himself will leave an appreciable margin for genuine activity.[3] But in the logic of the system the student's intellectual and moral activity remains heteronomous because it is inseparable from a continual constraint exercised by the teacher, even though that constraint may remain unperceived by the student or be accepted by him of his own free will. The new school, on the contrary, appeals to real activity, to spontaneous work based upon personal need and interest. This does not mean, as Claparede so succinctly put it, that active education requires that children should do anything they want; "it requires above all that they should will what they do; that they should act, not that they should be acted upon."[4] (*L' education fonctionnelle*, p.252) Need, the interest that is a resultant of need, "that is the factor that will make a reaction into an authentic act" (p.195). The law of interest is thus "the sole pivot around which the whole system should turn."[5] (p.197)

Such a conception implies, however, a very precise notion of the significance of childhood and its activities. For to repeat with Dewey and Dlaparede that compulsory work is an antipsychological anomaly and that all fruitful activity presupposes an interest, means the risk of appearing to be merely restating what all the great classical educators have already affirmed so often; on the other hand, by endowing the child with the possibility of a durable kind of personal work[6] one is postulating precisely what one is required to prove. Is childhood capable of this activity, characteristic of the highest forms of adult behavior[7]: diligent and continuous research, spring from a spontaneous need? —that is the central problem of the new education.

A decisive observation made by Claparede will help in throwing some light on the discussion of this point. If we make a distinction between the structure of thought and psychic operations on

13. Educational Principles and Psychological Data 教育的原则与心理学的论据

the one hand(in other words, everything that corresponds, from the psychological point of view, to the organs and the anatomy of the organism), and their functioning on the other hand(in other words all that corresponds with the functional relationships studied by physiology), then we may say that traditional pedagogy attributed to the child a mental structure identical with that of the adult, but a different mode of functioning[8]: "It liked to think of the child...as capable, for example, of grasping anything that is logically evident, or of understanding the deep significance of certain moral rules; but, at the same time, it also considered the child as functionally different from the adult, in the sense that whereas the hand is capable of laboring without a motive, of acquiring the most disparate forms of knowledge to order, of doing any work you like, simply because the school requires it, but without that work answering to any need arising within its child's self, within its child's life"(*L'education fonctionnelle*, pp.246—247).

In fact, it is the contrary that is true. The intellectual and moral structures of the child are not the same as ours; and consequently the new methods of education make every effort to present the subject matter to be taught informs assimilable to children of different ages in accordance withtheir mental structure and the various stages of their development.[9] But with regard to mental functioning, the child is in fact identical with the adult; like the adult, he is an active being whose action, controlled by the law of interest or need, is incapable of working at full stretch if no appeal is made to the autonomous motive forces of that activity.[10] Just as the tadpole already breathes, though with different organs from those of the frog, so the child acts like the adult, but employing a mentality whose structure varies according to the stages of its development.

What is childhood then? And how are we to adjust our educational techniques to beings at once so like and yet so unlike us?[11] Childhood, for the theorists of the new school, is not a necessary evil: it is a biologically useful phase whose significance is that of a progressive adaptation to a physical and social environment.

Moreover, this adaptation is a state of balance—an equilibrium whose achievement occupies the whole of childhood and adolescence and defines the structuration proper to those periods of existence—between two inseparable mechanisms: assimilation and accommodation.[12] We say, for example, that an organism is well-adapted when it can simultaneously preserve its structure by assimilating into it nourishment drawn from the external environment and also accommodate that structure to the various particularities of that environment: biological adaptation is thus a state of balance between an assimilation of the environment to the organism and an accommodation of the organism to the environment[13]. Similarly, it is possible to say that thought is well adapted to a particular reality when it has been successful in assimilating that reality into its own framework while also accommodating that framework to the new circumstances presented by the reality. Intellectual adaptation is thus a process of achieving a state of balance between the assimilation of experience into the deductive structures and the accommodation of those structures to the data of experience.[14] Generally speaking, adaptation presupposes an interaction between subject and object, such that the first can incorporate the second into itself while also taking account of[15] its particularities; and the more differentiated and the more complementary that assimilation and that accommodation are, the more thorough the adaptation[16].

The characteristic of childhood is precisely that it has to find this state of balance by means of a series of exercises or behavior patterns that are *sui generis*, by means of a continuous structuring activity beginning from a state of chaotic nondifferentiation between subject and object.[17] This means, in effect, that at the very beginning of its mental development the child is pulled in opposite directions by two tendencies that have still not been brought into harmony with one another and are still relatively undifferentiated, insofar as they have not yet found their equilibrium with regard to one another. Firstly, it is perpetually obliged to accommodate its sensorimotor, or intellectual, organs to external reality, to the particularities of things, about which it has everything to learn. And this continuous process of accommodation—which is extended in the form of imitation when the subject's movements are sufficiently applicable to the characteristics of the object—constitutes one primary necessity of its action.[18] Secondly, however—and this is something that has generally been less understood, except in fact by the practitioners and theorists of the new school-in order to accommodate its activity to the properties of things, the child needs to assimilate them and, in a very sense, to incorporate them into itself. Things have no interest in the initial stage of mental life except insofar as they constitute fuel for activity proper, and this continuous assimilation of the external world into the self, although antithetic in direction to accommodation, is so intimately fused with it during the earliest stages that the child is at first unable to establish any clear-cut dividing line between its own activity and external reality, between subject and object.[19]

However theoretical they may appear, these considerations are fundamental where schooling is concerned. For assimilation in its purest form—which is to say as long as it has not yet been brought into equilibrium with the process of accommodation to reality—is in effect nothing other than play; and play, which is one of the most characteristic infantile activities, has in fact found a use in the new techniques of education for young infants that remains inexplicable unless one clarifies the significance of this function in relation to the child's mental life as a whole and to its intellectual adaptation[20].

* * * *

Play is a typical case of the forms of behavior neglected by the traditional school because it appears to them to be devoid of functional significance.[21] In current educational theory it is no more than a form of relaxation or a reaction brought on by an excess of energy. But this over-simple view explains neither the importance that young children attribute to their games nor, above all, the invariability of form that children's games assume, symbolism and fiction, for example.[22]

After studying animals at play, Karl Groos arrived at a totally different conception of such behavior according to which play is a preparatory exercise, useful in the physical development of the organism. And just as the games of animals constitute a method of exercising particular instincts, such as fighting and hunting instincts, so the child when it plays is developing its perceptions, its intelligence, its impulses toward experiment, its social instincts, etc.[23] This is why play is such a powerful lever in the learning process of very young children, to such an extent that whenever anyone can succeed in transforming their first steps in reading, or arithmetic, or spelling into a game, you will see children become passionately absorbed in those occupations, which are ordinarily presented as dreary chores.

Karl Groos' interpretation, however, which goes no further than a simple functional description, only acquires its full significance to the degree in which it is reinforced by the notion of assimilation. During the first year, for example, alongside the behavioral patterns of adaptation proper, during which he child attempts to grasp whatever it sees—to rock, shake, rub, etc.—it is easy enough to distinguish other forms of behavior that are simply a kind of exercise, characterized by the fact that their objects have no interest whatever in themselves but are assimilated into those forms of activity proper purely and simply as functional raw material. In such cases, which must be looked upon as the origin of play, the behavior patterns develop by functioning—in conformity with the general law of functional assimilation—and the objects on which they bear have no other significance for the infant than that of providing an opportunity for that exercise.[24] In its sensorimotor origin play is nothing more than a pure assimilation of reality into the self, in the double sense of the term: in the biological sense of functional assimilation—which explains why these game-exercises really develop the organs and the behavior patterns—and in the psychological sense of incorporating objects into activity.

As for play at a higher level, that of imaginative and symbolic games, there is no doubt that Karl Groos failed to explain it adequately, since fiction in the child goes far beyond simple pre-exercise of particular instincts. Playing with dolls does not serve solely to develop the maternal instinct, but also provides a symbolic representation of all the realities the child has so far experienced but not yet assimilated in a form that it can relieve and therefore vary according to its needs.[25] So that in this respect symbolic play, like exercise play, is also to be explained as an assimilation of reality into the self: it is individual thought in its purest form; in its content, it is the unfolding and flowering of the self and a realization of desires, as opposed to rational socialized thought which adapts the self to reality and expresses shared truths;[26] in its structure, the symbol in play is to the individual what the verbal sign is to society.

Play then, in its two essential forms of sensorimotor exercise and symbolism, is an assimilation of reality into activity proper, providing the latter with its necessary sustenance and transforming reality in accordance with the self's complex of needs.[27] This is why the active methods of infant education all require that the children should be provided with suitable equipment, so that in playing they shall come to assimilate intellectual realities which would otherwise remain outside the infantile intelligence.[28]

Although assimilation is necessary to adaptation, it nevertheless constitutes only one aspect of it. The complete adaptation that it is childhood's task to achieve consists in a progressive synthesis of assimilation with accommodation.[29] This is why, in the course of its own internal development, the play of small children is gradually transformed into adapted constructions requiring an ever increasing amount of what is in effect work, to such an extent that in the infant classes of an active school every kind of spontaneous transition may be observed between play and work. But above all, from the very earliest months of life, the synthesis of assimilation and accommodation takes place through the agency of the intelligence itself, whose unifying labor increases with age and whose real activity it is now time to emphasize to the full, since it is upon this notion that the new education is ultimately based.[30]

注 释

1. To educate means to adapt the individual to the surrounding social environment. 施教的意思是使个体适应周围的社会环境。
   adapt...to 是"调整以适应"的意思,比如:She adapted herself quickly to the new climate. 她很快地适应了这种新的气候。

2. The new methods, however, seek to encourage this adaptation by making use of the impulses inherent in childhood itself, allied with the spontaneous activity that is inseparable from mental development. 而新方法企图利用儿童期本身固有的冲动,并与心理发展不可分割的自发活动结合起来去促进这种适应。
   that 引导的是定语从句修饰 activity。inherent in:是"内在的,固有的"意思,比如:This is the power inherent in the office of President. 这是总统任内固有的权利。
   ally with 是"与……结成联盟"意思,比如:Britain has allyed itself with other western powers for trade and defence. 英国与其他西方强国结成了贸易及防御联盟。

3. And it is doubtless true that the child is free to put a greater or lesser degree of interest and personal effort into that work, so that insofar as the teacher is a good one the collaboration that takes place between his students and himself will leave an appreciable margin for genuine activity. 千真万确的是,儿童对那种工作发生的兴趣和付出的个人努力的多寡是由他自己决定的。因此如果有一个好教师,师生之间的合作就可以给真正的活动留下明显的余地。
   第一个 that 从句是主语从句,it 是形式主语。so that 引导的是结果状语从句。第二个 that 从句是定语从句修饰 collaboration。

4. it requires above all that they should will what they do; that they should act, not that they should be acted upon. 最重要的是,它要求学生立意做他们要做的事;他们应该主动而不应当被动行动。
   本句中 that 从句用的是虚拟语气,should 可以省略。

5. The law of interest is thus "the sole pivot around which the whole system should turn." 因此,兴趣规律是整个体系随之运转的惟一枢纽。
   turn around 是"围绕着……运转"的意思,The earth turns around the sun. 地球绕着太阳转。

6. by endowing the child with the possibility of a durable kind of personal work:让儿童具有自个儿经久不懈的工作的可能性。

13. Educational Principles and Psychological Data 教育的原则与心理学的论据

endow sb. with sth. 是":使某人天生具有(任何好的品质或能力)"的意思,比如:She is endowed with intelligence as well as beauty. 她生来聪明貌美。

7 characteristic of the highest forms of adult behavior:代表着成人行为的最高形式的活动

8 If we make a distinction between the structure of thought and psychic operations on the one hand(in other words, everything that corresponds, from the psychological point of view, to the organs and the anatomy of the organism), and their functioning on the other hand(in other words all that corresponds with the functional relationships studied by physiology), then we may say that traditional pedagogy attributed to the child a mental structure identical with that of the adult, but a different mode of functioning. 如果我们把思维结构和心理运算这一方面(换言之,根据心理学的观点,一切与有机体的器官和组织相应的东西),同它们的机能作用那一方面(换言之,一切与生理学所研究的机能的关系相应的东西)区分开来的话,那么我们可以说,传统的教育学把儿童的心理结构等同于成人的心理结构,所不同的只是机能作用的形式。

9 …and consequently the new methods of education make every effort to present the subject matter to be taught informs assimilable to children of different ages in accordance with their mental structure and the various stages of their development. 因而新教育法尽一切努力按照儿童的心理结构和他们的不同发展阶段,将要教的材料以适应不同年龄的儿童的形式进行教学。

in accordance with 是"按照或依据某事物"的意思,比如:俄 Every citizen should act in accordance with the nation law. 每一个公民都应依法行事。

10 But with regard to mental functioning, the child is in fact identical with the adult; like the adult, he is an active being whose action, controlled by the law of interest or need, is incapable of working at full stretch if no appeal is made to the autonomous motive forces of that activity. 但是至于心理的机能作用,儿童事实上跟成人相同;像成人一样,他是个具有主动性的人,他的活动受兴趣或需要规律的支配,如果不能引起活动的自发动机和力量,是不可能全力工作的。

controlled by the law of interest or need 是分词短语作后置定语修饰 action。with regard to 是"关于"的意思,比如:I have nothing to say with regard to your complains. 对于你的投诉我无可奉告。

at full stretch 或者 at a stretch 是"竭尽全力"的意思,比如:She worked for six hours at a sretch. 他连续工作了六个小时。

11 And how are we to adjust our educational techniques to beings at once so like and yet so unlike us. 我们该如何调整教育技术,使它适应于既很像我们,又不太像我们的儿童呢?

adjust to:指"使适合",比如:The former soldiers have difficulty in adjusting to civilian life. 退伍军人很难适应平民生活。

12 Moreover, this adaptation is a state of balance—an equilibrium whose achievement occupies the whole of childhood and adolescence and defines the structuration proper to those periods of existence—between two inseparable mechanisms: assimilation and accommodation. 而且,这类适应是两种密切联系着的机制,即同化作用和调节作用的一种平衡状态,是一种在整

个儿童期和青年期起作用的、规定的与那些现存阶段相应的组织结构的平衡状态。
whose 引导的定语从句修饰 an equilibrium。

13 biological adaptation is thus a state of balance between an assimilation of the environment to the organism and an accommodation of the organism to the environment：所以生物的适应就是环境被有机体同化的作用和有机体调节环境的作用的一种平衡状态。

14 Intellectual adaptation is thus a process of achieving a state of balance between the assimilation of experience into the deductive structures and the accommodation of those structures to the data of experience. 智力的适应是把经验同化于推理结构之中，根据经验资料调节那些结构，因此，使这两种活动达成平衡状态的过程。

15 take account of 或者 take sth into account 是"考虑"的意思，比如：When judging her performance, don't take account of her age. 评定她的表现时不必考虑她的年纪。

16 and the more differentiated and the more complementary that assimilation and that accommodation are, the more thorough the adaptation. 同化作用和调节作用越是分化，越是补充，适应就越是完善。
The more..., the more... 是"越……，越……"的意思，比如：The more you practice, the more fluently you speak. 你练得越多，讲的就越熟练。

17 The characteristic of childhood is precisely that it has to find this state of balance by means of a series of exercises or behavior patterns that are *sui generis*, by means of a continuous structuring activity beginning from a state of chaotic nondifferentiation between subject and object. 儿童期的特征就是必须借助一系列本身独具的活动或行为模式，借助主体与客体间，以一种混沌的、未分化的状态为开端，连续不断地构造活动，寻找这种平衡状态。
这里 that 引导的是表语从句。

18 And this continuous process of accommodation—which is extended in the form of imitation when the subject's movements are sufficiently applicable to the characteristics of the object—constitutes one primary necessity of its action. 这个不断调节的过程——当主体的运动足以适用于客体的特征时，用模仿形式来扩大这一过程，构建其活动的最初需要。

19 Things have no interest in the initial stage of mental life except insofar as they constitute fuel for activity proper, and this continuous assimilation of the external world into the self, although antithetic in direction to accommodation, is so intimately fused with it during the earliest stages that the child is at first unable to establish any clear-cut dividing line between its own activity and external reality, between subject and object. 在心理活动的开始阶段，事物引不起儿童的兴趣，只不过构成活动本身的刺激。同时，儿童把外在世界不断同化为自我，尽管跟调节方向相反，但在儿童的初期它是与调节结合得如此密切。甚至儿童最初划不清自身活动与外界现实、主体与客体间的明确界限。
本句的 so...that 结构是结果状语从句。

20 and play, which is one of the most characteristic infantile activities, has in fact found a use in the new techniques of education for young infants that remains inexplicable unless one clarifies the significance of this function in relation to the child's mental life as a whole and to its intellectual adaptation：游戏是最能显示幼儿特性的活动之一，它已经在幼儿教育的新技

13. Educational Principles and Psychological Data 教育的原则与心理学的论据

术中得到运用,如果人们没有把儿童整个心理生活及与智力适应机能的意义搞清楚,人们仍旧难以说明它的用处。

which 引导的是非限制性定语从句修饰 play。that 从句修饰 use。

21 Play is a typical case of the forms of behavior neglected by the traditional school because it appears to them to be devoid of functional significance. 游戏是传统学校一直忽视的行为形式的一个典型例子,因为在他们看来游戏缺乏机能方面的重要作用。

neglected by the traditional school 是过去分词短语作后置定语修饰 behavior。be devoid of 指没有、空虚,比如:The criminal is completely devoid of conscience. 这个罪犯丧尽了天良。

22 But this over-simple view explains neither the importance that young children attribute to their games nor, above all, the invariability of form that children's games assume, symbolism and fiction, for example. 可是,这种过于简单化的观点既无法解释年幼儿童游戏的重要性,更不能说明儿童的游戏可以采取例如象征性和虚构性等不变的方式。

attribute to 指"认为某事物由某人或某事物引起",比如:She attributed her failure to her bad luck. 她认为是运气不好使她失败的。

23 And just as the games of animals constitute a method of exercising particular instincts, such as fighting and hunting instincts, so the child when it plays is developing its perceptions, its intelligence, its impulses toward experiment, its social instincts, etc. 正如动物游戏是练习某种本能——战斗本能和狩猎本能的方法一样,儿童在游戏活动中也发展了他的知觉、智力、试验的冲动和社交本能等等。

24 In such cases, which must be looked upon as the origin of play, the behavior patterns develop by functioning—in conformity with the general law of functional assimilation—and the objects on which they bear have no other significance for the infant than that of providing an opportunity for that exercise. 这种情况必须被看成是游戏的起源。行为模式因机能作用而发展——与机能同化的一般规律相符,有关的客体对幼儿来说没有什么别的意义,仅仅提供一种练习的机会而已。

in conformity with 指"与某事物相一致;顺从某失误",比如:Everything has been done in conformity with your instructions. 每件事情都是按照你的指示做的。

25 Playing with dolls does not serve solely to develop the maternal instinct, but also provides a symbolic representation of all the realities the child has so far experienced but not yet assimilated in a form that it can relieve and therefore vary according to its needs. 玩娃娃游戏不仅是为了发展母爱本能,而且还提供全部现实的、象征性的表象,这表明儿童早已经体验过,但还未同化到能再度体验,并根据需要给予变化的形式的程度。

the child has so far experienced but not yet assimilated in a form that it can relieve and therefore vary according to its needs 这是一个省略 that 的定语从句修饰 realities.

26 in its content, it is the unfolding and flowering of the self and a realization of desires, as opposed to rational socialized thought which adapts the self to reality and expresses shared truths: 就其内容来说,这是自我的扩大和展开以及欲望的实现,这和自我适应现实,与理性社会思维相反,这种理性社会思维表明了共同真理的现实性。

as opposed to 指"与……对照",比如:I am here on a holiday as opposed to on business. 我在

155

这里是度假不是办公事。

27 Play then, in its two essential forms of sensorimotor exercise and symbolism, is an assimilation of reality into activity proper, providing the latter with its necessary sustenance and transforming reality in accordance with the self's complex of needs. 因此，游戏在感知运动练习和象征表示两种重要形式方面，把现实同化于活动本身之中，给活动提供必要的原料，同时根据自身的复杂需要转化现实。

providing the latter with its necessary sustenance and transforming reality in accordance with the self's complex of needs 是分词短语作伴随状语。

28 This is why the active methods of infant education all require that the children should be provided with suitable equipment, so that in playing they shall come to assimilate intellectual realities which would otherwise remain outside the infantile intelligence. 这就是为什么幼儿教育的活动法都要求为儿童提供适宜的设备，儿童在游戏中实现同化智慧的现实，否则，这些现象就要被排斥在儿童的智慧之外。

why 引导的是表语从句。在表语从句中，又包含一个 that 引导的宾语从句和 so that 引导的目的状语从句。在目的状语从句中还有一个 which 引导的定语从句。

29 The complete adaptation that it is childhood's task to achieve consists in a progressive synthesis of assimilation with accommodation. 儿童期所要完成的工作，即完善适应，在于逐步综合同化作用与调节作用。

that it is childhood's task to achieve 是 adaptation 的同位语从句。consist in 指"存在于某事物之中"，比如：The advantage of the car consists in its speed. 这辆车的优势在于它的速度。

30 But above all, from the very earliest months of life, the synthesis of assimilation and accommodation takes place through the agency of the intelligence itself, whose unifying labor increases with age and whose real activity it is now time to emphasize to the full, since it is upon this notion that the new education is ultimately based. 但尤其重要的是，从生命的最初数月起，要通过智力本身的作用，综合同化作用与调节作用；智力的统一劳动随着年龄而增长，现在到了充分强调它的真实活动的时候了，因为新教育主要是建立在这种观点的基础上的。

两个 whose 定语从句修饰 intelligence. to the full. 指"充分"，比如：His musical talent was developed to the full. 他的音乐天赋被充分地挖掘出来了。

练　习

1. 回答问题

   (1) How to understand the methods and applications of the new education according to the author?

   (2) What is the highest forms of adult behavior according to the passage?

   (3) According to the new methods of education, how should the subject matter be taught to the children?

(4) What is biological adaptation?

(5) What is the purest form of assimilation?

2. 判断正误

(1) The traditional education forces the student to work without considering his interests.

(2) Active education means that children should do anything they want.

(3) The central problem of the new education is whether children can do diligent and continuous research, which is characteristic of the highest forms of adult behavior.

(4) The intellectual and moral structures of the child are the same as those of the adult.

(5) The new education thinks that interest is presupposition for all educational activities.

3. 选词填空

adapt...to, be endowed with, attribute to, with regard to, at full stretch, take account of, inherent in, ally with, make every effort to, turn around

(1) His musical talent _____ him was not developed until his adulthood.

(2) Once she decides to do something, she will _____ do it.

(3) After living here for a month, she _____ herself _____ the new climate.

(4) The earth _____ the sun, which is known to all.

(5) She _____ intelligence as well as beauty.

(6) She _____ her success _____ hard work and a bit of luck.

(7) I have nothing to say _____ your complaints.

(8) Britain has _____ itself _____ other western powers for trade and defense.

(9) You needn't regret not achieving it since you have worked _____.

(10) When judging his performance, do _____ his age.

4. 句型模拟

(1) the more... the more

(2) nothing other than

5. 英译汉

(1) But in the logic of the system the student's intellectual and moral activity remains heteronomous because it is inseparable from a continual constraint exercised by the teacher, even though that constraint may remain unperceived by the student or be accepted by him of his own free will.

(2) The new school, on the contrary, appeals to real activity, to spontaneous work based upon personal need and interest.

(3) But with regard to mental functioning, the child is in fact identical with the adult; like the adult, he is an active being whose action, controlled by the law of interest or need, is incapable of working at full stretch if no appeal is made to the autonomous motive forces of

that activity.

(4) Generally speaking, adaptation presupposes an interaction between subject and object, such that the first can incorporate the second into itself while also taking account of its particularities;

(5) For assimilation in its purest form—which is to say as long as it has not yet been brought into equilibrium with the process of accommodation to reality—is in effect nothing other than play;

6. 汉译英
   (1) 他们被迫卖房还债。(be obliged to)
   (2) 两公司因有共同利益而结合在一起。(fuse)
   (3) 对我们交谈所做的文字记录与我们的原话不符。(correspond with)
   (4) 身体迅速自行调节以适应气温的变化。(adjust to)
   (5) 他就是这么迟钝。(characteristic of)

7. 写作指导
   For this part, you are required to write a composition on the topic "How to educate the child." The following points taken from the text are useful expressions for your reference:
   - adapt the individual to the surrounding social environment
   - pay much attention to the significance of childhood, the structure of the child's thought, the laws of development, the mechanism of infantile social life
   - leave an appreciable margin for genuine activity
   - assign them work based upon personal need and interest
   - assimilate the environment to the organism
   - accommodate the organism to the environment

14. The Process of Education
教育过程

Jerome S. Bruner
杰罗姆·S. 布鲁纳

杰罗姆·布鲁纳(1915—?)是美国心理学家和教育家,是结构主义教育流派的代表人物之一。他 1937 年毕业于都克大学,1941 年获得哈佛大学心理学博士学位。1942 年担任普林斯顿公共舆论研究所副所长。从 1943 年至第二次世界大战结束在海外服役,在法国任政治情报工作。1945 年回到哈佛大学任教,并从事人的感知觉研究。此后,在瑞士心理学家皮亚杰(J. Piaget)的认知心理学影响下,他开始研究思维过程以及概念形成过程。1952 年起任哈佛大学教授。1956 年,访问欧洲时拜访了瑞士日内瓦发生认识论研究中心主任皮亚杰。1960 年,他与心理学家米勒(G. Miller)一起创办了"哈佛大学认知研究中心",并担任该中心主任(1961—1972),形成了以认知心理学研究为基础的教育思想。布鲁纳于 1959 年担任了美国科学院教育委员会主席。同年年底,美国科学院在伍兹霍尔召开讨论中小学数理学科教育改革会议,布鲁纳担任会议主席。会后,他在题为《教育过程》的小册子中综合了与会者的意见,阐述了结构主义教育思想。1972—1978 年,布鲁纳任英国牛津大学心理学教授。1978 年退休回国。他的主要教育著作有:《教育过程》(1960)、《论认知》、《教学论探讨》(1966)、《教育适合性》、《教育过程再探》(1971)等。

《教育过程》(1960)是布鲁纳的代表作,曾引起极大的反响,被誉为划时代的作品。

布鲁纳在《教育过程》一书中指出,"我们教什么？达到什么目的？"这种对教育质量和智育目的的关切集中地表现在中小学课程设置上。不论我们选教什么学科,务必使学生理解该学科的基本结构。任何学科都能够用在发展智力上,有效地教给任何儿童。分析思维的特征是一次前进一步,在此思维过程中,人们比较充分地意思到所包含的知识和运算。而直觉思维则不同,它倾向于对整个问题的内隐的感知为基础的那些活动。借助于发展学生的自信心和勇气去培养学生的直觉思维。学习动机应建立在唤起学生对所学知识的兴趣上,而且要有广泛性和多样性。现有的各种教学辅助装置帮助教师扩大学生的经验范围,促使学生理解学生所学材料的根本结构,并主动地理解他所学的东西的意义。

The Importance of Structure[1]

The first object of any act of learning, over and beyond the pleasure it may give, is that it should serve us in the future.[2] Learning should not only take us somewhere; it should allow us later to go further more easily. There are two ways in which learning serves the future. One is through its specific applicability to tasks that are highly similar to those we originally learned to perform.[3] Psychologists refer to this phenomenon as specific transfer of training; perhaps it should be called the extension of habits or associations.[4] Its utility appears to be limited in the main to what we usually speak of as skills. Having learned how to hammer nails, we are better able later to learn how to hammer tacks or chip wood. Learning in school undoubtedly creates skills of a kind that transfers to activities encountered later, either in school or after.[5] A second way in which earlier learning renders later performance more efficient is through what is conveniently called nonspecific transfer or, more accurately, the transfer of principles and attitudes.[6] In essence, it consists of learning initially not a skill but a general idea, which can then be used as a basis for recognizing subsequent problems as special cases of the idea originally mastered.[7] This type of transfer is at the heart of the educational process—the continual broadening and deepening of knowledge in terms of basic and general ideas.

The continuity of learning that is produced by the second type of transfer, transfer of principles, is dependent upon mastery of the structure of the subject matter, as structure was described in the preceding chapter.[8] That is to say, in order for a person to be able to recognize the applicability or inapplicability of an idea to a new situation and to broaden his learning thereby, he must have clearly in mind the general nature of the phenomenon with which he is dealing.[9] The more fundamental or basic is the idea he has learned, almost by definition, the greater will be its breadth of applicability to new problems. Indeed, this is almost a tautology; for what is meant by "fundamental" in this sense is precisely that an idea has wide as well as powerful applicability. It is simple enough to proclaim, of course, that school curricula and methods of teaching should be geared to the teaching of fundamental ideas in whatever subject is being taught.[10] But as soon as one makes such a statement a host of problems arise, many of which can be solved only with the aid of considerably more research. We turn to some of these now.

The first and most obvious problem is how to construct curricula that can be taught by ordinary teachers to ordinary students and that at the same time reflect clearly the basic or underlying principles of various fields of inquiry. The problem is twofold: first, how to have the basic subjects rewritten and their teaching materials revamped in such a way that the pervading and powerful ideas and attitudes relating to them are given a central role; second, how to match the levels of these materials to the capacities of students of different abilities at different grades in school.

The experience of the past several years has taught at least one important lesson about the design of a curriculum that is true to the underlying structure of its subject matter. It is that the best minds in any particular discipline must be put to work on the task.[11] The decision as to what should be taught in American history to elementary school children or what should be taught in arithmetic is a decision that can best be reached with the aid of those with a high degree of vision and competence in each of these fields. To decide that the elementary ideas of algebra depend upon the fundamentals of the commutative, distributive, and associative laws, one must be a mathematician in a position to appreciate and understand the fundamentals of mathematics. Whether schoolchildren require an understanding of Frederick Jackson Turner's ideas about the role of the frontier in American history before they can sort out the facts and trends of American history—this again is a decision that requires the help of the scholar who has a deep understanding of the American past.[12] Only by the use of our best minds in devising curricular will we bring the fruits of scholarship and wisdom to the student just beginning his studies.[13]

The question will be raised, "How enlist the aid of our most able scholars and scientists in designing curricular for primary and secondary schools?" The answer has already been given, at least in part. The School Mathematics Study Group, the University of Illinois mathematics projects, the Physical Science Study Committee, and the Biological Sciences Curriculum Study have indeed been enlisting the aid of eminent men in their various fields, doing so by means of summer projects, supplemented in part by year-long leaves of absence for certain key people involved.[14] They have been aided in these projects by understanding elementary and secondary school teachers and, for special purposes, by professional writers, film makers, designers, and others required in such a complex enterprise.

There is at least one major matter that is left unsettled even by a large-scale revision of curricula in the direction indicated. Mastery of the fundamental ideas of a field involves not only the grasping of general principles, but also the development of an attitude toward learning and inquiry, toward guessing and hunches, toward the possibility of solving problems on one's own.[15] Just as a physicists has certain attitudes about ultimate orderliness of nature and a conviction that order can be discovered, so a young physics student needs some working version of these attitudes if he is to organize his learning in such a way as to make what he learns usable and meaningful in his thinking.[16] To instill such attitudes by teaching requires something more than the mere presentation of fundamental ideas. Just what it takes to bring off such teaching is something on which a great deal of research is needed, but it would seem that an important ingredient is a sense of excitement about discovery-discovery of regularities of previously unrecognized relations and similarities between ideas, with a resulting sense of self-confidence in one's abilities.[17] Various people who have worked on curricula in science and mathematics have urged that it is possible to present the fundamental structure of a discipline in such a way as to preserve some of the exciting sequences that lead a student to discover for himself.[18]

Readiness for Learning

We begin with the hypothesis that any subject can be taught effectively in some, intellectually honest form to any child at any stage of development.[19] It is a bold hypothesis and an essential one in thinking about the nature of a curriculum.[20] No evidence exists to contradict it; considerable evidence is being amassed that supports it.[21]

To make clear what is implied, let us examine three general ideas. The first has to do with the process of intellectual development in children, the second with the act of learning, and the third with the notion of the "spiral curriculum" introduced earlier.

Intellectual Development

Research on the intellectual development of the child highlights the fact that at each stage of development the child has a characteristic way of viewing the world and explaining it to himself.[22] The task of teaching a subject to a child at any particular age is one of representing the structure of that subject in terms of the child's way of viewing things. The task can be thought of as one of translation.[23] The general hypothesis that has just been stated is premised on the considered judgment that any idea can be represented honestly and usefully in the thought forms of children of school age, and that these first representations can later be made more powerful and precise the more easily by virtue of this early learning.[24] To illustrate and support this view, we present here a somewhat detailed picture of the course of intellectual development, along with some suggestions about teaching at different stages of it.

The work of Piaget and others suggests that, roughly speaking, one may distinguish three stages in the intellectual development of the child.[25] The first stage need not concern us in detail, for it is characteristic principally of the pre-school child.[26] In this stage, which ends (at least for Swiss school children) around the fifth or sixth year, the child's mental work consists principally in establishing relationships between experience and action; his concern is with manipulating the world through action.[27] This stage corresponds roughly to the period from the first development of language to the point at which the child learns to manipulate symbols.[28] In this so-called preoperational stage, the principal symbolic achievement is that the child learns how to represent the external world through symbols established by simple generalization; things are represented as equivalent in terms of sharing some common property.[29] But the child's symbolic world does not make a clear separation between internal motives and feelings on the one hand and external reality on the other.[30] The sun moves because God pushes it, and the stars, like himself, have to go to bed. The child is little able to separate his own goals from the means for achieving them, and when he has to make corrections in his activity after unsuccessful attempts at manipulating reality, he does so by what are called intuitive regulations rather than by symbolic operations, the former being of a crude trail-and-error nature rather than the result of taking thought.[31]

What is principally lacking at this stage of development is what the Geneva school has called the concept of reversibility.[32] When the shape of an object is changed, as when one changes the shape of a ball of plasticene, the preoperational child cannot grasp the idea that it can be brought back readily to its original state. Because of this fundamental lack the child cannot understand certain fundamental ideas that lie at the basis of mathematics and physics—the mathematical idea that one conserves quantity even when one partitions a set of things into subgroups, or the physical idea that one conserves mass and weight even though one transforms the shape of an object.[33] It goes without saying that teachers are severely limited in transmitting concepts to a child at this age, even in a highly intuitive manner.[34]

注　释

1　本文选自杰罗姆·S.布鲁纳的教育过程。

2　The first object of any act of learning, over and beyond the pleasure it may give, is that it should serve us in the future. 任何学习行为的首要目的,不是限于它可能带来的乐趣中,而在于它将来会为我们服务。

3　One is through its specific applicability to tasks that are highly similar to those we originally learned to perform. 一种方式是通过与我们原先所学做的、十分相似任务的特殊应用性来实现的。
applicability to 是"应用于,适用于"的意思,比如:The applicability of the solution to the problem was not proved. 这个办法是否是用于解决那个问题尚未得到证明。
be similar to 是"与……相像,与……类似"的意思,比如:My problems are very similar to yours. 我的问题与你的差不多。

4　Psychologists refer to this phenomenon as specific transfer of training; perhaps it should be called the extension of habits or associations. 心理学家把这种现象称为训练的特殊迁移;或许他应被叫做习惯或联想的延伸。
refer to as 是"提到,谈到,指称"的意思,比如:The speaker referred to him as an up-and-coming politician. 演讲者称他是一位有为的政治新秀。

5　Learning in school undoubtedly creates skills of a kind that transfers to activities encountered later, either in school or after. 毫无疑问,学校里的学习创造了一种可以迁移到以后的技能,它可以迁移到无论在校内或离校后所遇到的任何活动上中去。
transfer to 是"迁移,传递"的意思,比如:The foot ballplayer is hoping to transfer to another team soon. 那名球员希望尽快转到另一个球队。

6　A second way in which earlier learning renders later performance more efficient is through what is conveniently called nonspecific transfer or, more accurately, the transfer of principles and attitudes. 先前的学习使日后工作更为有效的第二种方式则是通过所谓非特殊迁移,或更确切地说,是原理和态度的迁移。
本句主干部分是 A second way...is...through...。what 引导的从句作介词 through 的宾语。which 引导的是定语从句,修饰先行词是 a second way,在定语从句中主语是 learning,谓语是 render,宾语是 performance,more efficient 作宾语补足语。
Render 是"使得,使成为"的意思,比如:New technology has rendered my old computer obsolete. 新技术使我的旧电脑过时了。

7　In essence, it consists of learning initially not a skill but a general idea, which can then be used as a basis for recognizing subsequent problems as special cases of the idea originally mastered. 实质上,一开始学的不是技能而是一个普遍的观念,这个观念可以被当作一个基础,用来认识作为观念特例的后继问题。
in essence 是"本质上,实质上的"意思,比如:In essence, he just loves himself. 实质上他只爱

他自己。

8. The continuity of learning that is produced by the second type of transfer, transfer of principles, is dependent upon mastery of the structure of the subject matter, as structure was described in the preceding chapter. 由第二种类型的迁移及原理的迁移所产生的学习连续性，有赖于精通教材的结构。

   本句是一个带有方式状语从句的复合句，主句中的主语是 the continuity of learning，谓语是 is dependent upon，宾语是 mastery of the structure of the subject matter。that is produced by the second type of... 作 the continuity of learning 的定语。

9. That is to say, in order for a person to be able to recognize the applicability or inapplicability of an idea to a new situation and to broaden his learning thereby, he must have clearly in mind the general nature of the phenomenon with which he is dealing. 这就是说，一个人如能够认识到某一观念对新情境的适用性或不适用性，可以扩大他的学识，他对他所研究的普通本质，必须心中有数。

   in order to be able to recognize the applicability... 作目的状语，a person 在状语中作逻辑主语。主句中含有一个 which 引导的定语从句，修饰先行词 phenomenon。have sth. in mind 是"考虑"的意思，比如：Did you have anything in mind for Helen's present? 你有没有想过送什么礼物给海伦？

10. It is simple enough to proclaim, of course, that school curricula and methods of teaching should be geared to the teaching of fundamental ideas in whatever subject is being taught. 学校课程和教学方法应该适应所教学科里的基本观念的教学，当然，这样声明太简单了。

    本句是一个以 It 为形式主语，that 引导的从句为真正的主语的主语从句。

    be geared to 是"适应，与协调工作"的意思，比如：It is good for you to be geared to the new environment. 尽快熟悉环境对你有好处。

11. It is that the best minds in any particular discipline must be put to work on the task. 这个教训就是使任何特定学科的最优秀人才在课程设计工作中发挥作用。

    be put to work 是"起作用，发挥效果"的意思，比如：The machine should be put to work as soon as possible. 这台机器应该尽快发挥作用。

12. Whether schoolchildren require an understanding of Frederick Jackson Turner's ideas about the role of the frontier in American history before they can sort out the facts and trends of American history—this again is a decision that requires the help of the scholar who has a deep understanding of the American past. 美国的学龄儿童是否该先了解弗雷德里克·杰克逊·特纳关于历史上美国西进的理论，然后再了解那些历史事实和发展动向，该问题的答案又需求助于对美国历史造诣颇深的学者。

    sort out 是"把……分类，整理；拣出，拣选；弄清楚，解决"的意思，比如：We have to sort things out between us. 我们得把我们之间的事情弄弄清楚。

13. Only by the use of our best minds in devising curricular will we bring the fruits of scholarship and wisdom to the student just beginning his studies. 在设计课程时，只有使用我们最优秀的人事，才能把学识和智慧的果实带给刚开始学习的学生。

    本句是有＋介词短语提前，句子用倒装形式。Only in this way is it possible to explain their

14. The Process of Education   教育过程

actions. 只有如此才能解释他们的行为。

14 The School Mathematics Study Group, the University of Illinois mathematics projects, the Physical Science Study Committee, and the Biological Sciences Curriculum Study have indeed been enlisting the aid of eminent men in their various fields, doing so by means of summer projects, supplemented in part by year-long leaves of absence for certain key people involved. 数学教育研究组织,伊利诺伊大学数学工程,物理科学研究委员会,生物科学课程研究会实际上都在致力于取得各学科杰出人士的帮助,这些杰出人士会开办一些暑期课程。
eminent 是"文明的,显赫的,杰出的"的意思,比如:He is a man of eminent fairness. 他是个极其公正的人。

15 Mastery of the fundamental ideas of a field involves not only the grasping of general principles, but also the development of an attitude toward learning and inquiry, toward guessing and hunches, toward the possibility of solving problems on one's own. 对某一学术领域的基本观念的掌握,不但要掌握一般原理,而且还要培养对待学习和调查研究,对待猜想和预感,以及对待独立解决问题能力的态度。
not only...but also...是"不但……而且……"的意思,比如:He is not only mean but also cruel. 他不但吝啬,而且残忍。

16 Just as a physicists has certain attitudes about ultimate orderliness of nature and a conviction that order can be discovered, so a young physics student needs some working version of these attitudes if he is to organize his learning in such a way as to make what he learns usable and meaningful in his thinking. 正如物理学家对于自然界的终极次序抱着确定的态度并深信这种次序能够发现那样,年轻的物理学生如果想把自己的学习组织好,以至于所学到的东西在他的思想上有用和有意义,也需要对培养这些态度有一定工作见解。
just as...so...是"正如……一样"的意思,比如:Just as they must put aside their prejudices, so we must be prepared to accept their good faith. 正如他们必须抛掉偏见一样,我们必须准备好接受他们的意见。

17 Just what it takes to bring off such teaching is something on which a great deal of research is needed, but it would seem that an important ingredient is a sense of excitement about discovery-discovery of regularities of previously unrecognized relations and similarities between ideas, with a resulting sense of self-confidence in one's abilities. 要实现这样的教学任务需要大量的研究工作,但其要素之一是体会到发现思想间相似性及从未被发现的规律性的兴奋感,其结果是产生对自我能力的自信心。
bring off 是"使实现,成功地做"的意思,比如:It was a difficult task, but we brought it off. 这是一件困难的工作,但我们还是把它完成了。

18 Various people who have worked on curricula in science and mathematics have urged that it is possible to present the fundamental structure of a discipline in such a way as to preserve some of the exciting sequences that lead a student to discover for himself. 曾经从事于自然科学和数学课程工作的各方面人士,都极力主张在提出一个学科的基本结构时,不妨保留一些令人兴奋的有助于激发学生自主发现观念的系列材料。
本句是中 who 引导的从句为定语从句,修饰 people,that 引导的宾语从句作 have urged 的宾语。

19. We begin with the hypothesis that any subject can be taught effectively in some, intellectually honest form to any child at any stage of development. 我们首先提出这个假设，任何学科都能够以某一智慧上可靠的方式有效地教给任何发展阶段的任何儿童。

20. It is a bold hypothesis and an essential one in thinking about the nature of a curriculum. 它是在我们考虑课程本质时既大胆又必不可少的假设。

    bold 是"勇敢的，冒失的"的意思，比如：I admire you for you are bold to speak out your true feelings. 我佩服你敢于说出自己的真实的感觉。

21. No evidence exists to contradict it; considerable evidence is being amassed that supports it. 没有证据与之相悖；大量证据都支持此理论。

    contradict 是"反驳，与……发生矛盾/抵触"的意思，比如：The two versions contradict each other. 两种说法互相抵触。

22. Research on the intellectual development of the child highlights the fact that at each stage of development the child has a characteristic way of viewing the world and explaining it to himsel. 大量对儿童智力发展的研究证实，在每个发展阶段，孩子都有一个不同的看世界和理解世界的方式。

    highlights 是"使显著，使突出，强调"的意思，比如：Brisk exports highlight the upturn of economy. 出口活跃显出经济在好转。view 是"观看，看待，考虑"的意思，比如：We viewed a film last night. 昨天晚上我们看了一场电影。

23. The task can be thought of as one of translation. 这种做法可以被看作是一种翻译。

    be thought of 是"被认为"的意思，比如：The task can be thought of as one of translation. 这项任务可被看作是一种解释。

24. The general hypothesis that has just been stated is premised on the considered judgment that any idea can be represented honestly and usefully in the thought forms of children of school age, and that these first representations can later be made more powerful and precise the more easily by virtue of this early learning. 刚刚阐述的假设是经过深思熟虑判断的，任何思想都可以如实地以孩子们的思维形式展示出来，以备将来使用。而这些最初的表现形式通过最初的学习可以在将来变得更印象深刻，更准确，更容易。

    be premised on 是"以……为前提/假设"的意思，如：I will do it on the premise that I like it. 我会根据我喜欢某事的假设去做事。

    by virtue of 是"借助，凭借，因为，由于"的意思，比如：By virtue of your promise to advance me 500yuan, I bought it yesterday. 多亏你答应预支我 500 块钱我昨天才把这东西买下。

25. The work of Piaget and others suggests that, roughly speaking, one may distinguish three stages in the intellectual development of the child. 皮亚杰和其他人的研究表明，孩子的智力发展大体可分三个阶段。

    roughly speaking 是"一般来说，等同于"的意思，比如：Roughly speaking, there is no mother who dislikes her child. 一般说来没有不喜欢自己孩子的妈妈。

26. The first stage need not concern us in detail, for it is characteristic principally of the preschool child. 第一个阶段不需要我们详述，因为它主要是学前儿童的表现特征。

14. The Process of Education 教育过程

27. In this stage, which ends (at least for Swiss school children) around the fifth or sixth year, the child's mental work consists principally in establishing relationships between experience and action; his concern is with manipulating the world through action. 在这一阶段,到五六岁之前(至少是对瑞士学龄儿童而言)儿童的智力活动主要是确定经验和行为间的关系;他们最关心的是通过行为来操纵世界。

    consists in 是"在于,存在于"的意思,比如:Her charm does not consist only in her beauty. 她的魅力不仅仅在于她的美貌。

28. This stage corresponds roughly to the period from the first development of language to the point at which the child learns to manipulate symbols. 这个阶段大致相当于从语言的开始发展到儿童学会使用符号这段时期。

    correspond...to 是"相符,相当"的意思,比如:The money corresponds roughly to amount I need for my course. 这笔钱大致够我上学所需。

29. In this so-called preoperational stage, the principal symbolic achievement is that the child learns how to represent the external world through symbols established by simple generalization; things are represented as equivalent in terms of sharing some common property. 在这个所谓的操纵前阶段重要的标志性成就是孩子学会用简单的意义扩大来表示外部世界;所有物体都引起共有特性而被认作是同类事物。

    preoperational stage:前运算阶段

30. But the child's symbolic world does not make a clear separation between internal motives and feelings on the one hand and external reality on the other. 但儿童的符号世界并没有在儿童的内部动机和外部现实世界划分界限。

    make a clear separation 是"划分界限"的意思,比如:When the boy got his first salary, his parents made a clear separation with him in finance. 自从那个男孩拿到他的第一份工资,他的父母就在经济上与他划分了界限。

31. The child is little able to separate his own goals from the means for achieving them, and when he has to make corrections in his activity after unsuccessful attempts at manipulating reality, he does so by what are called intuitive regulations rather than by symbolic operations, the former being of a crude trail-and-error nature rather than the result of taking thought. 孩子还不太能够区分他自己的目标和实现目标的手段,在他多次尝试操纵现实无过而终时,他不得不改变自己的行为。引起他这样做是所谓的直觉规则,而非标志性操作,前者是自然而然的错了就改模式,而并非思考的结果。

    trail-and-error 是"尝试错误的"的意思,比如:Many experiments got their success in the trail-and-error way. 很多实验是在尝试错误中取得成功的。

32. What is principally lacking at this stage of development is what the Geneva school has called the concept of reversibility. 这一发展阶段主要所缺少的就是日内瓦学校所说的可逆转的概念。

    reversibility 是"可逆,可撤销,两面可用"的意思,比如:There is no reversibility of the material as it is said. 这种面料并不像所说的那样可以两面用。

33. Because of this fundamental lack the child cannot understand certain fundamental ideas that

lie at the basis of mathematics and physics—the mathematical idea that one conserves quantity even when one partitions a set of things into subgroups, or the physical idea that one conserves mass and weight even though one transforms the shape of an object. 由于缺乏这个基本概念，儿童就无法理解作为数学和物理学基础的某些基本观念——数学的观念，如即使他把一组东西分成若干小组时，他仍保持了它们的数量；物理的观念，如即使他改变了某物体的形状，他仍保持了它的质量和重量。

34 It goes without saying that teachers are severely limited in transmitting concepts to a child at this age, even in a highly intuitive manner. 不用说，教师向这个阶段的儿童灌溉概念受到很大限制，尽管采用高度直观的方法。

go without saying 是"不用说，不言而喻"的意思，比如：It goes without saying that they did not work well with each other as it was said. 显然他们合作的并不像所说的那样愉快。

练 习

1. 回答问题
   (1) What is the first object of learning act?
   (2) How could learning serve the future?
   (3) Who should be involved in the design of a curriculum?
   (4) What's the task of teaching a subject to a child at any age?
   (5) Why cannot the preoperational child grasp the idea that it can be brought back readily to its original state?

2. 判断正误
   (1) Learning should not only take us somewhere; it should allow us later to go further more easily.
   (2) Learning in school undoubtedly creates skills of a kind that transfers to activities encountered later in school.
   (3) Only by the use of our best minds in devising curricular will we bring the fruits of scholarship and wisdom to the student just beginning his studies.
   (4) Mastery of the fundamental ideas of a field involves mainly the development of an attitude toward learning and inquiry, toward guessing and hunches, toward the possibility of solving problems on one's own.
   (5) The work of Piaget and others suggests that, roughly speaking, one may distinguish four stages in the intellectual development of the child.

3. 选词填空
   be similar to, refer to as, in essence, sort out, bring off, contradict, highlights, be premised on, by virtue of, go without saying
   (1) The speaker _____ him as an up-and-coming politician.

(2) We have to _____ things between us.

(3) The two versions _____ each other.

(4) I will do it _____ that I like it.

(5) _____ that the exam is coming.

(6) My problems are very _____ yours.

(7) _____, he just loves himself.

(8) It was a difficult task, but we _____ it.

(9) Brisk exports _____ the upturn of economy.

(10) _____ your promise to advance me 500yuan, I bought it yesterday.

4. 句型模拟

(1) not only...but also...

(2) roughly speaking

5. 英译汉

(1) The first object of any act of learning, over and beyond the pleasure it may give, is that it should serve us in the future.

(2) Learning in school undoubtedly creates skills of a kind that transfers to activities encountered later, either in school or after.

(3) It is simple enough to proclaim, of course, that school curricula and methods of teaching should be geared to the teaching of fundamental ideas in whatever subject is being taught.

(4) We begin with the hypothesis that any subject can be taught effectively in some, intellectually honest form to any child at any stage of development.

(5) It goes without saying that teachers are severely limited in transmitting concepts to a child at this age, even in a highly intuitive manner.

6. 汉译英

(1) 这家公司已经迁到东部某地。(transfer to)

(2) 这里的所有人员都应发挥作用。(be put to work)

(3) 生产要适应需求。(Be geared to)

(4) 这是一个大胆的设想。(bold)

(5) 她的成功不仅仅在于机遇。(consists in)

7. 写作指导

For this part, you are required to write a composition on the topic "What's the Aim of Learning". The following points taken from the text are useful expressions for your reference:

- The first object of any act of learning, over and beyond the pleasure it may give, is that it should serve us in the future.
- Learning should not only take us somewhere; it should allow us later to go further more

easily.
- Learning in school undoubtedly creates skills of a kind that transfers to activities encountered later, either in school or after.
- In essence, learning consists of a general idea, which can then be used as a basis for recognizing subsequent problems as special cases of the idea originally mastered.
- The educational process is the continual broadening and deepening of knowledge in terms of basic and general ideas.
- In order for a person to be able to recognize the applicability or inapplicability of an idea to a new situation and to broaden his learning thereby, he must have clearly in mind the general nature of the phenomenon with which he is dealing.
- The more fundamental or basic is the idea he has learned, the greater will be its breadth of applicability to new problems.
- School curricula and methods of teaching should be geared to the teaching of fundamental ideas in whatever subject is being taught.

15. Nature of a Theory of Instruction
教学论的性质

Jerome S. Bruner
杰罗姆·S.布鲁纳

《教学论的性质》是美国心理学家布鲁纳在1972年发表的一篇论文。在这篇论文中布鲁纳指出,最理想的知识结构是相对的而不是绝对的。主要的条件应是:在同一个知识领域里不会产生两套相互矛盾的结构。他认为教学论具有四个主要特点:应当详细规定能使人最有效地牢固树立学习的心理倾向的经验;必须详细规定将大量知识组织起来使学习者易于掌握的方式;应当详细规定学习材料的最有效的序列;必须详细规定学习和教学过程中奖励和惩罚的性质和步调。由此,引出四条教学原则:动机原则;结构原则;序列原则;强化原则。

Nature of a Theory of Instruction

A theory of instruction is prescriptive in the sense that it sets forth rules concerning the most effective way of achieving knowledge or skill.[1] By the same token, such a theory provides a yardstick for criticizing or evaluating any particular way of teaching or learning.[2]

A theory of instruction is a normative theory. It sets up criteria and states the conditions for meeting them. The criteria must have a high degree of generality[3]: for example, a theory of instruction should not specify in an ad hoc fashion[4] the conditions for efficient learning of third-grade arithmetic. Rather, such conditions should be derivable from a more general view of mathematics learning.

One might ask why a theory of instruction is needed, since psychology already contains theories of learning and of development. But theories of learning and of development are descriptive rather than prescriptive.[5] They tell us what happened after the fact: for example, that most children of 6 do not yet possess the notion of reversibility. A theory of instruction, on the other hand, might attempt to set forth the best means of leading the child towards the notion of reversibility. A theory of instruction, in short, is concerned with how best to learn what one wishes to teach, with improving, rather than describing learning.[6]

This is not to say that learning and developmental theories are irrelevant to a theory of instruction. In fact, a theory of instruction must be concerned with both learning and development, as well as with the nature of particular subject-matter; and there must be congruence among the various theories, all of which have a complementary relation to each other[7].

A theory of instruction has four major features:

(1) A theory of instruction should specify the experiences which most effectively important

in the individual a predisposition towards learning—learning in general or a particular type of learning.[8] For example, what sorts of relationships towards people and things in the preschool environment will tend to make the child willing and able to learn when he enters school?

(2) Second, a theory of instruction must specify the ways in which a body of knowledge[9] should be structured so that it can be most readily grasped by the learner. Optimal structure refers to the set of propositions from which a larger body of knowledge can be generated, and it is characteristic that the formulation of such structure depends upon the state of advance in a particular field of knowledge[10]. In a later section, the nature of different optimal structures will be considered in more detail. Here it suffices to say that since the goodness of a structure depends upon its power for *simplifying information, for generating new propositions and for increasing the manipulability of a body of knowledge*, structure must always be related to the status and gifts of the learner.[11] Viewed in this way, the optimal structure of a body of knowledge is not absolute but relative. The major requirement is that no two sets of generating structures for the same field of knowledge be in contradiction.

(3) Third, the theory of instruction should specify the most effective sequences in which to present the materials to be learned. Given, for example, that one wishes to teach the structure of modern physical theory, how does one proceed? Does one present concrete materials first in such a way as to elicit questions about recurrent regularities? Or, does one begin with a formalized mathematical notation that makes it simpler to represent regularities later encountered? What results are in fact produced by the use of each? The question of sequence will be treated in more detail later.

(4) Finally, a theory of instruction should specify the *nature and pacing of rewards and punishments* in the process of learning and teaching.[12] Intuitively, it seems quite clear that as learning progresses there is a point at which it is better to shift away from extrinsic rewards, such as teacher's praise, towards the intrinsic rewards inherent in solving a complex problem for one's self. So, too, there is a point at which immediate reward for performance should be replaced by deferred reward. The shift rates from extrinsic to intrinsic and from immediate to deferred reward are poorly understood and obviously important.[13] Is it the case, for example, that wherever learning involves the integration of a long sequence of acts, the earliest shift should be made from immediate to deferred reward and from extrinsic to intrinsic reward?

It would be beyond the scope of any single paper to pursue in any detail all of the four aspects of a theory of instruction set forth above. What I shall attempt to do here is to explore a major theorem concerning each of the four. The object is not comprehensiveness but illustration.

Predispositions

It has been customary, in discussing predispositions to learn, to focus upon cultural, motivational and personal factors affecting the desire to learn and to undertake problem-solving.[14] And indeed, such factors are of enormous importance. But we shall concentrate here on a more cognitive level: upon the predisposition to explore alternative. For it is this predisposition that is often most affected by cultural and motivational factors.

Since learning and problem-solving depend upon the exploration of alternatives, instruction must facilitate and regulate the exploration of alternatives on the part of the learner.[15]

There are three aspects to the exploration of alternatives, each of them related to the regulation of search behavior. They can be described in shorthand terms as *activation*, *maintenance* and *direction*. To put it another way, exploration of alternatives requires something to get started, something to keep it going and something to keep it from being random.[16]

The major condition for *activating exploration* of alternatives in a task is the presence of some optimal level of uncertainty. Curiosity, it has been persuasively argued, is a response to uncertainty and ambiguity. A cut-and-dried routine task arouses little exploration; one that is too uncertain may arouse confusion and anxiety, with the effect of reducing exploration.[17]

The *maintenance of exploration*, once it has been activated, requires that the benefits from exploring alternatives exceed the risks incurred. Learning something with the aid of an instructor should, if instruction is effective, be less dangerous or risky or painful than learning on one's own. That is to say, the consequences of error-exploring *wrong* alternatives-should be rendered less grave under a regimen of instruction, and the yield from the exploration of *correct* alternatives should be correspondingly greater.[18]

The appropriate *direction of exploration* depends upon two interacting considerations: a sense of the goal of a task and a knowledge of the relevance of tested alternatives to the achievement of that goal. For exploration to have direction, in short, the goal of the task must be known in some approximate fashion, and the testing of alternatives must yield information as to where one is with respect to it.

Sequence and its Uses

Instruction consists of leading the learner through a sequence of statements and restatements of a problem or body of knowledge that increase the learner's ability to grasp, transform and transfer what he is learning. In short, the sequence in which a learner encounters materials within a domain of knowledge affects the difficulty he will have in achieving mastery.[19]

There are usually a variety of sequences that are equivalent in their ease and difficulty for learners. There is no unique sequence for all learners, and the optimum in any particular case will depend upon a variety of factors, including past learning, stage of development, nature of the material and individual differences.

If it is true that the course of intellectual development moves from enactive through ikonic to symbolic representation of the world, it is likely that an optimum sequence will progress in the same direction.[20] Obviously, this is a conservative doctrine. For when the learner has a well-developed symbolic system, it may be possible to by-pass the first two stages. But one does so always with the risk that the learner may not possess the imagery to fall back on[21] when his symbolic transformations fail to achieve a goal in problem-solving.

Sequencing must take into account the limited capacities of any organism to process information. In this sense. A sequence that begins economically will usually be advisable. This hypothesis is further premised on the assumption that more economically presented materials, learned first as a model, will serve to reduce the potential complexity of materials encountered later.[22]

Exploration of alternatives will necessarily be affected by the sequence in which material to be learned becomes available to the learner. It is an empirical question as to when the learner should be encouraged to explore alternatives widely and when he should be encouraged to concentrate on the implications of a single alternative hypothesis. To this subject we return in the next section.

Reverting to the earlier discussion of activation and the maintenance of interest, it is necessary to specify in any sequence the level of uncertainty and tension that must be present to initiate problem-solving behavior and what is necessary to keep active problem-solving going. This again is an empirical question.

Optimum sequences, as already stated, cannot be specified independent of the criterion in terms of which final learning is to be judged.[23] A classification of such criteria will include at least the following: (a) speed of learning, (b) resistance to forgetting, (c) transferability of what has been learned to new instances, (d) form of representation in terms of which what has been learned is to be expressed, (e) economy of what has been learned in terms of cognitive strain imposed, (f) effective power of what has been learned in terms of its generativeness for new hypotheses and combinations. Achieving one of these goals does not necessarily bring one closer to others.[24] Speed of learning is sometimes antithetical to transfer or to economy, and so forth.

注　释

1　A theory of instruction is prescriptive in the sense that it sets forth rules concerning the most effective way of achieving knowledge or skill. 教学论，在某种意义上说，是约定俗成的通例，它阐明有关有效地获得知识与技能的方法的规则。

set forth 是"公布某事物；宣布或提出某事物"的意思，比如：The Priminister set forth the aims of his government in a television broadcast. 首相在电视广播中公布了内阁的工作目标。

2　By the same token, such a theory provides a yardstick for criticizing or evaluating any particular way of teaching or learning. 相应地，这种理论可为批评或评定任何一种教学法或学习法提供一个尺度。

by the same token：相应地；基于同一理由

3　The criteria must have a high degree of generality：这些准则必须具有高度的概括性

4　in an ad hoc fashion：以特定方式

5　But theories of learning and of development are descriptive rather than prescriptive. 学习理论和发展理论是描述性的，不是规定性的。

rather than 指"宁愿"，比如：He resigned rather than take part in such a dishonest transaction. 他宁愿辞职也不愿参与这种欺诈的交易。

6　A theory of instruction, in short, is concerned with how best to learn what one wishes to teach, with improving, rather than describing learning. 简言之,教学论所关注的是如何用改善学习而不是描述学习的方法最好地学会人们想教的东西。

how best to learn 不定式短语作 with 的介词宾语。what 从句作 learn 的宾语。

7   and there must be congruence among the various theories, all of which have a complementary relation to each other：并且在各种不同的理论之间也必然是协调一致、彼此间又有互补关系的

8   A theory of instruction should specify the experiences which most effectively important in the individual a predisposition towards learning—learning in general or a particular type of learning. 教学论应当详细规定能使人最有效地牢固树立学习的心理倾向的经验———一般形式的学习和特殊类型的学习。

9   a body of sth：大量,如：a body of evidence 大量证据

10 and it is characteristic that the formulation of such structure depends upon the state of advance in a particular field of knowledge：显然,这种结构的系统化或公式化,取决于特定知识领域的进展状态。

11 Here it suffices to say that since the goodness of a structure depends upon its power for *simplifying information*, *for generating new propositions* and for *increasing the manipulability of a body of knowledge*, structure must always be related to the status and gifts of the learner. 这里只需说一说,因为一种结构的优越性取决于它在简化信息、产生新的命题和增强知识的可操作性等诸方面的力量,所以这种结构总是与学习者的状况和天赋有关的。

12 Finally, a theory of instruction should specify the *nature and pacing of rewards and punishments* in the process of learning and teaching. 最后,教学论必须详细规定学习和教学过程中奖励和惩罚的性质和步调。

13 The shift rates from extrinsic to intrinsic and from immediate to deferred reward are poorly understood and obviously important. 至于外来奖励向内在奖励和即时奖励向延缓奖励的转移速率,我们对此的了解少得可怜,但其重要性却是非常明显的。

14 It has been customary, in discussing predispositions to learn, to focus upon cultural, motivational and personal factors affecting the desire to learn and to undertake problem-solving. 在讨论学习的心理倾向时,焦点总是对准文化、动机和个性等因素对学习者渴望学习和解决问题的影响上的。

不定式短语 to focus upon...是句子的真正主语,主语后置是为了保持句子平衡。

15 Since learning and problem-solving depend upon the exploration of alternatives, instruction must facilitate and regulate the exploration of alternatives on the part of the learner. 既然学习与解决问题取决于个人做出选择的探索活动,那么教学就必须对学习者方面做出选择的探索活动起促进和调节作用。

on the part of sb/on sb's part：指"由某人做出",比如：It was an error on my part. 那是我的过失。

16 To put it another way, exploration of alternatives requires something to get started, something to keep it going and something to keep it from being random. 换句话说,做出选择的探索活动要求启动某件事情,能坚持持续不断的事情,能有的放矢不紊乱的事情。

17 A cut-and-dried routine task arouses little exploration; one that is too uncertain may arouse confusion and anxiety, with the effect of reducing exploration. 陈旧而呆板的常规工作不会激起探索活动。当然，一个寡断而多变的人也可能产生慌乱和焦虑，致使探索活动的效果减弱。

that 引导的是定语从句修饰 one。

18 That is to say, the consequences of error-exploring *wrong* alternatives-should be rendered less grave under a regimen of instruction, and the yield from the exploration of *correct* alternatives should be correspondingly greater. 也就是说，倘若有教学过程的控制，那么，误差，即做出错误选择的探索活动所造成的后果是不会太严重的；相应地说来，做出正确选择的探索活动所取得的好处则大得多了。

19 In short, the sequence in which a learner encounters materials within a domain of knowledge affects the difficulty he will have in achieving mastery. 简而言之，序列是学习者在某知识领域内所遇到的材料的程序，它影响着学习者在达到熟练掌握的程度时将会发生的难度。

he will have in achieving mastery 是一个省略 that 的定语从句修饰 difficulty。

20 If it is true that the course of intellectual development moves from enactive through ikonic to symbolic representation of the world, it is likely that an optimum sequence will progress in the same direction. 如果智力发展的正常历程确实是由表演式再现阶段经过肖像式再现阶段而达到象征式再现表象阶段，那么最理想的序列就多半要按照同一个方向进行。

在主句中 it 是形式主语，真正的主语是 that 从句。

21 fall back on：依靠某事物；比如：At least we can fall back on candles if the electricity fails. 停电时我们至少可以使用蜡烛。

22 This hypothesis is further premised on the assumption that more economically presented materials, learned first as a model, will serve to reduce the potential complexity of materials encountered later. 这个假设又是以下述的假定为前提的，即呈现材料的最经济法则乃是首先把它们作为一个模式来学习，这将会有助于减少以后遇到的材料所潜藏的复杂性。

that 从句是同位语从句，补充说明 assumption。

23 Optimum sequences, as already stated, cannot be specified independent of the criterion in terms of which final learning is to be judged. 正像上面业已表明的那样，最理想的序列是不能脱离以评判最后学习结果的准则而孤立地做出规定的。

这里 as 的用法是引导一个非限制性的关系子句，无显著的先行词，比如：Cyprus, as you all know, is in the Mediterranean. 塞浦路斯岛，你们大家都知道，是在地中海。

24 Achieving one of these goals does not necessarily bring one closer to others. 达到了这些目标中的一个目标，不一定能使人更接近其他目标。

练　习

1. 回答问题

（1）Why a theory of instruction is needed, since psychology already contains theories of learning and of development?

(2) What is optimal structure of knowledge according to the author?

(3) Which three aspects influence the exploration of alternatives?

(4) List some factors which influence the optimal sequence.

(5) Why is it advisable that a sequence should begin economically?

2. 判断正误

(1) A theory of instruction should describe in detail the way of efficient learning in any particular field.

(2) The optimal structure of a body of knowledge should be individually different.

(3) Learning and developmental theories are irrelevant to a theory of instruction.

(4) According to the author intrinsic rewards are more important than extrinsic rewards.

(5) Activating exploration of alternatives in a task needs uncertainty, but too much uncertainty may lead to confusion and anxiety.

3. 选词填空

set forth, derive from, by the same token, concentrate on, on one's own, on the part of, fall back on, take... into account, in terms of, be independent of

(1) The figures are expressed _____ a percentage.

(2) She must be more reasonable, but _____ you must try to understand her.

(3) The Prime Minister _____ the aims of his government in a television broadcast.

(4) She _____ no benefit _____ the course of drugs.

(5) I can't _____ my studies with all that noise going on.

(6) The agreement has been kept _____ me, but not of him.

(7) You should support yourself, since you are old enough to _____ your parents.

(8) When the teacher chooses teaching material, he should _____ the stage of the student's mental development _____.

(9) She is completely homeless—at least I have parents to _____.

(10) Although her father is in the firm she got the job _____.

4. 句型模拟

(1) It is characteristic that...

(2) It suffices to say that...

5. 英译汉

(1) A theory of instruction is prescriptive in the sense that it sets forth rules concerning the most effective way of achieving knowledge or skill.

(2) Intuitively, it seems quite clear that as learning progresses there is a point at which it is better to shift away from extrinsic rewards, such as teacher's praise, towards the intrinsic rewards inherent in solving a complex problem for one's self. So, too, there is a point at

which immediate reward for performance should be replaced by deferred reward.
(3) Instruction consists of leading the learner through a sequence of statements and restatements of a problem or body of knowledge that increase the learner's ability to grasp, transform and transfer what he is learning.
(4) There is no unique sequence for all learners, and the optimum in any particular case will depend upon a variety of factors, including past learning, stage of development, nature of the material and individual differences.
(5) The major condition for *activating exploration* of alternatives in a task is the presence of some optimal level of uncertainty.

6. 汉译英
(1) 他有喜欢挑人毛病的癖性。(predisposition)
(2) 他私下的行为跟公开的言论完全是两码事。(in contradiction to)
(3) 他的个性与她的相辅相成。(be complementary to)
(4) 政府已成立工作组调查滥用毒品问题。(set up)
(5) 我们的表现需要一个检验的标准。(yardstick)

7. 写作指导
For this part, you are required to write a composition on the topic "The Characteristics of a Theory of Instruction". The following points taken from the text are useful expressions for your reference:
- be prescriptive
- be normative
- be concerned with the most effective way of achieving knowledge or skill
- have a high degree of generality
- specify the experiences which most effectively implant in the individual a predisposition towards learning
- specify how a body of knowledge to be structured to be most readily grasped by the learner
- specify the most effective sequences in which to present the materials to be learned
- specify the nature and pacing of rewards and punishments in the process of learning and teaching

练习参考答案

1. My Pedagogic Creed

1. 回答问题
   (1) All education proceeds by the participation of the individual in the social consciousness of the race.
   (2) Through these demands he is stimulated to act as a member of a unity, to emerge from his original narrowness of action and feeling and to conceive of himself from the standpoint of the welfare of the group to which he belongs.
   (3) The educative process will be haphazard and arbitrary.
   (4) He can have the full and ready use of all his capacities.
   (5) If we eliminate the social factor from the child we are left only with an abstraction; if we eliminate the individual factor from society, we are left only with an inert and lifeless mass.

2. 判断正误
   (1) F　　(2) F　　(3) T　　(4) F　　(5) T

3. 选词填空
   (1) reference to
   (2) make of
   (3) adjusted to
   (4) with the advent of
   (5) from the standpoint of
   (6) departs from
   (7) has transformed...into
   (8) became reduced to
   (9) chanced to
   (10) sum up

4. 句型模拟
   (1) Save as he wrote a letter to me last year, we haven't communicated with each other any more.
   (2) It is urged that education reform must be carried out.

179

5. 英译汉

(1) 这个教育过程有两个方面：一个是心理学的，一个是社会学的。它们是平列并重的，那一方面也不能偏废。否则，不良的后果将随之而来。

(2) 我们为了要知道能力究竟是什么，我们就必须知道它的目的、用途或功能是什么；而这些，是无法知道的，除非我们认为个人是在社会关系中活动的。

(3) 准备儿童使其适应未来生活，那意思便是要使他能管理自己；要训练他能充分和随时地运用他的全部能量；他的眼、耳和手都成为随时听命令的工具，他的判断力能理解他必须在其中起作用的周围情况，他的动作能力被训练能达到经济和有效果地进行活动的程度。

(4) 总之，我相信，受教育的个人是社会的个人，而社会便是许多个人的有机结合。

(5) 因此，教育必须从心理学上探索儿童的能量、兴趣和习惯开始。它的每个方面，都必须参照这些考虑加以掌握。

6. 汉译英

(1) The blow caused him to lose consciousness.

(2) Most wage claims are settled by compromise.

(3) Make a careful examination to eliminate mistakes from your writing.

(4) The room was converted from a kitchen to a lavatory.

(5) The old man spend ten years turning this piece of barren land into oasis.

7. 写作指导

(略)

2. The School and Social Progress

1. 回答问题

(1) Because such work engages the full spontaneous interest and attention of the children; it keeps them alert and active, instead of passive and receptive; it makes them more useful, more capable, and hence more inclined to be helpful at home.

(2) At last he will become a selfish man and think helping others has become a school crime.

(3) A spirit of free communication, of interchange of ideas, suggestions, results, both successes and failures of previous experiences, becomes the dominating note of the recitation.

(4) We get it through life itself.

(5) Experience is the resource of the rewarding discipline and the place where children are sent for discipline is the place to get experience.

2. 判断正误

(1) T　　(2) T　　(3) T　　(4) F　　(5) T

3. 选词填空

(1) at his disposal

(2) open to

(3) At worst

(4) competing with

(5) Compared with

(6) was eliminated from

(7) contact with

(8) be devoted to

(9) in the process of

(10) relative to

4. 句型模拟

(1) Only in the spring do the flowers bloom.

(2) If green plants should disappear some day, there would hardly be any life on the earth.

5. 英译汉

(1) 最贤明的父母所希望于自己孩子的一定是社会所希望于一切儿童的。

(2) 这些取得的好处，对于今天在城市里成长的儿童极为重要。

(3) 它使得他们主动、活泼，而不是被动、呆板；

(4) 这种共同的需要和目的要求日益加强思想的交流和感情的和谐一致。

(5) 的确，对于那些把学校的形象僵化了的人来说，这样的改变必定使他们大为惊讶。

6. 汉译英

(1) I think that my uncle still conceives of me as a four-year-old.

(2) Let's not disagree for the sake of a few pounds.

(3) I'm afraid I have only a slight acquaintance with his works.

(4) We are sure that he will succeed in finishing that hard task.

(5) In view of the weather, we will cancel the outing.

7. 写作指导

（略）

3. Democratics and Education

1. 回答问题

(1) If we have the adult language, we can see the import of the babbling impulses of infancy.

(2) As a first consequence, the intelligence of the teacher is not free; it is confined to receiving the aims laid down from above.

(3) One is natural aim to their own experience at the time, and the other is the aim in which they are taught to acquiesce.

(4) Two: they are general ends and ultimate ends.

(5) A truly general aim broadens the outlook, and stimulates one to take more consequences into account.

2. 判断正误

(1) T   (2) F   (3) F   (4) F   (5) T

3. 选词填空

(1) on the part of

(2) as to

(3) root out

(4) bear, in mind

(5) size up

(6) square with

(7) imposed, on

(8) lay down

(9) acquiesce in

(10) on her guard against

4. 句型模拟

(1) His mother is more kind than intelligent.

(2) If it weren't for his wife's money, he would never be a director.

5. 英译汉

(1) 农民的目的,只不过是利用这种种环境,使他的活动和环境的力量,共同协作,而不相互对抗。

(2) 任何目的,只要能时时刻刻帮助我们观察、选择和计划,使我们的活动得以顺利进行,就是有价值的目的。

(3) 所以,他们的目的有无穷的变异,随着不同的儿童而不同,随着儿童的生长和教育者经验的增长而变化。

(4) 这种目的不但无助于具体的教学任务,并且阻碍教师应用平常的判断,观察和估量所面临的情境。

(5) 一个真正一般的目的,能开拓人们的眼界,激发他们考虑更多的结果。

6. 汉译英

(1) The laws apply to everyone irrespective of race, creed or color.

(2) At the age of nine he had the death of both parents to contend with.

(3) She's determined to succeed and she won't let anything get in her way.

(4) Money as such will seldom bring happiness.

(5) The computer lends itself to many different uses.

7. 写作指导

(略)

4. The Secret of Childhood

1. 回答问题

(1) Society showed not the smallest concern for the child. It left him where he was born, to the sole care of his family.

(2) The death of small children seemed so natural that families had accustomed themselves to it, comforting themselves with the thought that such little children went straight to heaven.

(3) Fathers and mothers must gain new knowledge and receive the instruction necessary for a proper care of the health of their babies.

(4) Tying placards to the children's backs, putting dunces' caps on their heads, putting them in a real pillory or standing in a corner for several hours, tired, bored by idleness, seeing nothing.

(5) The child who is punished in school must consign his sentence to his father, so that the father may join with the teacher in punishing him and scolding him. He is then forced to take back to school a writing from his father, as a proof that he has accused himself to his other executioner, who associated himself, at least in principle, with the persecution of his own son.

2. 判断正误

(1) T (2) F (3) F (4) T (5) F

3. 选词填空

(1) entrusted to

(2) as far as...is concerned

(3) resulted from

(4) in the midst of

(5) carried out

(6) appeal to

(7) substitute for

(8) subject...to

(9) deprive of

(10) in his place

4. 句型模拟

(1) He got up late, so he ran fast so as to catch the last bus.

(2) What with my tiredness and hunger, I decided to give it up.

5. 英译汉

(1) 在有利于成人的历史发展中，儿童成为不属于人类社会的生物，在社会以外，孤立无助，没有丝毫交流途径可以使社会了解他们的处境。他们可能成为牺牲品，而社会并不了解。

(2) 他们被关在学校里，和奴隶一般，受到社会强加的痛苦。儿童长时间伏案读书写字，使他们的胸膛受压而变得狭小，容易患肺病。

(3) 在他们上学以前，有些儿童已经步行好几英里去分送牛奶，或是奔走街头，叫卖报纸，或是在家里劳动。他们到达学校的时候感到饥饿、昏昏欲睡，惟一的愿望就是休息。

(4) 一个孩子，在学校受了惩罚，必须把判决送交给他的父亲，使父亲可以和教师一起惩罚和责骂孩子。然后孩子被迫把他父亲的字条送回学校，证明他已经自己向另一个刽子手投案，这另一个刽子手至少在原则上参与了对自己儿子的迫害。孩子就这样地被判背上自己的十字架。

(5) 推动机器的能量是从外部世界发出的，好像从整个社会来的一股巨大的非人格的力量，无情地作用着。向前！永远向前！

6. 汉译英

(1) She has been warned of the danger of driving the car in that state.

(2) We all condemn cruelty to children.

(3) After the death of his parents, the child was consigned to his uncle's care.

(4) Hatred often springs from fear.

(5) He quickly became accustomed to the local food.

7. 写作指导

(略)

5. Education and Good Life

1. 回答问题

(1) A higher standard of wealth; freedom from the danger of defeat in war; comparative absence of cramping traditions inherited from the Middle Ages.

(2) Because they found a generally diffused sentiment of democracy and an advanced stage of industrial technique.

(3) The attitude of the children is very largely determined by their school education.

(4) Those who possess a diffused form can be trusted to draw up schemes of education.

(5) He should love his students and also should have a right conception of human excellence.

2. 判断正误

   (1) F　　(2) F　　(3) F　　(4) F　　(5) T

3. 选词填空

   (1) retain

   (2) apart from

   (3) On the whole

   (4) was attributable to

   (5) deduced from

   (6) was confined to

   (7) likewise

   (8) belong to

   (9) make no distinction between

   (10) takes my brother's side

4. 句型模拟

   (1) This is the truth in so far as I know it.

   (2) No sulfur and no phosphorus is in this product.

5. 英译汉

   (1) 相反,他们的子女却丧失了对他们父母出生的国家的忠诚,简直完全成为美国人了。

   (2) 但是,在旧世界还比新世界优越的那些方面,逐渐灌输对真正优秀品质的一种轻视的思想就成为必然了。

   (3) 概括地说,好人有好的结果,坏人有坏的结果。

   (4) 凡是教师缺乏爱的地方,无论品格还是智慧都不能充分地或自由地发展。

   (5) 但是只有那些具有这种本能的人才能信托他们制订教育计划。

6. 汉译英

   (1) I always associate him with fast cars.

   (2) For her, happiness consists in watching television and reading magazine.

   (3) Your diet is deficient in vitamin D, so you may well get the disease rickets.

   (4) He tried without success to dismiss her from his thoughts.

   (5) We must be subject to the law of the land.

7. 写作指导

   (略)

6. The Aims of Education

1. 回答问题

   (1) Because education in the past has been radically infected with inert ideas, so for the uneducated clever women, they have been saved from this horrible burden of inert ideas.

   (2) One is "do not teach too many subjects," and the other is "what you teach, teach thoroughly."

   (3) The only use of knowledge of the past is to equip us for the present.

   (4) The theoretical ideas should always find important applications within the pupil's curriculum. This is not an easy doctrine to apply, but a very hard one. It contains within itself the problem of keeping knowledge alive, of preventing it from becoming inert, which is the central problem of all education.

   (5) The reason of dislike is that it kills the best part of culture. Because we are dealing with human minds, and not with dead matter. The evocation of curiosity, of judgment, of the power of mastering a complicated tangle of circumstances, the use of theory in giving foresight in special cases all these powers are not to be imparted by a set rule embodied in one schedule of examination subjects.

2. 判断正误

   (1) F   (2) T   (3) F   (4) T   (5) F

3. 选词填空

   (1) ferment
   (2) in isolation
   (3) apply to
   (4) inert
   (5) at intervals
   (6) worthy of
   (7) infect with
   (8) make any difference
   (9) sneer at
   (10) exception

4. 句型模拟

   (1) Nor could I do something to help her.
   (2) Nor sadder thing it is than to be hurt by the ones you love.

5. 英译汉

(1) 这就是为什么一些没有受过教育的有才智的妇女,她们饱经世故,到了中年却成为社会上最有教养的人的原因。

(2) 他必须发现,普通概念使他理解那倾注在他生活中的川流不息的事件,这川流不息的事件正是他的生活。

(3) 我略而不谈应该是文科教育所致力的那种理解。我也不愿被认为要对古典课程和限电课程哪个好表示意见。

(4) 没有比轻视现在对年轻人的心理造成更致命的损害了。

(5) 现在来谈谈科学的教育和逻辑的教育

6. 汉译英

(1) My papers are all muddled up with his.

(2) You must enunciate your intention clearly.

(3) How much he endeavored, the goal stayed unattained.

(4) I always have looked upon him in the light of my son.

(5) The theory should be applied to practice.

7. 写作指导

(略)

7. The Wasteland of Education

1. 回答问题

(1) Americans have unbounded faith in schools, but they seem to distrust the results of schooling. And they regard schooling as a mere experience, delightful to the recipient but hardly valuable to society.

(2) The public, seeing no point in much of what is done under the name of education, have developed a justifiable skepticism but not perverse opinion toward education.

(3) According to the education effects, the answer is no.

(4) Education is, first of all, the opposite of ignorance. Genuine education is intellectual training.

(5) Because compared with the vastly increased time, effort, and money, the achievements of the present-day students are exceedingly slight.

2. 判断对错

(1) F   (2) F   (3) F   (4) F   (5) T

3. 选词填空

(1) give due weight to

(2) adduced

(3) dismayed at

(4) amounts to

(5) deprived of

(6) engaged in

(7) vital to

(8) benevolence

(9) suspicious of

(10) conceive of

4. 句型模拟

(1) By the time of 2010, we will have had a big house.

(2) All but a lovely girl appeared on the stage.

5. 英译汉

(1) 普及的、免费的、公共的教育是民主信条的一部分,美国人接受这个信条,但是感到难于用合理的词语来解释。

(2) 原来,公共舆论是不会那么荒谬,以致无故就采取这一观点的。

(3) 这种对不信任的责任的正落在那些以教育工作为职业的男男女女身上。

(4) 公立学校行政人员和他们在大学教育系的同盟者为他们的管理职务所作的辩护那么软弱无力,等于承认失败。

(5) 在衡量这个证据时,让我们记着,今天,当一个学生读完某一年级时,他在校学习的时间是八十年前与他相当的学生学习时间的两倍。

6. 汉译英

(1) The big boy compelled his classmate to give the money to him.

(2) Before committing themselves to marriage, they did not know each other.

(3) A careless person is apt to make mistakes.

(4) We are privileged to live on a very precious planet.

(5) The salary is commensurate with the output.

7. 写作指导

(略)

8. Education and Freedom

1. 回答问题

(1) An atmosphere of personal independence and political liberty.

(2) Because it brings about drastic and long-overdue reforms in utilizing the nation's intellec-

tual resources.

(3) Because of its relation to missile weaponry and because of the potential military advantages of outer-space control.

(4) Social system and educational system.

(5) First, American must be awakened to the danger facing the nation-making public all the facts without soothing the impact of unpleasant truths; Second, their treatment of scientists and trained professionals must be reversed.

2. 判断正误

(1) T (2) T (3) F (4) F (5) F

3. 选词填空

(1) has done damaged to

(2) keep up with

(3) disregard of

(4) in terms of

(5) let alone

(6) take great effort to

(7) on my part

(8) at the cost of

(9) bring about

(10) concerned about

4. 句型模拟

(1) As you were concerned that she would forget the meeting, so I called her again.

(2) He was so nervous that he didn't know what to say.

5. 英译汉

(1) 它动摇了长期以来视为当然的认为高标准的物质福利乃是技术进步的外部表征和必要基础的信念。

(2) 第二,它证明一个现代专制国家能够制定一种仅仅符合国家利益而完全不顾儿童个人需要的教育制度,却能诱发全体儿童使他们的智能发展到极限。

(3) 也许太多的努力用于使美国生活快乐和舒适的东西,而用于保证不断的精神和物质的发展以及在任何战争中,不论热战还是冷战,保证军事和政治上胜利的东西则不足。

(4) 科学家们也有一切平常人共同的需要,所以俄国给他们有吸引力的住宅、乡村别墅、假期、保姆、轿车和汽车司机。

(5) 首先,我想,我们必须唤醒美国认清我们民族所面临的危险——公布一切事实,不减轻令人不愉快的真相的冲击。

6. 汉译英

(1) I take it for granted you have read this book.

(2) Don't lose your head in urgent case.

(3) Her sense of humor appealed to him enormously.

(4) She was always well ahead of the rest of the class.

(5) To his dismay, his young son often escapes the school.

7. 写作指导

(略)

9. General Education

1. 回答问题

(1) University must remain a series of disparate schools and departments, united by nothing except the fact that they have the same president and board of trustees.

(2) Having a common stock of fundamental ideas.

(3) It confuses immediate and final ends.

(4) Virtues of intuitive knowledge, of scientific knowledge, of philosophical wisdom, of art and of prudence.

(5) An education that consists of the cultivation of the intellectual virtues is the most useful education.

2. 判断正误

(1) T　　(2) T　　(3) F　　(4) F　　(5) T

3. 选词填空

(1) is divided up

(2) reminded me of

(3) cut off

(4) favorable to

(5) is foreign to

(6) succumbed to

(7) impressed with

(8) with respect to

(9) bring about

(10) insisted on

4. 句型模拟

(1) He takes it for granted that his parents support him.

(2) No matter why he was late, he should make apologies to his teacher.

5. 英译汉

(1) 物质上的成功和适应环境或多或少是有益的，但是它们本身不是有益的，而是在它们之外还有许多益处。

(2) 我们抛弃理智的传统，只阅读最近代的书，只讨论当前的失误，试图使学校与时代并肩前进，甚至超越时代，并写下关于教育和社会变迁的精心制作的论述。

(3) 教育意味着教学。教学意味着知识。知识是真理。真理在任何地方都是相同的。因此，教育在任何地方应当是相同的。

(4) 近年来这种看法已经由于世界范围内的不景气和大事宣扬由此引起的政治、社会和经济的变化而更为加强。

(5) 在普通教育中，我们所关心的是引出我们共同的人性中种种因素；我们所关心的是属于民族的而不是属于个人的不必需的东西。

6. 汉译英

(1) They seem ready to indulge his every whim.

(2) Jane and I have nothing in common.

(3) To me he embodies all the best qualities of a teacher.

(4) Many words have been added to this edition of the dictionary.

(5) Coming from a theatrical family, I was destined for a career on the stage..

7. 写作指导

(略)

10. How to Read a Book

1. 回答问题

(1) They complained about the schools for not teaching the young to write and speak well. And the complaints have focused mainly on the products of high school and college.

(2) Fewer than two young people in a hundred read.

(3) The school train their students not only to interpret but to criticize.

(4) He wants to tell us that most of able students can't do well in reading comprehension.

(5) Because the education do not know what to do about it, in addition, perhaps, because they do not realize how much time and effort must expected to teach students how to read, write, and speak well.

2. 判断正误

(1) F   (2) F   (3) F   (4) F   (5) F

3. 选词填空

(1) For the most part

(2) complaining of

(3) incompetence in

(4) rests on

(5) by means of

(6) nor

(7) incorporated into

(8) moreover

(9) apply to

(10) cluttered up

4. 句型模拟

(1) Either the offices or the classroom needs to be cleaned.

(2) Films these days aren't half as good as they used to be.

5. 英译汉

(1) 直到最近，大学一年英语也是每所大学的必修课程。

(2) 担任大学一年级英语课的教师，不得不重复在中学里就应该完成的工作。

(3) 不管阅读如何困难，总要比写好、说好容易一些。

(4) 不可能是因为职业的教育家们不知道这种情况。

(5) 在第一年年终，我向中学校长报告我们的进展情况。

6. 汉译英

(1) The film is based on a short story by Mark Twain.

(2) The path flattens out as it reaches the top of the hill.

(3) The children had no money, it was out of the question for them to go to the movies.

(4) Students who are already acquainted with one foreign language tend to find it easier to learn a new one.

(5) If you have any information concerning the recent incident at the station, place contact the police.

7. 写作指导

(略)

11. The Education of Character

1. 回答问题

(1) Personality is something which in its growth remains essentially outside the influence of

the educator. Personality is a completion, only character is a task. One may cultivate and enhance personality, but in education one can and one must aim at character.

(2) Because they will not let themselves be educated, or rather, they do not like the idea that somebody wants to educate them.

(3) Only in his whole being, in all his spontaneity can the educator truly affect the whole being of his pupil.

(4) By direct and ingenuous participation in the life of one's pupils and by assuming the responsibility which arises from such participation.

(5) A conflict with a pupil is the supreme test for the educator.

2. 判断正误

(1) F　　(2) F　　(3) T　　(4) F　　(5) T

3. 选词填空

(1) devoted...to

(2) springs from

(3) superior to

(4) ceased

(5) lay hold of

(6) gave way to

(7) in the midst of

(8) were deprived of

(9) feeding on

(10) is craving for

4. 句型模拟

(1) It is the bad weather that led to the cancellation of the match.

(2) Mary would like to do by herself rather than with others' help.

5. 英译汉

(1) 我试图向学生们解释妒忌是可鄙的,我立即就会感到那些比他们的同伴较穷的人的内心的反感。

(2) 然而,在这种具有塑造作用的无数力量中,教师不过是另一些不胜枚举的因素之一,但他又不同于其他一切因素,他具有参与施加烙印于品格的决心,他还具有这样的意识,即意识到就成长中的人看来他应表示某种抉择,抉择什么是"正确的"以及什么是应当的。

(3) 这种冲突不再单纯是两代人之间的冲突,而是几千年来深信有一种凌驾于人之上的真理的那种世界的人与不再相信——不再愿意相信或不再可能相信有这种真理的那一代人之间的冲突。

(4) 对于这一大堆矛盾只有通过个人的统一的再生,即整个人的统一,生活的统一,以及行动的统一即整个人、生活和行动的统一的再生,才能加以应付和克服。

(5) 对于这种个人的统一的深信和加以完成的意志,并不是"返回"到个人主义,而是超然于个人主义和集体主义的一切分歧之上的一个步骤。

6. 汉译英

(1) His achievements are worthy of the highest praise.

(2) Don't allow pleasure to interfere with duty.

(3) He's entrusted his children to me for the day.

(4) The only access to the farmhouse is across the fields.

(5) At first he refused to accept any responsibility but he ended up apologizing.

7. 写作指导

(略)

12. The Science of Learning and the Art of Teaching

1. 回答问题

(1) The traditional devices for the study of learning are the serial maze, for example, or the T-maze, the problem box, or the familiar discrimination apparatus.

(2) It should be emphasized that this has been achieved by analyzing the effects of reinforcement and by designing techniques, which manipulate reinforcement with considerable precision. Only in this way can the behavior of the individual organism be brought under such precise control.

(3) No, even the best schools are under criticism for their inefficiency in the teaching.

(4) Three of them have been mentioned.

(5) The teacher is seldom able to reinforce at each step in such a series because she cannot deal with the pupil's responses one at a time.

2. 判断正误

(1) T   (2) T   (3) T   (4) T   (5) F

3. 选词填空

(1) resort to

(2) under control

(3) In spite of

(4) in collaboration with

(5) promising

(6) optimal

(7) make sure

(8) Many a

(9) over and above

(10) at will

4. 句型模拟

(1) In none of the rooms have we found the lost child.

(2) I agree with you, but the teacher is on the contrary with our views, so we have to rethink it.

5. 英译汉

(1) 特殊的技术被设计来安排所谓的"强化的发现",即普遍存在于行为和行为结果之间的关系,从而更加有效地控制行为。

(2) 只要在恰当的时候给饥饿的鸽子食物,就可以在一段演示的时间内形成三、四个很明显的反应,诸如转圈、在地上走8字型、在演示器的一角站着不动、伸脖子或跺脚等。

(3) 当儿童学习数数,背计算表,边数数边给一堆物体做记号,对说出或写出的数目反应为"基数"、"偶数"、"质数"等时,这种情况就会发生。

(4) 第三个鲜明的缺点是缺乏一个巧妙的程序,这个程序可通过一系列递进的近似结果向所期望的最终复杂行为推进。

(5) 要使有机体最有效地掌握教学行为,需要有长长一连串的强化出现,但是教师在出现这样一长串强化的过程中,很难在每一步上都给予强化,因为她不可能一个一个地处理学生的反应。

6. 汉译英

(1) The struggle is far from over.

(2) Hunger and fear are in the wake of disaster.

(3) You should know the discrimination between right and wrong.

(4) The farm yields pears and apples. T

(5) The teacher permits them to have the football match this afternoon.

7. 写作指导

(略)

13. Educational Principles and Psychological Data

1. 回答问题

(1) One should take care to analyze its principles in detail and to check their psychological value on at least four points: the significance of childhood, the structure of the child's thought, the laws of development, and the mechanism of infantile social life.

(2) Diligent and continuous research, springs from a spontaneous need.

   (3) The subject matter should be taught in forms assimilable to children of different ages in accordance with their mental structure and the various stages of their development.

   (4) Biological adaptation is a state of balance between a assimilation of the environment to the organism and an accommodation of the organism to the environment.

   (5) Play

2. 判断正误

   (1) T　　　(2) F　　　(3) T　　　(4) F　　　(5) T

3. 选词填空

   (1) inherent in

   (2) make every effort to

   (3) adapted to

   (4) turns around

   (5) was endowed with

   (6) attributed to

   (7) with regard to

   (8) allied with

   (9) at full stretch

   (10) take account of

4. 句型模拟

   (1) The more you talk with him, the more you will admire him.

   (2) He speaks nothing to me other than to ask for money.

5. 英译汉

   (1) 但按照这种旧体制的逻辑，学生的智慧活动和道德活动不是服从其本身的发展规律的，因为这与教师不断施加的强制分不开，尽管那种强制可能未被学生觉察，也可能为学生自己的自由意志所接受。

   (2) 反之，新学校引起真正的活动，即以个人的需要和兴趣为基础的自发性工作。

   (3) 可是关于心理的机能作用，儿童事实上跟成人相同；像成人一样，他是个具有主动性的人，他的活动受兴趣或需要律的支配，如果不引起那种活动的自发的动机力量，是不可能全力工作的。

   (4) 总的来说，适应是以主体和客体的相互作用为前提，前者使后者融合进来，与此同时也顾到后者的特点。

   (5) 因为同化就其最单纯的形式来说，只要它与对现实的调节过程还未达到平衡，实际上就是游戏。

6. 汉译英

(1) They were obliged to sell their house in order to pay their debts.

(2) The two companies are fused by their common interests.

(3) The written record of our conversation doesn't correspond with what was actually said.

(4) The body quickly adjusts itself to changes in temperature.

(5) Such bluntness is characteristic of him.

7. 写作指导
(略)

14. The Process of Education

1. 回答问题

(1) The first object of any act of learning, over and beyond the pleasure it may give, is that it should serve us in the future. Learning should not only take us somewhere; it should allow us later to go further more easily.

(2) There are two ways in which learning serves the future. One is through its specific applicability to 3 tasks that are highly similar to4 those we originally learned to perform. Psychologists refer to this phenomenon as specific transfer of training; perhaps it should be called the extension of habits or associations5. A second way in which earlier learning renders later performance more efficient is through what is conveniently called nonspecific transfer or, more accurately, the transfer of principles and attitudes.

(3) It is that the best minds in any particular discipline must be put to work on the task of the design of a curriculum.

(4) The task of teaching a subject to a child at any particular age is one of representing the structure of that subject in terms of the child's way of viewing things.

(5) The preoperational child cannot t grasp the idea that it can be brought back readily to its original state because of the lack of the concept of reversibility called by the Geneva school.

2. 判断正误
(1) T   (2) F   (3) T   (4) F   (5) F

3. 选词填空
(1) referred to

(2) Sort out

(3) contradict

(4) on the premise

(5) It goes without saying

(6) similar to

(7) In essence

(8) bring off

(9) highlight

(10) by virtue of

4. 句型模拟

(1) Not only should you show your respect to your parents, but also you should take care of them since they are old now.

(2) Roughly speaking, I am quite satisfied with your achievements.

5. 英译汉

(1) 任何学习行为的首要目的，应该超过和不限于它可能带来的乐趣，而在于它将来为我们服务。

(2) 毫无疑问，学校里的学习创造了一种可以迁移到以后无论在校内或离校后所遇到的活动上去的技能。

(3) 课程和教学方法应该同所教学科里基本观念的教学密切地结合，当然，这样声明是够简单的。

(4) 我们一开始就提出这个假设：任何学科都能够以智育上是诚实的方式，有效地教给任何发展阶段的任何儿童。

(5) 不用说，教师向这个阶段的儿童灌溉概念受到很大限制，尽管采用高度直观的方法。

6. 汉译英

(1) The company has transferred to an eastern location.

(2) All the people here should be put to work.

(3) The production must be geared to demand.

(4) It's a bold enough hypothesis.

(5) Her success does not consist only in the chance.

7. 写作指导

(略)

15. Nature of a Theory of Instruction

1. 回答问题

(1) Because theories of learning and of development are descriptive rather than prescriptive and with how best to learn what one wishes to teach, with improving, rather than describing learning.

(2) Optimal structure refers to the set of propositions from which a larger body of knowledge

can be generated.

(3) Activation, maintenance and direction.

(4) Past learning, stage of development, nature of the material and individual differences.

(5) Because more economically presented materials, learned first as a model, will serve to reduce the potential complexity of materials encountered later.

2. 判断正误

 (1) F   (2) T   (3) F   (4) T   (5) T

3. 选词填空

 (1) in terms of

 (2) by the same token

 (3) set forth

 (4) derived from

 (5) concentrate on

 (6) on the part of

 (7) be independent of

 (8) take...into account

 (9) fall back on

 (10) on her own

4. 句型模拟

 (1) It is characteristic that Chinese people tend to be modest when they are praised.

 (2) No more needs to be said. It suffices to say that his failure resulted from his carelessness.

5. 英译汉

 (1) 教学论，在某种意义上说，是约定俗成的通例，它阐明有关最有效地获得知识与技能之方法的规则。

 (2) 从直观角度来讲，由于学习不断前进，因而有一个要点似乎是很清楚的，即最好将外来的奖励变为一个人在自行解决问题时所固有的内在的奖励。同理，还有一个要点似乎也是很清楚的，即学生完成作业后的即时的奖励应当代之以延缓的奖励。

 (3) 教学就是引导学习者通过一系列有条不紊地陈述一个问题或大量知识，以提高他们对所学事物的掌握、转换和迁移的。

 (4) 独一无二的序列是没有的。在任何特定条件下，最理想的序列则随着多种因素而定，这些因素包括过去的学习、发展的阶段、材料的性质和个别差异等。

 (5) 人在进行工作时，做出选择的探索活动得以激起的主要条件，在于具有最适度的不确定性。

6. 汉译英

(1) He has a predisposition to criticize others.

(2) His private actions are in direct contradiction to his publicly expressed opinions.

(3) His personality is complementary to hers.

(4) The government has set up a working party to look into the problem of drug abuse.

(5) We need a yardstick to measure our performance.

7. 写作指导

(略)

词 汇 表

A

abandon v. 放弃
abase v. 降低身分
abembryonic adj. 雏形的
abreast adv. 并列
abstraction n. 抽象物
accentuate v. 突出;强调
accommodation n. 调节
accumulate v. 积累
acquire v. 获得,得到
adduce v. 引证,举证
adjust v. 调节,对准,调整,适应
administrative adj. 行政的;经营的
administrator n. 管理者,行政官员
advent n. 来临;到来
adversary n. 对手;敌手
affectionate adj. 亲爱的,亲切的
affirm v. 肯定;断言
agency n. 代办,代理处,经销处
aisle n. 走道,走廊
alertness n. 警觉,灵活
algebra n. 代数(学)
algebraic adj. 代数学的,代数上的,代数的
allege v. 宣称,控诉
alley n. 巷,小径;(保龄馆)球道
alternative n. 选择余地
ambiguity n. 模棱两可
amenity n. 愉快,温柔,适宜,宜人
amplify v. 放大,增强
anomaly n. 异常事物;不合规则
anticipation n. 预计,预测
antipsychological adj. 违反心理学的
antithetic adj. 相反的;对立的
antithetical adj. 对照的;相反的
apparatus n. 机构;仪器

application n. 用途,应用
approximate adj. 大约的;大概的
approximation n. 接近,类似
apt adj. 恰当的,适宜的
arbitrary adj. 任意的,武断的,专断的
arithmetic adj. 算术的
articulate v. 表达
articulate adj. 发音清晰的
ascertain v. 弄清;确定
asphyxiated adj. 窒息而死的
assemblage n. 集会,集合物,装配
assertion n. 主张,断言,维护
assessor n. 财产估价人,技术顾问
assimilation n. 同化
asylum n. 避难所,收容所
attributable adj. 可归因的
atypical adj. 非典型的,不规则的,不正常的
authentic adj. 真实的
authoritarian adj. 权力主义的
authoritative adj. 权威性的
authority n. 权力;权威
autonomous adj. 自治的;自主的
aversive adj. 厌恶的,促使退避的
avert v. 防止;避免

B

babble v. 唠叨,咿呀学语
babbling n. 咿牙学语
bafflement n. 困惑
barren adj. 贫瘠的;不结果实的
bemoan v. 悲叹,哀泣
beneficent adj. 行善的,慈善的
benevolence n. 善意,仁慈,善行
betray v. 辜负,不忠,出卖,显示,泄漏
blast v. 炸毁
blight n. 枯萎

bluntly *adj*. 迟钝的,率直的
bold *adj*. 勇敢的;冒失的
breadth *n*. 广度,宽宏
bully *v*. 胁迫,欺负
buoyant *adj*. 飘浮的

C

candidate *n*. 参加考试的人
capacity *n*. 容纳力,生产力
catalyst *n*. 催化剂
certify *v*. 证明
chaotic *adj*. 处于混乱状态的
characteristic *n*. 特征,特点 *adj*. 特有的,性格上的
chastise *v*. 严惩
chastisement *n*. 严惩
chauffeur *n*. 司机
citation *n*. 引用,引述
civilization *n*. 文明
coercive *adj*. 强迫的,抑制的,高压的
cognitive *adj*. 认知的
coincide *v*. 同时发生
collaboration *n*. 合作
commerce *n*. 商业
commutative *adj*. 互相的,交替的,交换的
comparative *adj*. 比较的,比较而言的
compatriot *n*. 同胞
competence *n*. 能力,胜任
complacent *adj*. 自满的;自鸣得意的
complementary *adj*. 互补的
compound *v*. 使化合,使混合,增加
compromise *n*. 折中
compulsory *adj*. 必须做的;义务的
concede *v*. 承认
conception *n*. 概念,思想
concurrently *adv*. 同时地,共同地
condemn *v*. 谴责
congruence *n*. 一致性
conscience *n*. 良知
consciousness *n*. 意识
consequence *n*. 结果,后果
conservative *adj*. 保守的,守旧的,传统的
consign *v*. 交付

consistent *adj*. 一贯的,前后一致的
consolation *n*. 安慰
consolidated *adj*. 合并的;联合的
contemporary *adj*. 当代的;现代的
contingency *n*. 偶然性,意外事件
continuity *n*. 连续,关联
continuous *adj*. 连续的,持续的,重复的
continuously *adv*. 连续不断地
contradict *v*. 反驳,与……发生矛盾/相抵触
correlation *n*. 相互关联
cramp *v*. 妨碍
crank *n*. 怪人,奇思妙想
creed *n*. 教条,信条,信念
critical *adj*. 决定性的,关键的
cultivate *v*. 培养
currency *n*. 通用,流传
curriculum *n*. 课程,全部课程,路线,途径
curve *n*. 曲线

D

deaden *v*. 减轻(某物)的力量或强度
decent *adj*. 令人满意的
deduce *v*. 推断,推论
deductive *adj*. 演绎的,推论的,推理的
defeat *n*. 击败,失败
defect *n*. 缺点,毛病
deferred *adj*. 延期的
deformed *adj*. 畸形的
delectation *n*. 欢娱,享乐
democratic *adj*. 民主的
denounce *v*. 当众指责,告发,公然抨击
dent *n*. 凹陷
deplorable *adj*. 可悲可叹的
descriptive *adj*. 描述性的
despotism *n*. 暴政
destined *adj*. 命中注定的
detach *v*. 分开
detached *adj*. 分离的,独立的
detachment *n*. 冷静;超然
devour *v*. 狼吞虎咽,吞食
differentiate *v*. 区别;区分
diffuse *v*. 散布,传播

diffusion n. 散布,普及,传播
dignity n. 尊严
digression n. 离开本题,脱轨,题外话,闲话
diligent adj. 勤奋的;刻苦的
diploma n. 文凭,毕业证书
discipline v. 控制,惩戒
disciplined adj. 守纪律的
discord n. 不和;争吵
discretion n. 谨慎,明辨,自由选择或决定
discriminate v. 区别,辨别
discrimination n. 辨别,识别,辨别力
disgrace n. 丢脸
disintegrated adj. 分裂的
disintegration n. 瓦解;崩裂
disparaging adj. 贬低性的(言语、评论等)
disparate adj. 迥然不同的;无法比较的
dissatisfaction with/at 对……不满
distinct adj. 清楚的,明晰的
distraction n. 心烦意乱
distribute v. 发送;分发
distributive adj. 分配的,普及的,(语言)个别的
divinity n. 神学
division n. 分工
doctrine n. 教义,教条,学说,主义,方针
domination n. 统治
dramatic adj. 戏剧的,戏剧性的,表情丰富的
dryrot n. 干腐,腐败

E

editorial n. 社论
effectively adv. 有效地
efficient adj. 有效率的,最经济的,有能力的
elaborate adj. 精心的,精巧的,复杂的
elapse v. (时间)消逝
elementary adj. 基本的;初步的
elicit v. 诱出;探出
eliminate v. 除去,剔除,淘汰
eliminate v. 除掉
eloquence n. 口才,雄辩
emanate v. 来自
eminent adj. 文明的,显赫的,杰出的
eminently adv. 著名地,卓越地,优良地

emphatically adv. 用力地,强调地,显著地
empirical adj. 实证的
emulation n. 竞争,争胜
enactive adj. 表演式的
encase v. 将某物置于箱、盒、套等之中
endeavor v. 努力,企图,尽力
endow v. 赋予
enrollment n. 登记(人数),注册(人数)
enterprise n. 企业
entitle v. 给……取名
entrust v. 委托
enunciate v. 宣布,发表
equilibrium n. 平衡
equivalent adj. 相等的,相当的 // n. 相等物
equivalent n. 对应词;等同物
err v. 犯错误,出差错
errand n. 使命,出差
ethical adj. 伦理的
evocation n. 引起,唤起(灵魂等)
exceedingly adv. 非常,极端地,胜过地
exception n. 例外,异议,排除在外
exclude v. 排除
exclusive adj. 绝对的,惟一的
exhortation n. 劝告,劝诫
exorbitant adj. 过分的,不合理的
explicit adj. 明确的,明白表示的,直爽的
external adj. 外在的,外面的
extract v. 选录,夺取,摘取,榨取,摘录
extrinsic adj. 外在的

F

fad n. 时尚,一时流行的嗜好
ferment n. 蓬勃发展,激动,骚动,纷扰
flourish v. 昌盛
fluctuating adj. 被动的
flux n. 接连不断的变化
folly n. 愚蠢,愚行,[pl] 轻松歌舞剧
formidable adj. 可怕的;难以应付的
fortify v. 设立防御工事,加强,坚固,确证
foundation n. 建立,创立,基础
friction n. 摩擦;冲突
frivolous adj. 轻浮的,不严肃的

fruitfully *adv*. 有成效地
fundamental *adj*. 基本的
fuse *v*. 融合

G

gaiety *n*. 快乐
generality *n*. 概括
generalization *n*. 一般化
generic *adj*. 类的;一般的
geometric *adj*. 几何图形的

H

handicap *n*. 障碍
haphazard *adj*. 无秩序的;任意的
head *v*. 注意,听从
heritage *n*. 遗产;继承物
heterogeneous *adj*. 各种各样的
heteronomous *adj*. 异质的
highlight *v*. 使显著,使突出,强调
homogeneous *adj*. 同类的,相似的
humanity *n*. 人类
humanity *n*. 人性;人道
humiliate *v*. 使丧失尊严
hunch *n*. 肉峰,瘤,块,[俗语]预感
hygiene *n*. 卫生学

I

ignominious *adj*. 可耻的,没面子的
ignorance *n*. 无知
ikonic *adj*. 肖像式的
illiteracy *n*. 文盲;无知
illiterate *adj*. 文盲
illumine *v*. 启明,照耀
impart *v*. 传授,告知,揭发
implicit *adj*. 暗示的,含蓄的
impose *v*. 强加于某人
imposition *n*. 强加,(惩罚的)给予
impulse *n*. 冲动
impulse *n*. 推动力;刺激
inapplicability *n*. 不适用

incentive *n*. 刺激;奖励
inclination *n*. 倾向,爱好,意向
incoherent *adj*. 思想不连贯的,语无伦次的
inculcation *n*. 反复灌输,谆谆教诲
incurred *adj*. 所遭受的
indefinitely *adv*. 无限期地
individualistic *adj*. 个人主义的;利己主义的
ineptitude *n*. 不称职
inert *adj*. 无生命的
inert *adj*. 迟钝的;迟缓的
inexorably *adv*. 坚持不懈地;不可阻挡地
inexplicable *adj*. 无法解释的
infantile *adj*. 婴儿的,幼儿的
infect *v*. 传染,使腐化,使影响
infectious *adj*. 传染的
ingenuity *n*. 足智多谋,善于创造发明
ingredient *n*. (混合物)成分
ingredient *n*. 成分,原料,要素
inherent *adj*. 内在的;固有的
inheritor *n*. 继承者
initial *adj*. 最初的;开始的
initiate *v*. 开始,传授知识
insistent *adj*. 坚持的,强求的,显著的,强烈的
instill *v*. 逐渐地灌输,一点一滴地滴入
instinctively *adv*. 本能地,直觉地
instrumentality *n*. 方法
integral *adj*. 构成整体所必需的,完整的,整体
intellectual *n*. 知识分子
intellectual *adj*. 智力的
intelligence *n*. 智力
interact *v*. 相互作用
intercourse *n*. 交往;交际
interpretation *n*. 解释,表明,体现
intimacy *n*. 亲密,亲近
intricacy *n*. 纷杂,复杂,[pl]纷乱的事物
intrinsic *adj*. 内在的
intrinsically *adv*. 固有地,本质地
irrelevant *adj*. 不相关的
irrespective *adj*. 不考虑,不顾

J

jive *n*. 摇摆乐;摇摆舞

jointly *adv*. 共同地,联合地
justifiable *adj*. 正当的,可证明的
justify *v*. 证明……正当(或有理)

L

lapse *n*. 堕落,终止,暂停
lassitude *n*. 厌倦;疲乏
legitimate *adj*. 正当的,真实的,合理的
leverage *n*. 影响;力量
likewise *adv*. 同样地
lofty *adj*. 高尚的

M

malevolent *adj*. 恶意的,恶毒的
manipulability *n*. 可操作性
manipulate *v*. 操纵,使用;窜改,假造
margin *n*. 边缘;余地
maximum *adj*. 最高的、最大的
meager *adj*. 缺乏的
mechanism *n*. 机制;构造
mediocre *adj*. 平庸的,二流的
mercantile *adj*. 贸易的,商业的
merit *n*. 优点,价值
meticulous *adj*. 极精细的,极注意细节的
militarist *n*. 军国主义者
misguided *adj*. 被误导的
mitigate *v*. 减轻;和缓
modification *n*. 变化
mortality *n*. 死亡率
multiplication *n*. 增加,增值
multiplicity *n*. 多样性

N

napkin *n*. 餐巾,餐纸,毛巾,布,(英)尿布
normative *adj*. 标准的;规范的
nourishment *n*. 食物;营养

O

obedience *n*. 驯服

obsession *n*. 困扰;牵挂
obstacle *n*. 障碍物
obstinacy *n*. 顽固
offspring *n*. 孩子;子女
optimal *adj*. 最佳的,最理想的
orbit *n*. 轨道
original *adj*. 起初的,原先的 *n*. 原稿,原件
originally *adv*. 起初地,原先地
ornamental *adj*. 装饰的,装饰用品的,装饰过渡的
outspoken *adj*. 直言无隐的,率直的,坦白的
outward *adj*. 外面的,向外的,表面的

P

pedagogy *n*. 教学法;教育学
palliative *n*. 缓和物;缓解剂
pamper *v*. 纵容;娇养
parental *adj*. 父母的
pathetic *adj*. 可怜的,情感的,可悲的,乏味的
patriotism *n*. 爱国主义
pedantry *n*. 迂腐,拘泥形式
penetrate *v*. 穿透
perceive *v*. 察觉,理解
perception *n*. 感觉,知觉
peril *n*. 严重危险
pervade *v*. 遍布,弥漫,扩大,渗透
perverse *adj*. 任性的,荒谬的
physiology *n*. 生理学
pivot *n*. 中心点;枢轴
placard *n*. 布告;海报
plasticine *n*. [商标](塑像用的)黏土,彩泥,橡皮泥
plethora *n*. 太多,过剩
postulate *v*. 假定;假设
potency *n*. 效力;威力
precede *v*. 先于(某事物)
predecessor *n*. 某职位的前任,前任者
predict *v*. 预言,预测
predisposition *n*. 倾向
prematurely *adv*. 过早地;提前地
preoccupation *n*. 抢先占据(占有),入神,专心
preoperational *adj*. 前运算的
prescribe *v*. 规定,指定
prescriptive *adj*. 规定性的

prevail v. 盛行,流行
prevail v. 流行,说服,盛行,成功,获胜
prevalent adj. 普遍的,流行的
primrose n. 樱草花
priority n. 优先权
proclaim v. 宣布,宣言,声明,赞扬
productive adj. 多产的
promising adj. 有前途的,大有可为的
promptness n. 迅速,敏捷,即时
propaganda n. 宣传
propaganda n. 宣传;传播
propensity n. 倾向;习性
proportion n. 比例,比率,均匀,相称,容积
proposition n. 主张,建议,陈述,命题,提出
propound v. 提议,提出(问题)供考虑
prospect n. 景色,展望,期望
prosperity n. 繁华
prudence n. 审慎
psychic adj. 灵魂的;心灵的
psychological adj. 心理学的,心灵的
psychologist n. 心理学家,心理学者
psychology n. 心理学,心理状态,心理学著作
purvey v. 供应,承办

Q

qualification n. 资格,证书,资格事物
qualitative adj. 性质上的,质量上的
quantitative adj. 数量的
quote v. 引用

R

radical adj. 根本的,基本的
ramified adj. 复杂的
rational adj. 理智的,有理性的,合理的,推理的
rationality n. 理智;理性
reactionary adj. 反动的,保守的 // n. 反动者
reams [pl] n. 许多
reappraisal n. 重新评价;重新考虑
receptive adj. 善于接受新建议,新思想等的
recipiency n. 接受
recipient adj. 容纳的,领受的,易于接受的

recognition n. 承认,认出
recruitment n. 征收;招募
recurrent adj. 经常发生的
redemption n. 补救;赎回
regiment n. 大量的
reinforcement n. 援助,增强,补给品
reiteration n. 重复,反复,重说
relic n. 遗物;遗骸
render v. 使(某人/某事物)处于某种状况
repertoire n. 戏目,演唱目录,电脑的指令表
representation n. 描述,表示
restraint n. 克制,抑制,约束
retain v. 保留,保存
retort v. 反驳,回嘴
revamp v. 给(鞋等)换新面,(口语)修理
reverence n. 尊敬
reverse v. 彻底转变
reversibility n. 可逆,可撤销,两面可用
reversibility n. 可转变性
ridicule v. 讥笑,嘲弄
rigid adj. 严格的,精确的,僵硬的
rigorous adj. 严厉的;严格的
rock'n'roll n. 摇滚乐

S

sacrosanct adj. 神圣不可侵犯的
salient adj. 显著的
sample n. 样品,(抽样调查的)人或物
sanction n. 处罚措施;制裁
sanity n. 明智;理智
saturate v. 浸湿;浸透
seamstress n. 女裁缝
segment n. 部分
sensorimotor n. 感知运动
sequence n. 顺序,连续
shrewdly adv. 精明地、准确地
significance n. 重要性
skepticism n. 怀疑态度
slaughter n. 屠杀
sloppy adj. 草率的
sneer at 嘲笑,讥讽
solace n. 慰藉

specialist n. 专家
speculative adj. 思考的;思索的
spontaneous adj. 自发的;主动的
sputnik n. (俄国的)人造卫星
squarely adv. 明确地,直截了当地
standpoint n. 立场,见地,角度
staple adj. 主要的 n. 主要产品
stewardship n. 乘务员(或服务员等)的职位
stimulation n. 激发;刺激
stimuli n. (stimulus 的复数) 刺激物,激励
stringent adj. 严格的,苛峻的
stuff n. 东西,材料
subordinated adj. 次要的;附属的
substitute n. 代替物
subtraction n. 减去,扣除,消减
succinctly adv. 简明地;简洁地
succumb v. 屈从
superimposition n. 将某物置于另一物上
supersede v. 替代,更换,充任,接替
superstition n. 迷信
supervise v. 监督,管理,指导,审阅,审查
supplement n. 附刊,补充,追加,补足之物
supremacy n. 至高无上
suspend v. 暂停,延缓
sustain v. 支撑,维持,持续
symbol n. 符号
sympathetic adj. 同情的,相怜的
synonym n. 同义词

T

tadpole n. 蝌蚪
tangle v. 缠结,(使)纠缠,(使)陷入
tautology n. 同义语之重复
taxation n. 征税,关税
temperament n. 气质,性情,性格
tendency n. 倾向
testimony n. 证词,见证,证明
theological adj. 智力发达的,知识的
theorem n. 定理;命题
torment n. 折磨;痛苦
totalitarian adj. 极权主义的

trail-and-error adj. 尝试错误的
transferability n. 可转移;可转变
transitory adj. 短暂的,片刻的
transmit v. 传播;传送
treble adj. 三倍的
tribunal n. 审理团;特别法庭
trustee n. 管理班子成员
tyrant n. 暴君

U

ultimate adj. 最终的
unanimous adj. 全体一致的,全体同意的,和谐的
unbounded adj. 无限制的,无边际的,压抑不住的
uncertainty n. 不确定性
underestimate v. 不充分如实地陈述
undergo v. 经历,遭受
unduly adv. 过分地;过度地
uniformity n. 一律,同样
utilitarian adj. 实用的、功利的
utilize v. 利用,派上用场
utmost adj. 最大的,极度的

V

valid adj. 令人信服的,有效的
vertebrate n. 脊椎动物
victim n. 牺牲品
view v. 观看,看待,考虑
vitality n. 生命力,生机,活力

W

wager v. 打赌
weaponry n. 武器、兵器
welfare n. 福利
whim n. 突然的念头,心血来潮
woefully adv. 不合意地,悲哀地

Y

yardstick n. 标准,尺度
yield v. 出产,屈服,放弃